Julie Miller-Cribbs
Editor

New Advances in Technology for Social Work Education and Practice

New Advances in Technology for Social Work Education and Practice has been co-published simultaneously as *Journal of Technology in Human Services*, Volume 18, Numbers 3/4, 2001.

The Haworth Press, Inc.

New Advances in Technology for Social Work Education and Practice

New Advances in Technology for Social Work Education and Practice has been co-published simultaneously as *Journal of Technology in Human Services*, Volume 18, Numbers 3/4 2001.

The *Journal of Technology in Human Services* Monographic "Separates"

(formerly the *Computers in Human Services* series)*

Below is a list of " separates," which in serials librarianship means a special issue simultaneously published as a special journal issue or double-issue *and* as a "separate" hardbound monograph. (This is a format which we also call a "DocuSerial.")

"Separates" are published because specialized libraries or professionals may wish to purchase a specific thematic issue by itself in a format which can be separately cataloged and shelved, as opposed to purchasing the journal on an on-going basis. Faculty members may also more easily consider a "separate" for classroom adoption.

"Separates" are carefully classified separately with the major book jobbers so that the journal tie-in can be noted on new book order slips to avoid duplicate purchasing.

You may wish to visit Haworth's website at . . .

http://www.haworthpress.com

. . . to search our online catalog for complete tables of contents of these separates and related publications.

You may also call 1-800-HAWORTH (outside US/Canada: 607-722-5857), or Fax 1-800-895-0582 (outside US/Canada: 607-771-0012), or e-mail at:

getinfo@haworthpressinc.com

New Advances in Technology for Social Work Education and Practice, *edited by Julie Miller-Cribbs, PhD (Vol. 18, 3/4, 2001). "A valuable tool for educators who want to introduce students of social work to the numerous applications of technology within the field . . . . Goes a long way toward helping social work become proactive in its approach to technology integration within the field." (Sharon D. Johnson, PhD, Assistant Professor, Department of Social Work, University of Missouri, St. Louis)*

Using Technology in Human Services Education: Going the Distance, *edited by Goutham M. Menon, PhD, and Nancy K. Brown, PhD (Vol. 18, No. 1/2, 2001). "A REFRESHINGLY REALISTIC AND BALANCED COLLECTION . . . . Highlights many innovative efforts in both education and practice. Will be extremely valuable in courses on technology in social work, or for courses examining emerging trends in social work practice." Paul P. Freddolino, PhD, Professor and Coordinator of Distance Education, School of Social Work, Michigan State University, East Lansing*

Human Services Online: A New Arena for Service Delivery, *edited by Jerry Finn, PhD, and Gary Holden, DSW (Vol. 17, 1/2/3, 2000). Focuses on the ways that human services are using the Internet for service delivery, social change, and resource development as more and more agencies can be found on the Internet.*

Computers and Information Technology in Social Work: Education, Training, and Practice, *edited by Jo Ann R. Coe, PhD, and Goutham M. Menon, PhD (Vol. 16, No. 2/3, 1999). Discusses the impact that recent technological advances have had on social work practice and education. Social workers and educators will discover ideas and projects that were presented at a week long conference presented at the University of South Carolina College of Social Work. This unique book covers a wide range of topics, such as different aspects of technology applied to assist those in helping professions, how computers can be used in child protective cases in order to practice more effectively, social services via videoconferencing, and much more.*

Information Technologies: Teaching to Use–Using to Teach, *edited by Frank B. Raymond III, DSW, Leon Ginsberg, PhD, and Debra Gohagan, MSW, ACSW, LISW* (Vol. 15, No. 2/3, 1998). Explores examples of the use of technology to teach social work knowledge, values, and skills across the curriculum.*

The History and Function of the Target Cities Management Information Systems, *edited by Matthew G. Hile, PhD* (Vol. 14, No. 3/4, 1998). "Essential Reading for anyone invested in improving the coordination and delivery of substance abuse services in large metropolitan areas."*

(Albert D. Farrell, PhD, Professor of Psychology, Virginia Commonwealth University, Richmond)

Human Services in the Information Age, edited by Jackie Rafferty, MS, Jan Steyaert, and David Colombi* (Vol. 12, No. 1/2/3/4, 1996). *Anyone interested in the current state of the development of human service information systems of all types needs to read this book." (Walter F. LaMendola, PhD, Consultant, Wheat Ridge, CO)*

Electronic Tools for Social Work Practice and Education, edited by Hy Resnick, PhD* (Vol. 11, No. 1/2/3/4, 1994). *"Opens a new world of opportunities for readers by introducing a variety of electronic tools available when working with various clients." (Ram A Cnaan, PhD, Associate Professor, School of Social Work, University of Pennsylvania)*

Technology in People Services: Research, Theory, and Applications, edited by Marcos Leiderman, MSW, Charles Guzzetta, EdD, Leny Struminger, PhD, and Menachem Monnickendam, PhD, MSW* (Vol. 9, No. 1/2/3/4, 1993). *"Honest reporting and inquiry into the opportunities and limitations for administrators, managers, supervisors, clinicians, service providers, consumers, and clients . . . A well-integrated and in-depth examination." (John P. Flynn, PhD, Associate Director for Instructional Computing, University Computing Services and Professor of Social Work, Western Michigan University)*

Computer Applications in Mental Health: Education and Evaluation, edited by Marvin J. Miller, MD* (Vol. 8, No. 3/4, 1992). *"Describes computer programs designed specifically for mental health clinicians and their work in both private practice and institutional treatment settings." (SciTech Book News)*

Computers for Social Change and Community Organizing, edited by John Downing, PhD, Robert Fasano, MSW, Patricia Friedland, MLS, Michael McCullough, AM, Terry Mizrahi, PhD, and Jeremy Shapiro, PhD* (Vol. 8, No. 1, 1991). *This landmark volume presents an original and-until now-unavailable perspective on the uses of computers for community- and social-change-based organizations.*

Computer Literacy in Human Services Education, edited by Richard L. Reinoehl and B. Jeanne Mueller* (Vol. 7, No. 1/2/3/4, 1990). *This volume provides a unique and notable contribution to the investigation and exemplification of computer literacy in human services education.*

Computer Literacy in Human Services, edited by Richard L. Reinoehl and Thomas Hanna* (Vol. 6, No. 1/2/3/4, 1990) *"Includes a diversity of articles on many of the most important practical and conceptual issues associated with the use of computer technology in the human services." (Adult Residential Care)*

The Impact of Information Technology on Social Work Practice, edited by Ram A. Cnaan, PhD, and Phyllida Parsloe, PhD* (Vol. 5, No. 1/2, 1989). *International experts confront the urgent need for social work practice to move into the computer age.*

A Casebook of Computer Applications in the Social and Human Services, edited by Walter LaMendola, PhD, Bryan Glastonbury, and Stuart Toole* (Vol. 4, No. 1/2/3/4, 1989). *"Makes for engaging and enlightening reading in the rapidly expanding field of information technology in the human services." (Wallace Gingerich, PhD, Associate Professor, School of Social Welfare, University of Wisconsin-Milwaukee)*

Technology and Human Service Delivery: Challenges and a Critical Perspective, edited by John W. Murphy, PhD, and John T. Pardeck, PhD, MSW* (Vol. 3, No. 1/2, 1988). *"A much-needed, critical examination of whether and how computers can improve social services . . . Essential reading for social workers in the field and for scholars interested in how computers alter social systems." (Charles Ess, PhD, Assistant Professor of Philosophy, Morningside College)*

Research in Mental Health Computing: The Next Five Years, edited by John H. Greist, MD, Judith A. Carroll, PhD, Harold P. Erdman, PhD, Marjorie H. Klein, PhD, and Cecil R. Wurster, MA* (Vol. 2, No. 3/4, 1988). *"Provides a clear and lucid perspective on the state of research in mental health computing." (David Servan-Schreiber, MD, Western Psychiatric Institute & Clinic and Department of Computer Science, Carnegie Mellon University)*

New Advances in Technology for Social Work Education and Practice

Julie Miller-Cribbs, PhD
Editor

New Advances in Technology for Social Work Education and Practice has been co-published simultaneously as Journal of Technology in Human Services, Volume 18, Numbers 3/4 2001.

The Haworth Press, Inc.
New York • London • Oxford

New Advances in Technology for Social Work Education and Practice has been co-published simultaneously as *Journal of Technology in Human Services*, Volume 18, Numbers 3/4 2001.

The development, preparation, and publication of this work has been undertaken with great care. However, the publisher, employees, editors, and agents of The Haworth Press and all imprints of The Haworth Press, Inc., including The Haworth Medical Press® and The Pharmaceutical Products Press®, are not responsible for any errors contained herein or for consequences that may ensue from use of materials or information contained in this work. Opinions expressed by the author(s) are not necessarily those of The Haworth Press, Inc.

Cover design by Thomas J. Mayshock Jr.

Library of Congress Cataloging-in-Publication Data

New Advances in Technology for Social Work Education and Practice / Julie Miller-Cribbs, editor.
    p. cm.
    Published also as v. 18, number 3/4, 2001 of the Journal of technology in human services.
    Includes bibliographical references and index.
    ISBN 0-7890-1433-5 (alk. paper)
    1. Social work education--Computer network resources. 2. Social service--Computer network resources. I. Miller-Cribbs, Julie II. Journal of technology in human services.
HV11 .N484 2001
361.3′2′0285--dc21
                                      2001039400

Indexing, Abstracting & Website/Internet Coverage

This section provides you with a list of major indexing & abstracting services. That is to say, each service began covering this periodical during the year noted in the right column. Most Websites which are listed below have indicated that they will either post, disseminate, compile, archive, cite or alert their own Website users with research-based content from this work. (This list is as current as the copyright date of this publication.)

Abstracting, Website/Indexing Coverage . . . . Year When Coverage Began

- *ACM Guide to Computer Literature* **1992**

- *Applied Social Sciences Index & Abstracts (ASSIA)*
  (Online: ASSI via Data–Star) (CDRom: ASSIA Plus) **1993**

- *Behavioral Medicine Abstracts* **1996**

- *BUBL Information Service, an Internet-based Information*
  Service for the UK higher education community
  <URL:http://bubl.ac.uk> **1995**

- *caredata CD: the social and community care database* **1994**

- *CNPIEC Reference Guide: Chinese National Directory*
  of Foreign Periodicals **1995**

- *Computer Abstracts* **1995**

- *Computer Literature Index* **1994**

(continued)

(continued)

Special Bibliographic Notes related to special journal issues
(separates) and indexing/abstracting:

- indexing/abstracting services in this list will also cover material in any "separate" that is co-published simultaneously with Haworth's special thematic journal issue or DocuSerial. Indexing/abstracting usually covers material at the article/chapter level.
- monographic co-editions are intended for either non-subscribers or libraries which intend to purchase a second copy for their circulating collections.
- monographic co-editions are reported to all jobbers/wholesalers/approval plans. The source journal is listed as the "series" to assist the prevention of duplicate purchasing in the same manner utilized for books-in-series.
- to facilitate user/access services all indexing/abstracting services are encouraged to utilize the co-indexing entry note indicated at the bottom of the first page of each article/chapter/contribution.
- this is intended to assist a library user of any reference tool (whether print, electronic, online, or CD-ROM) to locate the monographic version if the library has purchased this version but not a subscription to the source journal.
- individual articles/chapters in any Haworth publication are also available through the Haworth Document Delivery Service (HDDS).

New Advances in Technology for Social Work Education and Practice

CONTENTS

ABOUT THE EDITOR

Julie Miller-Cribbs, PhD, is Assistant Professor in the University of South Carolina College of Social Work and an affiliated faculty member of the University of South Carolina Women's Studies Program. She has an extensive background in social work and is currently working on a project that investigates welfare reform and kin networks of rural, southern African-Americans. Her publications have appeared in various journals, including *Journal of Adolescent Research, Computers in Human Services*, and *Journal of Technology in Human Services*, and she has authored educational material used in textbooks and course outlines dealing with racial, ethnic, and cultural diversity. Dr. Miller-Cribbs is a member of numerous professional societies, including Society for Social Work Research, National Association of Social Workers, Council on Social Work Education, and the National Council on Family Relations. She is a Mentor in the African-American Scholars Program at the University of South Carolina and teaches Advanced Social Work Practice, Policy and Research.

Introduction

Advances in technology continue to influence social work research, practice and education. As a result, social workers have become more aware of the wide impact of information technology in these domains. In social work education, the continued development and refinement of course management software, web-based course delivery systems, and distance education provide a tremendous array of options for classroom and non-classroom teaching. While the choices of such technological tools are awesome, many agencies continue to struggle with issues of data management, research, and evaluation of practice. Social workers find themselves in an environment where they must adapt to constantly changing and emerging technology.

Because technology continues to outpace our ability to absorb it, conferences where dialogue and dissemination of information and research that address the evaluation and development of technological tools are essential to the field. The College of Social Work at the University of South Carolina continues to hold an annual conference on the use of information technology in the field of social work. In August 1997, the 4th Annual Technology Conference, titled Social Work Education and Practice, was held in Charleston, South Carolina. This compilation is a selection of the best papers that represented the ideas and projects that were presented at this conference. The text is divided into four sections: information management in social work, distance education evaluation, video and web-based learning and training, and technology and vulnerable populations.

Julie Miller-Cribbs, PhD, is Assistant Professor at the College of Social Work, University of South Carolina. She has an MA in social work from the University of Chicago and received her PhD from Washington University George Warren Brown School of Social Work.

[Haworth co-indexing entry note]: "Introduction." Miller-Cribbs, Julie. Co-published simultaneously in *Journal of Technology in Human Services* (The Haworth Press, Inc.) Vol. 18, No. 3/4, 2001, pp. 1-3; and: *New Advances in Technology for Social Work Education and Practice* (ed: Julie Miller-Cribbs) The Haworth Press, Inc., 2001, pp. 1-3. Single or multiple copies of this article are available for a fee from The Haworth Document Delivery Service [1-800-342-9678, 9:00 a.m. - 5:00 p.m. (EST). E-mail address: getinfo@haworthpressinc.com].

Information Management in Social Work

Johnson, Hinterlong, and Sherraden have written an article that highlights the connection between research, practice and evaluation–all while applying an innovative information management system. They emphasize the importance of the involvement of practitioners in the development of databases and evaluation. Patterson's article describes a unique application of technology in an international rural setting. The author highlights many of the challenges that were encountered as well as offers solutions to the problems that were faced. Wasko explores a hypothetical model of a clinical information system for behavioral health services. She describes the political feasibility of such a task.

Distance Education Evaluation

Macy, Rooney, Hollister, and Freddolino provide a solid overview of the literature on distance education that ends with important suggestions regarding the development of stronger research in this area. The authors review both television and web-based distance education studies. Potts and Kleinpeter provide a unique contribution to the distance education literature by focusing on distance education alumni. This provides an examination of more distal outcomes uncommon in the literature. Dalton's research compares classes taught in person and classes taught on television. He compares students on dimensions of student satisfaction and educational outcome. Controlling for the instructor variable is a strength of his research design that has not been part of many prior evaluations of distance education.

Video and Web-Based Learning and Training

Schoech describes the development and use of multimedia testing that assessed supervisor training. The author takes the reader through the process of development of the multimedia testing which includes both the successes and pitfalls of the program. He concludes with an overview of "lessons learned" that will be informative to those interested in developing similar projects. Robin, Reardon, and Strand also explore web casting or video streaming as a tool for enhancing both social work education and training. Barnett-Queen's article also provides information on a population not often studied, that is, licensed social workers. He describes both the attitudes and use of the Internet for license-related continuing education. Knowles describes the use of course management software in a mental health course. He addresses the advantages and disadvantages of web-based learning for both students and faculty.

Technology and Vulnerable Populations

Sarnoff provides an interesting paper on a topic that is not frequently addressed in the social work or technology literature, the development of ADA compliant web pages. At a time when increasingly more agencies and schools are developing websites, this article is especially appropriate. Opalinski addresses the increasing importance of technology in the lives of older adults. She describes her findings of a web survey of older adults as well as provides the reader with an excellent summary of the literature on the potential of Internet use to aid older adults.

The papers published herein highlight the many innovative and important uses of technology in social work education and practice. Many of them point to further research in the area of social work and technology. It is important for social workers to understand how to use technology in the best interest of students and clients. We must remain cognizant of our commitment to social justice and continue to develop technological tools that are consistent with social work values.

Julie Miller-Cribbs

INFORMATION MANAGEMENT IN SOCIAL WORK

Strategies for Creating MIS Technology to Improve Social Work Practice and Research

Elizabeth Johnson
James Hinterlong
Michael Sherraden

SUMMARY. This paper illustrates the potential for Management Information System (MIS) technology to integrate information collection, management and reporting within a single program or network of organizations. Properly devised and created, MIS applications can improve administration, service delivery and practice evaluation. Three strategies

Elizabeth Johnson, MSW, is Project Director, Center for Social Development, George Warren Brown School of Social Work, Washington University, Campus Box 1196, St. Louis, MO 63130 (E-mail: ejohnson@gwbmail.wustl.edu).

James Hinterlong, MSW, is Research Associate, Center for Social Development, George Warren Brown School of Social Work, Washington University, Campus Box 1196, St. Louis, MO 63130 (E-mail: hinterj@gwbmail.wustl.edu).

Michael Sherraden, PhD, is Director, Center for Social Development, George Warren Brown School of Social Work, Washington University, Campus Box 1196, St. Louis, MO 63130 (E-mail: sherrad@gwbmail.wustl.edu).

[Haworth co-indexing entry note]: "Strategies for Creating MIS Technology to Improve Social Work Practice and Research." Johnson, Elizabeth, James Hinterlong, and Michael Sherraden. Co-published simultaneously in *Journal of Technology in Human Services* (The Haworth Press, Inc.) Vol. 18, No. 3/4, 2001, pp. 5-22; and: *New Advances in Technology for Social Work Education and Practice* (ed: Julie Miller-Cribbs) The Haworth Press, Inc., 2001, pp. 5-22. Single or multiple copies of this article are available for a fee from The Haworth Document Delivery Service [1-800-342-9678, 9:00 a.m. - 5:00 p.m. (EST). E-mail address: getinfo@haworthpressinc.com].

are offered to guide the design and development of MIS software. This paper is based on lessons from the production and implementation of MIS software that serves as a management and evaluation tool for a nationwide policy demonstration. Data from the MIS have helped to shape state and federal policy. *[Article copies available for a fee from The Haworth Document Delivery Service: 1-800-342-9678. E-mail address: <getinfo@haworthpressinc.com> Website: <http://www.HaworthPress.com> © 2001 by The Haworth Press, Inc. All rights reserved.]*

KEYWORDS. Management information system, program administration, evaluation research

The Center for Social Development (CSD) at Washington University in St. Louis created an MIS application to serve both as an administrative support and evaluation tool for a network of thirteen Community-Based Organizations (CBO) offering matched savings programs throughout the United States. The goal of these Individual Development Account (IDA) programs is to assist low-income individuals and households to accumulate sufficient savings to invest in assets, such as homes or small-businesses, which have the potential to generate benefits over the long term. This Management Information System for Individual Development Accounts (MIS IDA) was then redesigned for release as a commercial-grade application. Currently, more than 230 IDA programs are using the software. MIS IDA has helped to shape and accelerate the growth of the IDA field, and may serve as a model for enhancing practice and policy with technology.

In the first half of this paper, we discuss how MIS technology can integrate areas or components of practice into a single practice system. By incorporating the information collection, storage, and reporting needs of administrators, service delivery staff, and evaluators into the same system, work in each area is more readily linked with that in others. In the second section, we offer three strategies that were used in the design, development, and dissemination of MIS IDA. These strategies may help ensure that the final product enhances the efficacy and efficiency of service delivery and evaluation within a single or network of organizations.

USING MIS TECHNOLOGY TO CREATE A PRACTICE SYSTEM

Information management is a critical aspect of social work practice, administration, and evaluation. Relationships between the practitioner and client, the organization and its funding sources, and researchers and practitioners, are characterized by the exchange of information. Therefore it is not surprising that MIS technology increasingly is being used to improve the collection, management, and distribution of information within community-based human service organizations. The potential benefits from developing MIS applications to support practice and research are substantial and the greatest impacts are achieved when MIS applications are created through a collaboration of stakeholders and crafted as an administrative and evaluation tool. When this occurs, the MIS can integrate practice, administration, and evaluation into a single system.

Component-Based Practice

At risk of oversimplification, work within a single organization can be viewed as comprised of three distinct components: service delivery, program administration, and sometimes evaluation. Information management for each component typically occurs in relative isolation, though some degree of overlap may exist. In other words, an MIS may be introduced to assist in one area with little impact on other areas. For example, a program may use in-house expertise or contract with an outside consultant to produce an MIS to support case management. This may be carried out with some thought as to the types of information that would be useful to administrators of the program, i.e., demographics. But, it is less common for programs to consider what the key evaluation questions are that could shed light on the efficacy and efficiency of program operations. Thus, this case management application may be unconnected to a second application used to record intake information, client contact hours, or staff time and budget expenditures. As a result, the organization has incurred significant time and financial costs to produce an MIS that does not support work across these three components.

When not carefully planned, the development and use of MIS technology to support discrete types of work within an organization can introduce inefficiencies. For example, if different software platforms are used in each area (i.e., spreadsheet and relational database), the data may be stored in inconsistent formats. Many agencies store information in a flat-file (spreadsheet) format, i.e., Microsoft Excel™ and data in this format are not easily recorded, managed, or merged. Relational database technology, such as was used to create MIS IDA (Microsoft Access™), is far more efficient and flexible for these tasks (Nurius, Berger, and VanDerWeele, 1988). The use of separate MIS applications increases costs when discrepant data must be merged or missing data entered for use in operational reports or for program evaluation (Mutschler, 1990).

Creating a Practice System

MIS technology makes it possible to manage within a single application information that is from different areas of practice. The adoption and use of MIS IDA has made it possible for more than 230 IDA programs to enhance their practice through the use of integrated information management, which is available at a lower cost to each program than would be a proprietary system purchased or developed internally. As an integrated system, MIS IDA can benefit individuals working within each area (Goodhue, Wybo, & Kirsch, 1992). For example, program administrators can merge trend data on client contact hours with program expenditures in order to produce better budget estimates. In terms of service delivery, MIS applications such as MIS IDA can also serve as tools to support evidence-based practice. For example, if the appropriate data are recorded, it may be possible to identify the most efficacious types of services for particular types of clients. Even in very large programs with complex service options and considerable client populations, MIS technology can assist in monitoring the effect of program-level factors on client outcomes (Rupp, Driessen, & Kornfeld, 1999). These data are most likely to be collected when the MIS is designed to serve simultaneously as an administrative, service delivery, and evaluation tool.

MIS technology can best support evaluation by folding the collection of standardized evaluation data into routine service delivery and program administration tasks. If an organization wishes to design an application that accomplishes this, it is important that an evaluation agenda be developed early in the design process and used as the core of the MIS. This allows the organization and its partners (i.e., funding sources, local partner institutions, etc.) to discuss and refine the agenda so that it addresses the information needs of each. This point is more fully discussed in the section on strategies of MIS design and development. We first offer a brief overview of Individual Development Accounts (IDAs) and of the MIS created for use by organizations sponsoring IDA programs.

DESCRIPTION OF AN INDIVIDUAL DEVELOPMENT ACCOUNT PROGRAM

IDAs are matched savings accounts for low-income persons and are restricted for specific asset purchases such as purchase of a home, post-secondary education, or business start-up (Sherraden, 1991). IDA participants receive a passbook savings account at a local financial institution and are required to attend financial education courses offered by the program. Deposits are matched up to a maximum savings goal by private and/or public funding sources.

The Management Information System for Individual Development Accounts (MIS IDA) is a Microsoft Access™ database application with links to Microsoft Word™ and Excel™ (Johnson, Hinterlong, Sherraden, Clancy, & O'Brien, 2000). The database may be run on a single workstation or in a local area network environment. MIS IDA keeps track of both programmatic and participant information. Program information includes: program design structure, funding partner contributions, and program costs. Participant information includes demographics, asset and income, account deposit/withdrawal behavior, asset purchases, and economic literacy class attendance. MIS IDA features over 30 reports that can be customized by sorting and filtering on various fields. Database administration functions are available through a readily-accessible menu system so that users do not need knowledge of Microsoft Access™ prior to using the application.

MIS IDA was designed to support both single and multi-site administration. As such, practitioners can collect and report on data for one or more IDA program sites in a single database. IDA programs involved in evaluations send a copy of their data (via an Excel™ file) to the research team who also aggregate the data into one database, and later export it to statistical analysis software for further analysis.

STRATEGIES OF MIS DESIGN AND DEVELOPMENT

The initial impetus for creating MIS IDA was the need to obtain timely, reliable, clean data to evaluate a national policy demonstration (Sherraden, Page-Adams, & Johnson, 1999). Once the decision was made to release the application to the broader IDA field, CSD facilitated a collaborative process that focused on creating a tool that would facilitate the operation of IDA programs and their evaluation (Premkumar & King, 1994). The timing of this process allowed the MIS application to evolve along with and help guide the growth of the IDA field.

CSD followed an MIS development life-cycle to create MIS IDA, which included needs assessment, design, development, operation, and evaluation (Gore & Stubbe, 1981). However, we highlight three strategies within these processes that may distinguish this effort from other MIS implementations.

Collaborative Development Process

Efficient and effective MIS development requires the involvement of those who understand MIS design, those who understand the technology involved in coding such applications, and those who understand the program or service area. A team of social work researchers familiar with both MIS technology and human service delivery led MIS IDA's development effort. And the collaborative process extended beyond one agency to include human service practitioners from multiple types of organizations (e.g., housing service agency, community development agency, state agency) as well as non-traditional partners such as financial institutions.

CSD facilitated a collaborative process throughout the MIS life-cycle. Prior to beginning the development of MIS IDA, researchers from CSD and an advisory research group posed questions about the impact of IDA program and participant characteristics on saving behavior.[1] This research agenda was then used to create a monitoring instrument that would collect the data needed to answer these questions. CSD's initial intent was to migrate the monitoring instrument from paper forms to a Microsoft Access™ database application for use by IDA program administrators in the field. The goal was simply to create an electronic version of the evaluation instrument. However, as the instrument was being refined and discussed with field practitioners, CSD was asked to expand the functionality of the application to assist with program and account management.

Practitioner insight was critical to the design process and helped to expand the scope of MIS IDA's capabilities. Recognizing that other organizational partners of an IDA program community would also have information management and reporting requirements, the design process was expanded to include: representatives from funding sources and financial institutions, policymakers, and other program practitioners. This ensured that the final MIS IDA product would effectively serve all constituents of an IDA program (Wood & Gray, 1991; Landsberger, Coursey, & Loveless, 1997).

Human service organizations commonly form partnerships with other community institutions. In the case of IDA programs, these partners include financial, consumer credit, and housing organizations. Therefore, the collaborative approach to designing MIS IDA solicited input from these stakeholders. To illustrate, MIS IDA can be used to facilitate the transfer of information between financial institutions that hold the IDA accounts and the IDA program. Periodic transfers of account data may also build stronger institutional linkages between the financial institution and the program. In this example, close collaboration enabled practitioners and researchers to jointly decide what information would be important to collect, and what information could be easily obtained from a financial institution. The account information then had to be standardized to facilitate electronic file transfers from financial institutions to MIS IDA. At the time of development, few financial institutions provided real-time access; practitioners requested such connectivity for later versions.

Collaboration should occur, not only in the design phase, but also through development and implementation (Hartwick & Barki, 1994). Field practitioners continued to make suggestions via e-mail and phone calls regarding data to be collected and reports that would be required in the field. The software was refined accordingly.[2] Field practitioners also performed beta testing of the application prior to its release, giving them a critical role in the actual development of the system. Pre-adoption involvement of users in the design and development process fostered positive perceptions of the software's potential (Karahanna, Straub, & Chervany, 1999). An important consequence of this was the later reduction in the amount of time to train practitioners on the use of the software. Moreover, their involvement reduced the incidence of "technology shock," which can occur when new technologies are suddenly introduced into the practice setting.[3]

Practice guidelines and evidence-based practice guided MIS design. The evolution and use of these guidelines can be traced through the versions of MIS IDA. Version 1, released in 1997, was a beta product provided to the 13 ADD sites, which focused on obtaining research data to answer theoretical questions regarding the implementation and impact of IDAs on participants rather than on supporting program administration and account management. CSD released Version 2 the following year as a commercial-grade product. Version 2 was developed with the assistance of Microsoft-certified programmers. It was a system designed to support the daily tasks of practitioners as well as the collection of data necessary for research. In this release, greater attention was paid to "best-practice standards," as they were called at the time. As IDA programs became more prevalent, CSD received many more requests for functionality revisions and for updated best-practice standards. The release of Version 3 in late 1999 included updated account structure standards as well as data collection fields to track information specific to certain client sub-populations, such as individuals with disabilities. The late addition of these questions did introduce some gaps in baseline information for previously enrolled clients; however, the resultant data set is invaluable, since it is to our knowledge the most comprehensive, longitudinal data available on the saving behavior of low-income individuals.

CSD continues to compile feedback on MIS IDA's usability for consideration in future versions. In designing a system to support evaluation research, there is a tension between the data collection requirements of the researcher versus those of the practitioner. Although the research team favored including more data fields and more extensive field and record edit criteria (to prevent changes to previously collected and analyzed data), practitioners felt this would make MIS IDA's use cumbersome. Even so, practitioner feedback has indicated that, while there is preference for less required data collection in MIS IDA, there is also a desire for more extensive error-checking on certain fields. In addition, heightened use of the World Wide Web has led practitioners to request the next generation of the software to be web-based. As noted above, such feedback is critical to field usage, and highlights the importance of updating software applications with the latest technology.

Collaboration during the design and development process was integral in creating a more robust MIS with integrated capabilities. The guiding vision was that a data collection instrument must be capable of providing information relevant to all program stakeholders: program administrators, counselors, researchers, funders, and policymakers, as well as program participants.

Integrated Practice Components

In human service organizations, data management activities are often logically divided among applications for participant (client) services, administration, and evaluation. However, a properly designed MIS can integrate the information requirements of all three areas within one system. To this end, an integrated system must gather data in a manner consistent with daily program operations and casework protocols, and make that data available in a variety of formats. One way in which MIS IDA accomplishes this task is by merging information about program design and costs with participant characteristics and account activity. This enables the IDA program to provide timely, accurate reports to each stakeholder, which enhances the program's accountability (Austin et al., 1982; Freel & Epstein, 1993). Below is a description of each of the main components in MIS IDA, categorized by the three practice areas noted above, illustrating how data can be integrated into one system for use by all constituents.

Client Services

Client services in an IDA program, at a minimum, include assisting the participant in opening a matched savings account at a partnering financial institution, providing economic education, and assisting in purchasing the desired asset. Program workers use MIS IDA to enroll participants, collecting demographic and contact information as well as current levels of income, assets, and liabilities. This information is updated semi-annually to track changes in demographics, income, and net worth. A case notes function in MIS IDA allows program caseworkers to note the completion of economic education classes and record narrative comments.

Participant account information from the partnering financial institution(s) is entered or electronically transferred into MIS IDA to track account statement activity (monthly or quarterly) and to calculate the matched savings for each participant. An account statement is periodically generated for the participant showing the personal savings plus the accrued match amount. Account tracking allows program workers to monitor participant savings behavior. Clients can then be counseled on how best to maximize the benefits of participating in the IDA program, namely, how to establish and sustain a saving pattern that will lead to the receipt of the highest possible match dollar amount during a particular savings period.[4]

Administration

MIS IDA divides administrative data into three main components: program design characteristics, expenditures, and funding sources. Program design data describe the context within which the participants interact with the caseworkers, administrators, and other program partners. For example, when users first install and run MIS IDA, they are asked to provide information concerning host organization characteristics, rules for the design and use of IDAs, and the types and amounts of economic literacy training provided to participants. These questions reflect factors that may contribute to program success. Semi-annual updates of this information are then recorded to track changes over time, which, in turn, can be used to identify programmatic factors linked to successful implementation and desired participant outcomes.

Program expenditures, such as salaries, staff time, and utilities, are entered periodically to track the costs of running an IDA program. Marketing and participant recruitment techniques are also recorded to track factors of enrollment success. Reports may be generated to show such information for a given time period or aggregated over time.

Funding sources and contribution amounts are recorded, as are the distributions obligated and made to participants when assets are purchased. Thus, MIS IDA serves the information needs of both participants and the administrator by tracking participant account activity, match fund obligations to individual accounts, and use of participant and match savings to purchase assets. By integrating the funding obligations with individual account information, MIS IDA generates reports that are also useful to foundations and other funding partners that track and project utilization of grant dollars by IDA program participants. These reports can be provided on demand to external funders, which enables the IDA program to be highly responsive and accountable to the information needs of its partners (Eggertsson, 1997).

Evaluation

The integrative aspect of MIS IDA's database is that key evaluation questions are blended into forms that record program design and participant information. This means that programs accumulate evaluation data while using the software for day-to-day operations. For example, questions about program structure are included to help researchers answer questions regarding institutional theories of saving. The data collected about participants provide the information to assess saving patterns for particular demographic and program structure characteristics. One of the biggest theoretical questions is whether the poor can save. Data collected on participant characteristics such as income, assets, and liabilities compared to data about account activity assist in answering such questions. Additionally, certain programmatic and participant information, such as changes in program match rate and changes in participant demographics, are updated periodically to produce longitudinal measurements.

Two levels of reporting are generated from MIS IDA. First is the custom report generation capability within the structure of MIS IDA that allows program workers to run reports at any time for all of the data that have been collected. For example, a program administrator can run reports to view the demographics of the client base, or calculate IDA program costs for a particular time period. In addition, funding sources often request reports showing how the match dollars are being used and amount of match dollars accrued by participants. Program administrators use date-stamped information collected and stored in MIS IDA within the application's dynamic reporting system to generate both current and historical reports (Appendix A). The reporting system of MIS IDA places this information at the fingertips of program administrators and frontline workers. As noted previously, an important feature of MIS IDA is that the various stakeholders in an IDA program benefit from this information as well. The application contains numerous reports that were designed to meet the different information needs of funders, policymakers, program administrators, counselors, and participants. Reports generated by the system enable IDA program administrators to be accountable to external partner organizations and to feed information on demand to internal decision-makers (Austin, 1982; Freel & Epstein, 1993).

The second level of reporting is use of the dataset from MIS IDA's database that can be transferred to statistical analysis software for more extensive analyses that relate program characteristics, participant characteristics, and savings performance. By combining information about the program with that of participants and savings activity, MIS IDA's reporting system can answer the key evaluative questions regarding the interactions between program implementation, participant characteristics, and IDA account structure.

One major challenge in creating an MIS is providing for its usability across program settings. To this end, two design features are employed. First, data are collected by MIS IDA in a standardized format using lists of values where possible, i.e., categories for race and ethnicity. However, users may customize the values for some fields within the participant information section of the system, which provides greater flexibility in reporting on subsets of participants without sacrificing standardization.

Second, a set of best practice guidelines is integrated into the functional structure of MIS IDA (Hinterlong, Johnson, & Sherraden, 1999). In early discussions among researchers, practitioners, funders, and policymakers, decisions were made regarding what was considered to be best practice for IDA implementation. These guidelines are primarily concerned with IDA program design and account structure. Program design questions and possible responses assist the program administrator in determining how to set up the IDA program structure. For example, questions on number of hours and type of financial education prompt the administrator to consider the design of the financial curriculum. In discussions about account structure, practitioners running the early IDA programs were employing different methods in tracking deposits and matches. It was clear that saving outcomes could not be analyzed and program lessons could not be learned if accounting methods were not standardized. The design team developed a flexible structure that provided a standard accounting structure with options from which administrators could choose for various types of program implementation. As IDA programs have evolved, modifications to the best practice guidelines have been incorporated into subsequent versions of MIS IDA. For example, additional methods in account calculations have been added to support variations in IDA account structure.

Program administrators have the freedom to customize the software to suit their programmatic designs without facing constraints on how their programs are organized or operated. Yet, by using MIS IDA to establish general account structure and management guidelines, the IDA concept is implemented similarly across sites. These embedded standards and research focus offer the ability for MIS IDA to be used in a variety of program settings with positive implications for the growth of the field and evaluation. As IDA programs have grown into larger statewide networks, it is important to collect comparable data across sites. MIS IDA's design provides the ability to aggregate data across different sites for more extensive data analyses. Thus far, MIS IDA has been used to create reports based on data from IDA programs in 13 different organizations (for example, see Sherraden et al., 2000).

Proactive Development and Distribution

In addition to collaborative design and integrated practice functions, MIS IDA's widespread use has been in large part due to the timing of its development and release to the field (Nurius, Berger, and VanDerWeele, 1988). In 1997, federal, state, and local governments, in collaboration with community-based organizations, were just beginning to implement IDA programs, but lacked systems that could assist in evaluation and program management. Thus, development of MIS IDA interacted with program and policy development in the field. By incorporating "best practice" guidelines for IDA program design into MIS IDA, and making the software available at an early stage, the IDA field grew at a faster pace. Indeed, we believe that MIS IDA, in use in over three-quarters of all IDA programs in the United States, has played a significant role in advancing this emerging practice and policy innovation.

MIS development, and especially evaluation tools, often trails program design and implementation. In this case however, theoretical propositions regarding the factors likely to influence participant saving behavior and asset accumulation were articulated well in advance of program implementation. Likewise, the potential effects of saving through an IDA on the individual, her family and community were also proposed prior to program development (Sherraden, 1991). As mentioned above, these theoretical perspectives provided the impetus and design for the core functions of MIS IDA, in part in their articulation through the best practice guidelines.

Developing a system in advance of or early in the process of program implementation has several advantages. It improves data integrity, reduces program costs, and enhances the extent to which data can be evaluated. Systems that are thoughtfully designed upfront can reduce data redundancy and long-term system maintenance by planning for the information needs of each component in a program. Moreover, developing a single MIS application enables integration of data collection, management, and reporting functions. The more typical pattern is that new systems are added on to existing systems or simply stand alone, requiring additional resources to develop and maintain. Developing one system to serve the needs of administration, service delivery, and evaluation reduces program costs. And the earlier a system is developed, the sooner program workers are able to use it, facilitating program implementation and growth. Finally, baseline information is much more likely to be collected and to be accurate if the data collection system is ready at the start of the program.

CHALLENGES IN THE DEVELOPMENT OF MIS IDA

A collaborative process requires balancing competing requirements. CSD's open and inclusive approach was satisfactory until resources limited the amount of changes that could be made. A level of expectation had been set that was difficult to alter, especially as IDA programs expanded to populations not previously served. Requests for revisions exceeded the resources available to make such changes. In addition, some IDA practitioners wanted to modify MIS IDA for their particular IDA program rules that did not agree with the established best-practice standards on which MIS IDA was built. The flexibility of MIS IDA's design allowed practitioners to modify how the system was intended to be used. For example, practitioners who did not agree with the established practice of "matching the interest" on participant deposits simply did not record in MIS IDA the interest shown on the financial account statement. In another example, limited error-checking allowed practitioners to bypass some client asset and liability questions that the practitioner felt unnecessary to collect. These modifications compromised the use of the data for evaluation, but satisfied MIS IDA's use for the practitioner.

In using an evaluation tool, it is important to consider client confidentiality and to obtain informed consent. CSD developed a statement of release that was approved by Washington University's Institutional Review Board for organizations to use in the IDA policy demonstration. A more generic version of this document was included as an appendix in the operations manual accompanying the software (Johnson, Hinterlong, & Sherraden, 1998). However, we cannot be sure that it is used in all cases by other evaluators.

The level of financial resources that went toward MIS IDA's development was higher than anticipated. Part of the reason for this cost was that few had ever implemented an IDA program. Therefore, the MIS design continued to change as best practice guidelines were discussed, revised, and revised again. For practices that are well-established, this iterative process in MIS development may be less time-consuming. However, an important lesson in evidence-based practice is to budget resources for future maintenance and upgrades as technology changes and practitioners discover new information.

CONCLUSION

The example of MIS IDA may be useful for several reasons. First, MIS design and development was conceived and led by social work researchers then expanded to include stakeholders of IDA programs. While it is advantageous to have social workers who understand computer technology, it is important to stress that technology is not a substitute for social work skills. MIS IDA's design process was heavily dependent upon community development techniques and an understanding of the role of the caseworker in assisting program participants. In addition, the availability of MIS IDA has created a stronger link between practice and research, with innovations in each area influencing the other. MIS IDA's commercial adoption by organizations beyond the ADD is due to its ability to integrate the information management needs of IDA programs into a single system. Collaboration led to the creation of practice guidelines and an evaluation agenda, which in turn was used to drive the structure and function of MIS IDA.

Second, collection, management, and retrieval of information are critical tasks within any practice setting. When information processes are incorporated within a single MIS application that supports all areas of work, including administration, service delivery, and program evaluation, a practice system can emerge. MIS IDA is also an example of how a fully integrated system can be duplicated across a network of users. MIS IDA provides guidelines for program design, administration, and service delivery that are flexible yet offer some degree of standardization, which will allow for the application to function across settings and still provide quality aggregate data for evaluation. These "best practice guidelines" can be developed out of findings from previous evaluations and/or can be more theoretical in nature. By using best practice guidelines as the parameters for various functions within the MIS, it is possible to distribute them widely to the field. Where best practice guidelines do not exist, findings from previous evaluations may be useful in developing draft guidelines that can be reviewed by practitioners and other stakeholders and incorporated into existing systems.

Finally, to our knowledge this is the first time an MIS was developed and released proactively to evaluate a large-scale policy demonstration. The information collected through MIS IDA is currently aggregated to generate reports useful to policymakers (e.g., Sherraden et al., 2000). Non-profit community organizations use such reports to develop stronger links to state and national policymakers and to attract more and larger funding resources.

MIS IDA is currently in use at most of the approximately 250 IDA programs operating throughout the United States and in use by at least 14 state-supported IDA programs. Reports from MIS IDA data have played a role in influencing many of the 29 states that have passed IDA legislation. In fact, several states have modeled their statewide program designs based on MIS IDA's embedded "best practice" design guidelines and many specify the use of MIS IDA to meet their program evaluation requirements (e.g., Task Force on Individual Development Accounts, 2000).

The impact of MIS IDA has reached beyond state initiatives. Federal IDA legislation was enacted through the Assets for Independence Act of 1998, calling for a five year IDA demonstration with $125 million in funding (U.S. Congress, 1998). MIS IDA (or comparable software) was included in the regulations as a requirement for programs seeking to participate in this demonstration. Most significantly, MIS IDA data influenced President Clinton's (2000) expanded proposal for matched savings.[5]

The example of MIS IDA highlights the potential for social workers to merge social work practice and public policy innovation through technology. The strategies offered can also be used to improve the conceptualization, development, and distribution of other technology innovations within social work.

NOTES

1. The Evaluation Advisory Committee assists in the evaluation design of the American Dream Policy Demonstration, and is comprised of: Drs. Margaret Clark (Aspen Institute), Claudia Coulton (Case Western University), Kathryn Edin (University of Pennsylvania), John Else (Institute for Social and Economic Development), Irving Garfinkel (Columbia University), Karen Holden (LaFollette Institute of Public Affairs), Laurence Kotlikoff (Boston University), Robert Plotnick (University of Washington), Salome Raheim (University of Iowa), Marguerite Robinson (Harvard University), Clemente Ruiz Duran (National University of Mexico), Thomas Shapiro (Northeastern University), Michael Sherraden (Washington University), and Mr. Robert Friedman (Corporation for Enterprise Development).

2. MIS IDA Version 2 was developed by Lissa Johnson, Jim Hinterlong, and Michael Sherraden of CSD, and Ross Baker and Mark Kombrink of System Service Enterprises, Inc. Modifications to Version 3 were completed by staff at CSD: Patrick O'Brien, Lissa Johnson, and Margaret Clancy.

3. Following the application's commercial release to the broader field, CSD addressed this problem by instituting a training service to assist users for whom MIS IDA is new or who desire additional preparation. Technical support is also available.

4. IDA programs generally cap the amount of match dollars available to any one account. Thus, participants obtain the maximum benefit by making deposits up to but not exceeding a clearly defined limit.

5. At the request of the White House and Treasury Department during Fall 1999, CSD provided MIS IDA data to the Clinton Administration. The findings from the first two years of the American Dream Demonstration, published in a report by Sherraden and colleagues (2000), showed that low-income IDA participants saved an average of $33 per month, and the very poorest saved a higher proportion of their income than other participants. Subsequently, Clinton said in his State of the Union Address (2000):

Tens of millions of Americans live from paycheck to paycheck. As hard as they work, they still don't have the opportunity to save. Too few can make use of IRAs and 401(k) plans. We should do more to help all working families save and accumulate wealth. That's the idea behind the Individual Development Accounts, the IDAs. I ask you to take that idea to a new level, with new retirement savings accounts that enable every low- and moderate-income family in America to save for retirement, a first home, a medical emergency, or a college education. I propose to match their contributions, however small, dollar for dollar, every year they save.

Thus, data on IDAs from MIS IDA directly contributed to a major proposal on progressive savings policy. Connections between IDA research and policy are described in Sherraden et al. (2000).

REFERENCES

Austin, Michael J. (1982). *Evaluating your agency's programs*. Beverly Hills, CA: Sage Human Services.

Clinton, W. (2000). *State of the Union Address*. Washington: U.S. Government Printing Office.

Eggertsson, T. (1997). The old theory of economic policy and the new institutionalism. *World Development, 25(8), 1187*-1203.

Freel, C., & Epstein, I. (1993). Principles for using management information data for programmatic decision making. *Child & Youth Services*, 16(1), 77-93.

Goodhue, D. L., Wybo, M. D., & Kirsch, L. J. (1992). The impact of data integration on the costs and benefits of information-systems. *MIS Quarterly, 16(3)*, 293-311.

Gore, M., & Stubbe, J. (1981). *Elements of systems analysis for business data processing. Dubuque, Iowa: Wm. C. Brown Company Publishers.*

Hartwick, J., & Barki, H. (1994). Explaining the role of user participation in information-system use. Management Science, 40(4), 440-465.

Hinterlong, J., Johnson, E., & Sherraden, M. (1999). Strengthening policy and practice innovations with management information system technology. Paper presented at 45th Annual Program Meeting, Council on Social Work Education, San Francisco, CA, March 1999.

Johnson, E., Hinterlong, J., Sherraden, M., Clancy, M., O'Brien, P. (2000). MIS IDA: Management Information System for Individual Development Accounts, (Version 3.05) [Computer software]. St. Louis: Center for Social Development, Washington University.

Johnson, E., Hinterlong, J., & Sherraden, M. (1998). *Operations Manual: Management Information System for Individual Development Accounts*, Version 2.0. St. Louis, MO: Center for Social Development at Washington University.

Karahanna, E., Straub, D. W., & Chervany, N. L. (1994). Information technology adoption across time: A cross-sectional comparison of pre-adoption and post-adoption beliefs. *MIS Quarterly*, 23(2), 183-213.

Landsberger, D., Coursey, D.H., & Loveless, S. (1997). Decision quality, confidence, and commitment with expert systems: An experimental study. *Journal of Public Administration Research and Theory*, 7(Jan.), 131-157.

Mutschler, E. (1990). Computerized information systems for social workers in health care. *Health and Social Work, 15,* 191-196.

Nurius, P.S., Berger, C., VanDerWeele, T. (1988). ASSIST: An alternative management information system for social services in health care. *Social Work in Health Care*, 13(4), 99-113.

Premkumar, G., & King, W. R. (1994). Organizational characteristics and information-system planning: An empirical study. *Information Systems Research*, 5(2), 75-109.

Rupp, K., Driessen, D., & Kornfeld, R. (1999). The development of the project network administration database for policy evaluation. *Social Security Bulletin, 62(2)* 30-42.

Sherraden, M. W. (1991). *Assets and the poor: A new American welfare policy.* Armonk, NY: M. E. Sharpe, Inc.

Sherraden, M., Johnson L., Clancy M., Beverly, S., Schreiner, M., Zhan, M., Curley, J. (2000). *Saving patterns in IDA programs.* St. Louis: Center for Social Development, Washington University.

Sherraden, M. (2000). *From research to policy: Lessons for individual development accounts.* Colston Warner Lecture, American Council on Consumer Interests, San Antonio, March 23.

Sherraden, M., Page-Adams, D., & Johnson, L. (1999). *Downpayments on the American Dream Policy Demonstration: A National Demonstration of Individual Development Accounts, Start-Up Evaluation Report.* St. Louis, MO: Center for Social Development at Washington University.

Task Force on Individual Development Accounts (2000). *Report and Recommendations.* Hartford: Treasurer's Office, State of Connecticut.

U.S. Congress (1998). *Assets for Independence Act.* Washington: U.S. Government Printing Office.

APPENDIX A. Sample MIS IDA Report Distribution

MIS IDA Reports	Distribution to Stakeholders						
	Program Administrators	Participants	Funding Partners	Financial Institutions	Vendors	Researchers	Policy makers
Participant account statement	X	X					
Cumulative account activity	X		X	X		X	X
Account history	X	X		X		X	
Matched withdrawals	X	X	X	X	X	X	X
Participant demographics	X	X	X	X		X	X
Program design characteristics	X		X			X	X
Funder obligation dollars	X		X				
Program expenses	X					X	
Account discrepancies	X					X	
Monthly deposit patterns	X	X				X	
Closed accounts	X			X		X	
Case Notes	X	X					
Mailing labels	X						

The Deployment of Information Technology in an International Rural Health Care Project

David A. Patterson

SUMMARY. This paper presents a case study of the utilization of Information Technology (IT) in a cataract surgery eye camp held outside a remote village in India. Detailed here are the organizational and technological context of the project, the steps taken in the development and deployment of a patient medical database, the data collection procedures employed during the eye camp, and the resultant information products of these endeavors. Discussed are the implications for the application of IT in the documentation and evaluation of time-limited health and social service delivery projects. *[Article copies available for a fee from The Haworth Document Delivery Service: 1-800-342-9678. E-mail address: <getinfo@haworthpressinc.com> Website: <http://www.HaworthPress.com> © 2001 by The Haworth Press, Inc. All rights reserved.]*

KEYWORDS. International health care, database development, cataract surgery eye camp

---

David A. Patterson, PhD, is Associate Professor in the College of Social Work at The University of Tennessee, Knoxville, TN 37996-3333 (E-mail: dpatter2@utk.edu).

The author wishes to acknowledge and thank the College of Social Work at The University of Tennessee for providing the release time that made his participation in the project possible, each of the volunteers who served on the Clinical Statistics team during Netraprakash 99 and without whose tireless efforts this paper would not have been possible, the staff of PRASAD, and the great beings who founded and sustain the PRASAD Project in its efforts to ease suffering and uplift humanity.

[Haworth co-indexing entry note]: "The Deployment of Information Technology in an International Rural Health Care Project." Patterson, David A. Co-published simultaneously in *Journal of Technology in Human Services* (The Haworth Press, Inc.) Vol. 18, No. 3/4, 2001, pp. 23-40; and: *New Advances in Technology for Social Work Education and Practice* (ed: Julie Miller-Cribbs) The Haworth Press, Inc., 2001, pp. 23-40. Single or multiple copies of this article are available for a fee from The Haworth Document Delivery Service [1-800-342-9678, 9:00 a.m. - 5:00 p.m. (EST). E-mail address: getinfo@haworthpressinc.com].

23

The social work profession has a long history of involvement in international health and social service projects in the developing world (Cagan & Julia, 1998; Chandler, 1995; Mba, 1985). Similarly, there is a growing history of the profession's use of computers and Information Technology (IT) to document, support, and facilitate social service delivery (Collins, Epstein, Barbarin, & Savas, 1996; Patterson & Cloud, 1999; Shank, Roesch, Murphy-Breman, Wright, 1996). There is, however, in the social work literature, and more broadly in the medical and healthcare literature, a striking absence of reports of the application of IT in international health and social service projects. Moreover, descriptions of the use of information systems for the collection and analysis of information from time-limited, rural healthcare projects were absent from the medical, healthcare, social work, and social science literature databases reviewed.

Despite the inattention to the problem of how to reliably collect medical, demographic, and social information in short-term social service and healthcare delivery settings, the challenge of this endeavor is to provide both accurate and timely information that supports the delivery services and the subsequent evaluation of the outcomes of such undertakings. Examples of time-limited health and social service delivery projects include disaster relief operations, specialized medical care delivery such as cataract surgery or orthopedic surgery in developing nations, health education projects, and school crisis intervention. In each of these examples, the collection, analysis, and reporting of service delivery and associated outcomes would be facilitated by health information systems adapted to the specific information needs of the project. Time-limited health and social service delivery projects have historically relied on paper-based data collection methods and have suffered from limited or nonexistent evaluation of services provided (Lwanga, 2000; WHO, 2000).

One medical problem in developing countries around the globe with significant social implications addressed by time-limited healthcare interventions is cataract blindness (Angra, Murthy, Gupta, & Angra, 1997; Ruit, Tabin, Nissman, Paudyal, & Gurang, 1999). Worldwide, cataracts are the leading cause of blindness, with a majority of cases concentrated in the developing world. It is estimated that cataract blindness afflicts 16 million people, leaving them unable to count fingers at a distance of three meters (approximately 10 feet). This is a visual acuity of less than 20/400. This level of visual impairment impacts the blind individual in the psychosocial domains of self-care, mobility, social functioning, and emotional well-being (Fletcher, Ellwein, Selvaraj, Vijaykumar,

Rahmathullah, & Thulasiraj, 1997). The effects of blindness are not limited to the afflicted individual, but extend to their families, communities and nations. Angra et al. (1997) have pointed out that in the developing world the cataract blind commonly live with family members. Their blindness and consequential inability to contribute their labor to the household poses a dual burden on the family providing care for the blind family member, due to the loss of productivity of the blind family member, and the partial or complete loss of productivity of the family member primarily responsible for care provision. This diminished productivity of the family impacts not only their own economic well-being, but has social and economic consequences for the community as well. The lack of mobility of blind individuals often removes them from the social fabric of the community. Their blindness also subjects them and their families to taunts and ridicule in rural communities where the etiology of cataract blindness is not understood. The economic impact of blindness on communities and nations is a function of the lost productivity of the blind individual and the costs associated with their care. In India, it has been estimated that the 12 million blind cost the country $28 billion a year in lost productivity and care costs (Angra et al., 1997). From this analysis it is apparent that while cataract blindness can be viewed solely as a medical condition, a more comprehensive perspective is to understand it as a condition with broad psychosocial, familial, and economic implications. Consequently, the positive effects of the treatment of cataract blindness have implications beyond the restoration of sight to blind individuals; they extend to families, communities, and nations.

Modern cataract surgery typically entails the removal of the clouded or opaque lens of the eye and the insertion of an intraocular lens to restore vision (American Academy of Ophthalmology, 2000). In the developing world, medical resources for the delivery of intraocular lens surgery are typically either unavailable or economically unaffordable to most individuals in need of care (Angra et al., 1997). One response to the growing number of people in the developing world blinded by cataracts has been the use of eye camps to delivery intraocular lens surgery. Eye camps were pioneered in India in the mid-1970's in a national effort to combat blindness (Limburg, Kumar, & Bachani, 1996). Eye camps provide time-limited, eye care services to underserved and/or economically disadvantaged populations, often in geographically remote regions. Eye camps may be operated by government agencies providing free care or by non-governmental organizations that provide care on a free or subsidized basis. There are some eye camps operated by commercial enterprises offering eye care on a for-fee basis. The recommended minimal duration of eyes camps is seven days with follow-up examination one to two months post surgery (Nagpal, 2000).

The purpose of this paper is to present a case study of the application of IT in a geographically remote Indian cataract surgery eye camp. This paper describes the development and management of an electronic medical database in this rural Indian eye camp. Detailed here are the organizational and technological context of the project, the steps taken in the database's development, the organization of data collection procedures during the eye camp, and the resultant information products of these endeavors. The author served as the Director of Clinical Statistics for the eye camp and coordinated the activities of an international team of volunteers responsible for the collection, management, analysis, and reporting of medical data from the camp. One goal of this case study is to present the technological and organizational challenges encountered in this undertaking and the solutions developed over the course of this time-limited, healthcare project. A second goal is to convey how the lessons learned at this healthcare setting are applicable to the use of information technology in social work practice settings.

ORGANIZATIONAL AND TECHNOLOGICAL CONTEXT

For ten days in March 1999, the fifth Netraprakash (meaning light of the eye) eye camp was held near Ganeshpuri, India, providing free-of-charge cataract surgery to 1190 people of the Tansa Valley. The Tansa Valley is a largely rural area of the Maharashtra State of India, located about 50 miles north of Mumbai (Bombay). The prior Netraprakash eye camps are described elsewhere (Civerchia, Apoorvananda, Natchiar, Balent, Ramakrishnan, & Green, 1993; Civerchia, Ravindran, Apoorvananda, Ramakrishnan, Balent, Spencer, & Green, 1996).

The Netraprakash 99 (NP 99) eye camp was held in a temporary field hospital established for the provision of vision screening and cataract surgery for a time-limited period. The PRASAD Project, an international, not-for-profit, philanthropic organization, sponsored this eye camp. More than 700 volunteers from 22 countries participated in NP 99. The camp was held in a large agricultural research center. Six very large tents erected in former rice paddies served as the field hospital wards and a former tractor showroom was transformed into a surgical theater with twelve operating tables. Onsite food service facilities served over 20,000 meals during the course of the camp. Safe water, sanitation facilities, and electrical generation were all provided onsite as a function of the eye camp's operation.

Preparation and planning for NP 99 began more than a year in advance of the camp's opening. Work on the initial development of the patient database and planning for data collection for the eye camp began in July of 1998. Documentation and statistical reports from previous Netraprakash eye camps were reviewed to determine what outcomes were important for organizational and governmental reporting purposes. The results of Netraprakash eye camps in 1993 and 1996 were described in ophthalmology journals (Civerchia et al., 1993; Civerchia, 1996). As a result, surgeons were asked to comment on the types of data they wished to ensure were collected. Programmers and other volunteers who had worked on databases used for the 1993 and 1996 eye camps were interviewed about both the development of the previous databases and the problems encountered in the process of data collection, storage, and analysis during the camps. A copy of the Netraprakash 1996 patient database was obtained and reviewed. It was written in Microsoft Access 1995 and had a primary data entry form that displayed basic admissions data including name and demographic data. On this form were labeled buttons that when clicked displayed subforms for the entry of information regarding pre-operative status, surgical procedures and outcome, discharge evaluation, and follow-up camp examination results. It was initially planned that the Netraprakash 1996 patient database would be updated for use at NP 99. As described below, an entirely new database was subsequently developed immediately prior to the 1999 eye camp.

The larger planning for NP 99 and the data collection preparation was an endeavor requiring communications between PRASAD staff and volunteers around the globe. The PRASAD Project headquarters is in Hurleyville, New York and the office of the Indian arm of PRASAD, Prasad Chitkitsa, is in Ganeshpuri, India. Much of the communication between staff and volunteers in these two locations and other volunteers was via e-mail. This process was partially confounded by both the slow speed of Internet access in Ganeshpuri at that time and its occasional disruption due to monsoon flooding and line breakage. Consequently, Prasad staffers in Ganeshpuri occasionally had to make a four-hour round trip to Bombay in order to send and receive e-mail related to the camp preparations.

PRASAD provided an IT infrastructure to support the data collection and analysis for the camp. The basic IT infrastructure consisted of a Novell Network running on a 200 megahertz dedicated network server with a system for backup data storage and seven ports available for other computers. The network server was housed in air-conditioned room (a rarity in this area of India) with four networked computers and an additional available port. The other two network ports were in an adjacent room. There was a backup power supply for the network to guard against crashes and data loss during frequent power outages. All the computers ran Windows 95 and had at least 32 megs of RAM. Only one of the networked machines was faster than 200 megahertz. Each machine had a licensed copy of Microsoft Office Professional that includes Microsoft Access.

These computing resources were shared with other departments involved in the eye camp's operations. Volunteer Coordination had its own Microsoft Access database for managing information of the 700 volunteers. Graphics and Promotions were responsible for production and printing all the signs for the camp. Nursing staff needed computing resources to generate rosters, forms, and memorandums for distribution. The office staff of Prasad Chitkitsa required computer time for their normal office functions. Consequently, there was the need for considerable coordination and cooperation in sharing the limited available information technology resources.

One of the planning problems for the eye camp's data collection was the fact that the camp would be held at a location approximately 1.2 miles from the Prasad Chitkitsa compound where the computer network was housed. Early in the planning process, it was recommended that all data collection take place onsite at the eye camp with direct data entry into computers located at key data collection points such as the admissions tent, pre-operative evaluations, outside the surgical theater, and in the discharge tent. The intention behind direct data entry was to attempt to minimize data entry errors associated with first recording data on paper and then entering it into the database. About three weeks before the opening of the camp, it was decided that data entry at the camp was not feasible due to the database being housed on the server, the dust and heat expected at the camp, and the inability to create a network to link computers geographically distributed around the camp. As will be described below, a middle ground solution for electronic data entry was developed over the course of the camp.

In the pre-camp planning process a number of information management challenges were identified that would have to be addressed across the pre-camp, operational, and post-camp phases. These health service data management challenges included, (a) development and deployment of a fully functional networked database within a time-constrained interval, (b) training and coordination of an international team of volunteers with highly varied IT skills, (c) data entry of information collected prior to the development of the database, (d) the ongoing operation of a computer network for data entry that was geographically separate from the eye camp, (e) daily capture of data from multiple sites within the eye camp, (f) specification, development, and production of necessary daily medical and camp operational reports, (g) ad-hoc report production, (h) follow-up camp data collection, and (i) statistical analysis of clinical outcomes. The ways in which these challenges were met are detailed in the discussion that follows.

DATABASE DEVELOPMENT

A Microsoft Access programmer and a PhD-level chemist with extensive information management experience developed the NP 99 patient database over a two-week period, approximately two weeks before the opening of the eye camp. The tight timeframe was due to the brief window of time the programmer was available to be in India and work on the project. A second reason was that the NP 99 patient database is carefully linked to information captured on the forms created for the patient medical record. The development of these forms was completed during this same time period and only then became available to the database designers.

After reviewing the Netraprakash 1996 patient database, the programmer concluded it would be easier and less time consuming to create a new database than to modify the existing one. The NP 99 Patient Database is composed of four basic elements: (1) data tables, (2) forms, (3) queries, and (4) reports. All the data contained in the database are held in the data tables. There are a total of fourteen data tables in the NP 99 database. Each data table contains data fields reflecting categories of information collected in medical record form used over the course of the eye camp's operation. The data sources on the right side of Figure 1 represent the key stages/functions of the camp's operation from which data were collected.

Data input from the medical record and searches for individual patient data occur in the forms section of the database. The NP 99 database was designed so that all the data for a patient are available on a single screen. This was accomplished by using subforms with tabs that create the appearance of stacked note cards. Each subform's tab identifies the form's contents that are revealed when the tab is clicked. The subform tabs correspond to the data sources in Figure 1. Figure 2 displays the Screening Camp subform. Contained in the Screening Camp subform are eight additional subforms representing elements of the Screening Camp medical form. Note also that the subforms are alphabetically labeled and that some letters of the alphabet sequence are absent. The missing letters were on sections of the Screening Camp medical form that contained infrequently used fields and were deemed by medical staff to not be necessary for the patient database.

Three other elements of the data entry form are worth noting. First, in the upper left hand corner the patient's name, case number, and age are always displayed irregardless of which subform is present. This allows

FIGURE 1. Data Sources and Data Products from the Netraprakash 1999 Eye Camp Patient Database.

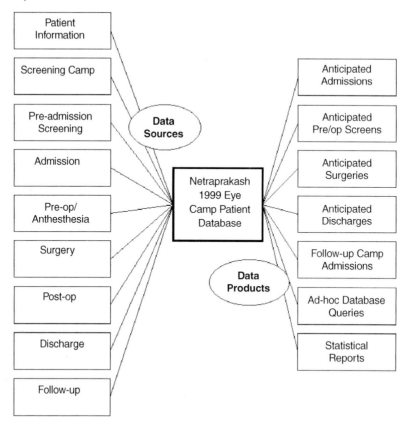

FIGURE 2. NP 99 Patient Database Data Entry Form with Screening Camp Subform Displayed.

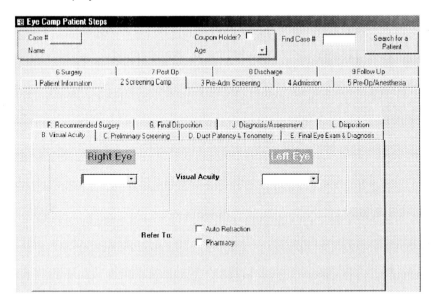

volunteers doing data entry to check the correspondence between the patient identification number on the medical form and in the database. Second, in the upper right hand corner there is the "Find Case #" field that can be used to search for a particular patient. Patient case number was selected, instead of patient name, as the search element in order to reduce errors associated with duplicate names or spelling errors. The third noteworthy feature in Figure 2 are the fields under the labels Right Eye and Left Eye. Though these fields in Figure 2 are blank, clicking on the down arrow of either of these fields in the database produces drop-down list box from which to select the appropriate visual acuity for the patient. This feature eliminates the need to type in the actual text. These drop-down list boxes are used throughout the subforms of the data entry form to speed data entry, reduce data entry error, and insure greater uniformity in the labeling of categories of information within the database.

Queries and reports while present as functional options within any Microsoft Access database were not directly used as operational elements of the NP 99 patient database. Queries are a means to ask questions of the database and retrieve specified information from one or more data tables. Queries are a highly versatile tool for extracting information meeting designated criteria from the database. In order to avoid the possible corruption of data files in the NP 99 patient database and upon the recommendation of the programmer, a second database called New Queries was created. New Queries was created with linkages to all the data tables in the NP 99 database, thus allowing it to interact with the NP 99 patient data without the risk of inadvertently altering the NP 99 patient data. New Queries was used to retrieve information from one or more tables across multiple fields. Each of the data products in Figure 1 was created through queries designed in New Queries.

EYE CAMP DATA COLLECTION AND REPORTING

Clinical Statistics Team

The volunteers assigned to the Clinical Statistics team were a diverse, international group with a wide range of professional backgrounds. Members of the team included a retired PhD chemist from Australia, a New Zealand businessman and actor with considerable hardware and software skills, a Mexican economist, an Indian computer technician and his wife, a Texas environmental engineer, and Indian graduate students working on degrees in computer science and economics. Other Indian volunteers with a range of computer skills also took part in the data entry at various phases of the eye camp. Though a majority of the volunteers had not worked with Access databases prior to the eye camp, most were more than proficient in standard skills required to work in a Windows operating system environment. English was the common language of the team. All team members read English without difficulty and most spoke it with little trouble. Training of the team members was informal with team members working in pairs. Experienced team members trained inexperienced team members in the necessary data entry skills and other associated tasks.

Data Capture Procedures

Once the NP 99 database was ready, data from the screening camp had to be entered prior to the start of the camp. In the first phase of NP 99, 60 Indian volunteer health workers canvassed the Tansa Valley in an outreach program designed to identify potential cataract surgery candidates. Identified candidates were given a "coupon" inviting them to the screening camp that was held in early February. At the screening camp, medical staff assessed the coupon holders and other walk-ins both on medical and ophthalmological grounds for cataract surgery. Those deemed to be surgical candidates were invited to NP 99 and given an arrival date on which they were to come to the camp. Consequently, the first data entry task prior to the opening of the NP 99 eye camp on March 3rd, 1999, was the input of all the data from the Screening Camp forms of over 1200 patients invited to come to NP 99 for cataract surgery. This was necessary in order to both create daily lists of expected admissions for the admitting team and to prepare for the subsequent input of other data on these expected patients. It was anticipated that 200 patients a day would be admitted over the course of the six days the camp was open for admissions. As it turned out, there were 1204 patients admitted to the camp at a rate of approximately 200 per day.

One of the most important questions the Clinical Statistics team had to address prior to the camp's opening was how we would capture data out at the field hospital. The answer to this question was complicated by the fact that once a patient was admitted to the eye camp, they carried their medical record with them throughout the time they were in the camp. When they went for an evaluation or for surgery, they presented their medical record to the medical staff and it was returned to them once the procedure was complete. Thus, the challenge was to capture necessary medical information from the patient's medical record before it was returned to them.

There were four key data collection points identified where critical information would need to be obtained. The first was the admissions tent where patient who had passed medical and surgical screenings were assigned a bed in one of the wards and admitted to the camp. The second was the pre-operative scanning area (aka A-scan) where the shape and length of the patient's eye that was to be operated on was measured. Knowing which patients had received pre-operative scanning allowed us to generate daily reports on which and how many patients were ready for surgery the following day. The third area for critical data collection was surgery. We wanted to capture on a daily basis what types of surgical procedures were preformed by which surgeons and at what rate per day. The fourth key data collection point was discharge. Knowing which patients were discharged and the daily discharge rate was important for the camp's resource management. At the height of the camp's operation, we were collecting, processing, and reporting on data from all four areas each day.

On the evening prior to the opening of the camp the chief of surgeons asked the Clinical Statistics team if we could create a computer program to calculate the power of the lens to be implanted. In pre-operative scanning, measurement of the eye's length and shape produces three numbers. These three numbers needed to be entered into an equation along with a constant to calculate the power of the intraocular lens implanted in the cataract surgery. We responded to this request by creating a spreadsheet with seven columns containing the patient's ID number, the pre-operative scanning date, the surgical eye, columns for entering each of the three measures, and a final column that contained the equation to calculate the lens power. Each day a laptop with a spreadsheet containing information in the first three columns on patients anticipated for pre-op scanning for that day was taken to the pre-operative scanning location at the camp. As patients were examined, the data from their pre-op scans were entered into the spreadsheet and the lens power automatically calculated. Additionally, this information was printed out each evening and given to the technician who was responsible for selecting the appropriate lenses for the next day's surgery. Each evening the data from the pre-op scan spreadsheets was merged into the patient database. As stated above, patients who had been pre-op scanned were then eligible for surgery. A report was produced each evening and provided to the chief surgical nurse in the early morning listing anticipated surgeries for the day.

This innovation of downloading lists of patients expected in pre-op scan each day to a laptop and then uploading the captured pre-op evaluation data at the end of the day to the database, was one of several developed by the Clinical Statistics team to overcome the lack of onsite network connection to the medical database. In order to capture post-surgical data two options were tested. Because patients kept their records with them and because we wanted to have post-operative information, it seemed important to collect information from the patients as they exited the surgical theater. Postoperatively, patients were under the influence of the sedating medication given to them prior to the operation. Patients were assisted to a wheelchair as they exited the surgical theater and aides were given their medical records. The problem we faced was collecting the post surgical information from patients' medical records without slowing the flow of patients exiting the surgical theater. It was estimated by the surgical staff that the flow would be approximate 36 patients per hour. One idea considered and tested in the first days of the camp was to place one of the Prasad Chitkitsa desktop computers, a scanner, and a printer in a room directly across from the surgical theater. As a patient left surgery, the portion of their medical record containing the surgical information was scanned and printed. Surgical information from the printed copies was subsequently entered into the patient database. Scanning the medical records quickly proved to be excessively time-consuming and prone to computer crashes. The team then elected to do direct data entry of the key fields from the surgical record into a spreadsheet listing anticipated surgical candidates for the day. At the end of the day's data collection, this spreadsheet was then uploaded to the patient database in much the same manner as the pre-op scanning information. This solution required two to three team members working at this data collection point at any one time, but allowed for the capture of this critical information without constraining the flow of patients from the surgical theater. Knowing which patients had received surgery allowed us to project the anticipated discharge dates based on a standard three day period of time for recovery.

We initially provided the staff of the admissions tent with a daily printout of anticipated admissions based on screening camp data. At the end of each day, admission's information was entered from the paper record into the patient database. This provided us information on who had been admitted that day. The downside of this procedure was that the data had to be reentered from the paper record. When an extra laptop became available, anticipated admissions for the day were downloaded to a spreadsheet and placed on the laptop. The laptop was then placed in the admissions tent and volunteers were trained on how to find patients in a spreadsheet record and note their admission. Each evening the admission's data from the laptop was merged into the patient database.

Following surgery and a three to four day recovery period, patients to be discharged from the camp were processed through the Discharge Tent. It was at this point that their medical record was retrieved from them and became available for the collection of additional information for the NP 99 patient database. The Discharge Tent was the one key data collection point where we were unable to electronically capture data. This was due to a shortage of available laptops to place in the Discharge Tent. We did provide the staff in the Discharge Tent with a daily list of anticipated discharges. This proved to be of only marginal assistance since a patient's discharge on a particular day was dependent on the doctor's examination of the patient's surgical eye each morning and the physician's assessment of the patient's readiness for discharge. Consequently, our attempts to predict daily discharges based on standard recovery periods were less than entirely satisfactory.

During the ten days of NP 99, the data entry and reporting tasks of the Clinical Team and other computer tasks of the eye camp, as described above, placed considerable stress on the Prasad Chitkitsa computer network. Several of the network machines failed at some point prior to, during, or after the eye camp. Because of the remote location, there was often a two to three day delay before a computer technician could come from Mumbai and make the necessary repairs. The limited number of available computers on the network and the significant quantities of data that had to be entered into the patient database within a brief time period necessitated the limitation of certain machines only for data entry. Moreover, the operations of the Clinical Statistics team had to be extended from 7 a.m. to 11p.m. during the peak of the camp's operation.

Post-Camp Evaluation

Following the eye camp, members of the Clinical Statistics team met and evaluated the data collection and management processes of the eye camp. A number of observations and recommendations were made for the improvement of data collection, management, and reporting in future eye camps. These recommendations are presented here as they may prove useful for other time-limited health and social service delivery projects.

- Data errors were noted in paper-based data collected by volunteers who were not part of the Clinical Statistics team. Additional data entry training was recommended in order to assure data integrity.
- The patient database should be on a network located at the eye camp. This would allow greater integration of the patient database into the activities of the nursing and medical staff.
- The Clinical Statistics team was organizationally located under Administrative services. It was recommended that in order to increase the utilization of information available in the patient database by the medical staff, that the Clinical Statistics team be placed under the administrative purview of Clinical services.
- In the database development and during data collection, a number of medical questions arose regarding diagnoses, medical conditions, surgical complications, and procedures. It was recommended that a single physician be assigned as a liaison to the Clinical Statistics team.

- There was a need for more laptops for remote data collection and more networked computers for data entry.
- It was recommended that brief team meetings during shift changes and logs for noting completed work would have facilitated clarification of what tasks had been completed and which tasks remained to be done.

Follow-Up Camp Data Collection and Reporting

At the time of their discharge NP 99 patients were invited to return to the site of the eye camp in sixty days for a post-surgical evaluation. A total of 1057 patients from NP 99 returned for the follow-up camp. During the follow-up camp, each patient's visual acuity was retested and the patient's eye examined for any surgical complications. If additional visual correction was required, patients were given a referral to a local ophthalmologist who would fit them with glasses paid for by PRASAD.

I returned to India in early May of 1999 for the follow-up camp in order to coordinate the collection of follow-up data and produce the eye camp's Clinical Statistics report. Two challenges of this endeavor were soon evident. First, a new team of volunteers with limited computer experience had to be trained to enter the data from the follow-up camp medical form into the NP 99 patient database. The second was the fact that the follow-up camp data entry subform in the patient database was never created, despite the fact that there was a tab on the data entry form indicating its location. The follow-up camp subform was omitted during the creation of the patient database due to both time constraints on the programmer and the fact that the associated follow-up camp medical form had not been developed.

A follow-up camp medical form was ready in May. This paper-based form was used to create a database table containing the key fields from the follow-up camp form. A Microsoft Access data entry form was produced from the follow-up camp database table. Unfortunately, several hours of efforts by two different Access programmers were unsuccessful in achieving the integration of this data entry form into the NP 99 patient database as a subform. Due to the press to enter the follow-up camp while there were volunteers available, an alternative solution was devised. Instead of using a data entry form in the patient database, follow-up camp data were entered directly into the follow-up camp database table. This alternative method required data entry volunteers to tab across columns representing fields from the medical form as they entered data for each patient, much as one would do in entering data in a spreadsheet. This task was accomplished without significant data errors. Once the follow-up camp data was in the NP 99 patient database, the Clinical Statistics report was produced with a series of database queries to extract specific information. This report was used as the basis of a subsequent manuscript reporting the surgical results of the NP 99 (Balent, Narendrum, Patel, & Patterson, in review).

IMPLICATIONS FOR SOCIAL WORK PRACTICE

Social workers world wide are involved in health and social service delivery projects, both time-limited and ongoing, that either require or would benefit from the collection of service delivery and evaluation data. Too often such data are either not collected or are collected on paper forms, thereby impeding subsequent data analysis due to the necessity to re-enter the data into an electronic database. This case study demonstrates the potential and utility of capturing essential data at the point of service delivery and then merging it into a patient database. On this project, a bi-directional flow of data was established. Laptop computers were employed to capture data at the field hospital. These data were downloaded to the network database and resultant reports that enabled the next day's data collection were uploaded to the laptops. This process of remote data collection with laptops eliminated the need for redundant paper-based data entry and furthered the efforts to document and evaluate the service delivery of this international, rural, health care project.

This case study also illustrates the adaptability of current IT systems to meet the complex health and social services data collection challenges. Widely available software suites such as Microsoft Office are underutilized in social work practice settings for data collection and analysis (Patterson, 2000). This case study describes how a relatively inexpensive, off-the-shelf database application was used in the creation of a complex patient database that was rapidly developed and adapted for the unique data collection needs of an international healthcare project. The processes and findings described here are applicable to social service agencies faced with the nontrivial challenge of developing and deploying, with limited fiscal resources, information systems in dynamic environments. Many agencies, especially those operating in rapidly changing service demand environments, would be well served to adopt a strategy of incremental development for information systems using integrated software suites instead of opting to purchase a fully formed, off-the-shelf database. Further, the development and deployment of such systems is facilitated by clear specification of requisite data sources and necessary data products.

The IT and organizational lessons learned on this project have implications both for the deployment of IT systems in the developing world and their use in the developed world on time-limited, health and social service delivery projects. At a more fundamental level, the international healthcare delivery project described here, Netraprakash 99, represents a shining example of the capacity and potential of individuals and organizations uniting to ease suffering and uplift humanity.

REFERENCES

American Academy of Ophthalmology (2000). History of cataracts: Developments this century. *Eye Net,* Retrieved August 6, 2000 from the World Wide Web. (http://www.eyenet.org/public/museum/hist_century.html).

Angra, S. K., Murthy, G. V. S., Gupta, S. K., & Angra, V. (1997). Cataract related blindness in India and its social implications. *Indian Journal of Medical Residency,* 106, 312-324.

Balent, L. C., Narendrum, K., Patel, S., & Patterson, D. A. (in review). *Ophthalmic Surgery and Lasers.*

Cagan, B. & Julia, M. (1998). Maintaining wartime gains for women: Lessons from El Salvador. *International Social Work.* 41(4): 405-415.

Chandler, S.K. (1995). "That biting, stinging thing which ever shadows us": African-American social workers in France during World War I. *Social Service Review.* 69(3): 498-14.

Civerchia, L., Apoorvananda, S. W., Natchiar, G., Balent, A., Ramakrishnan, R.,& Green, D. (1993). Intraocular lens implantation in rural India. *Ophthalmic Surgery,* 24(10), 648-653.

Civerchia, L., Ravindran, R. D., Apoorvananda, S. W., Ramakrishnan, R., Balent, A., Spencer, M. H. & Green, D. (1993). High-volume intraocular lens surgery in a rural eye camp in India. *Ophthalmic Surgery and Lasers,* 27(3), 200-208.

Collins, M. E., Epstein, I., Barbarin, O. & Savas, S. A. (1996). Re-designing a clinical information system: A description of the process in a human service agency. *Computers in Human Services,* 13(3), 19-36.

Fletcher, A. E., Ellwein, L. B., Selvaraj, S., Vijaykumar, V., Rahmathullah, R., & Thulasiraj, R. D. (1997). Meausures of vision function and quality of life in patients with cataracts in southern India. *Archives of Ophthalmology,* 115, 767-774.

Limburg, H., Kumar, R., & Bachani, D. (1996). Monitoring and evaluating cataract intervention in India. *British Journal of Ophthamology,* 80, 951-955.

Lwanga, S. (2000). Health information systems. *World Health Organization.* Retrieved August 4th, 2000 from the World Wide Web: http://www.who.int/health-services-delivery/information/index.htm.

Mba, P. O. (1985). Social welfare services for disabled children in schools in developing countries. *International-Social-Work*, 28(1): 30-33.

Nagpal, P. N. (2000). Indian ophthalmology past, present, and future. *Eye Net*, Retrieved August 6, 2000 from the World Wide Web. (http://www.eyenet.org/public/whats_new/nagpal.html).

Patterson, D. A. & Cloud, R. N. (1999). The application of artificial neural networks outcome prediction in a cohort of severely mentally ill outpatients. *Journal of Technology in Human Services*. 16(2/3), 47-61.

Patterson, D. A. (2000). *Personal Computer Applications in the Social Services*, Boston: Allyn & Bacon.

Ruit, S., Tabin, G. C., Nissman, S. A., Paudyal, G. & Gurang, R. (1999). Low-cost high-volume extracapsular cataract extraction with posterior chamber intraocular lens implantation in Nepal. *Ophthalmology*, 106(10), 1887-1892.

Shank, N. C., Roesch, S. C., Murphy-Breman, V. A., Wright, G. F. (1996). The use of the Internet for at-risk families receiving services co-ordination. *Dreams and Realities: Information Technology in the Human Services*, In B. Glastonbury (Ed.), *Dreams and Realities: Information Technology in the Human Services*. Stakes National Research and Development Centre for Welfare and Health: Helsinki, Finland.

World Health Organization (2000, July 12). Investing in evidence and information base: A WHO strategy to support member states. New York, NY: Author. Retrieved August 1, 2000, from the World Wide Web: http://www.who.int/health-services-delivery/information/20000629b.htm.

Internet Technology
Makes Clinical Data Systems
Technically and Economically Practical:
Are They Politically Feasible?

Norma H. Wasko

SUMMARY. The creation of data systems capable of tracking health service inputs and outcomes were a major thrust of health reform. It proved neither technically nor politically feasible. Recent advances in software, communication technologies and measurement tools suggest integrated information systems, reliable at the individual case level, are now practical. This paper explores one possible model of a clinical information system for behavioral health services and asks, "Is implementation of such a model now politically feasible?" *[Article copies available for a fee from The Haworth Document Delivery Service: 1-800-342-9678. E-mail address: <getinfo@haworthpressinc.com> Website: <http://www.HaworthPress.com> © 2001 by The Haworth Press, Inc. All rights reserved.]*

Norma H. Wasko, MSW, PhD, is Assistant Professor, Division of Social Work, School of Applied Social Sciences, West Virginia University. Previous experience includes seven years with the Health Care Authority, State of Vermont, where she worked on health reform and quality assurance in managed care, and sixteen years as a clinical social worker in Burlington, Vermont. Research interests include health and mental health policy, client experience of service delivery and accountability in health care services.

Correspondence should be directed to: Norma H. Wasko, Division of Social Work, West Virginia University, Post Office Box 6830, Morgantown, West Virginia 26506-6830 (NorWasko@aol.com).

[Haworth co-indexing entry note]: "Internet Technology Makes Clinical Data Systems Technically and Economically Practical: Are They Politically Feasible?" Wasko, Norma H. Co-published simultaneously in *Journal of Technology in Human Services* (The Haworth Press, Inc.) Vol. 18, No. 3/4, 2001, pp. 41-62; and: *New Advances in Technology for Social Work Education and Practice* (ed: Julie Miller-Cribbs) The Haworth Press, Inc., 2001, pp. 41-62. Single or multiple copies of this article are available for a fee from The Haworth Document Delivery Service [1-800-342-9678, 9:00 a.m. - 5:00 p.m. (EST). E-mail address: getinfo@haworthpressinc.com].

KEYWORDS. Internet, technology, clinical, data, systems

In health policy the relationship between technical and political feasibility is complex and difficult to separate. Technical capacity (the practical ability to solve a service delivery problem with the existing technology) may create the possibility for different political relationships among stakeholder groups, as occurred when consumer satisfaction ratings of health plan services achieved a reasonable degree of reliability and validity. The use of satisfaction data became a means of politically leveraging changes in health plan practices such as standards for client appointment wait-times and consumer grievance processes (National Committee for Quality Assurance, 2000; Thompson et al., 1998). In this case technical feasibility fostered political acceptance of a policy change. Without the instrument and the data it generated, plans could well have continued resisting pressure to change.

Technical feasibility does not always mean that a proposal will achieve political acceptance. The current difficulty in securing federal legislation to protect confidentiality of individually identifiable economic information (credit card, social security numbers, etc.) is a case in point. The software capacity to secure this information exists but, so far, the political will to require uniform application of security standards is lacking. At the same time, political feasibility may abound but a problem remains unsolved because the technical capacity to solve it is lacking.

In health policy the technical capacity to solve a problem frequently exists but political conflict prevents resolution because some or all of the stakeholders perceive they will lose advantage. The evolution from technical feasibility to political feasibility seems to require that major players conclude that they have more to lose by *not* adopting a technological innovation. Health care data systems have presented particularly difficult issues of technical and political feasibility. Technical problems have tended to be easier to resolve than the political issues of who will control the data, who will have access to it and how it will be used. In an open, high tech society information equates to dollars, power, and market and political advantage. This has made discussion of integrated data systems a focal point for ideological and political dispute.

Health Reform and Data Systems. The creation of data systems capable of tracking health service inputs and outcomes was both the managerial dream and the political nightmare of health reform planners. The dream, spurred by the promise of sophisticated software and computer enabled analysis of large data sets, envisioned a system that would permit the matching of individual client case data with empirically grounded information about the most effective intervention technologies. It would have allowed monitoring of client progress through the treatment system, permitted analysis of service quality and fostered the collection of data on cost and clinical outcomes across population groups. Aggregated population data would then be used to conduct research to improve service quality and promote cost-efficiency. All participants were to benefit from the wealth of shared information (Debating health care reform, 1993).

The dream died on the rocks of technical difficulty, high cost and political and economic competition. As major stakeholders involved in state health reform activities realized the practical consequences of integrated data systems–e.g., loss of control over the data and such potential effects as publication of data on service quality, liability for adverse outcomes, breach of confidentiality and public access to what was considered proprietary information–enthusiasm for participation in such systems rapidly cooled. However, in the context of reform forthright refusal to participate was not a viable political option. Thus reformers came to understand that despite participation in a host of planning activities, the major players had little intention of participating in large data systems that they could not control (Oliver & Dowell, 1994; Weir, 1995). Both public and private sector data initiatives that attempted to establish broad-based stakeholder involvement encountered major political and technical difficulties. While gains were made in increased understanding of the issues, and technical development did occur in both sectors, the vision of a unified data base remained unfulfilled (Mathematica Policy Research, Inc., August 29, 1994; April, 1996; July, 1996; Gold, Burnbauer & Chu, 1996; John A. Hartford Foundation, Inc., 1997; Leichter, 1993, 1994).

INTEGRATED INFORMATION SYSTEMS ARE NOW TECHNICALLY FEASIBLE

Although the political effort to achieve health reform failed, innovation in information technology, driven by market competition, is making the creation of integrated clinical support and managerial systems technically feasible (Eddy, 1998). Clinical support systems are information systems designed to enhance clinical decision-making and treatment intervention. Data in these systems is focused at the level of individual patient care and links treatment protocols and recommended best practices with individual case assessments, diagnoses, interventions and outcomes. The unit of attention is the individual client. In contrast, managerial information systems focus on populations and use aggregated data to answer questions about the performance of delivery systems in achieving access, accountability, quality, cost effectiveness and cost efficiency. Internet technology now offers the possibility of integrated information systems capable of providing individualized information about the probable best treatment options for particular clients and permitting real-time monitoring of the results (Quality Metric, 1999, 2000; Ware, 1997; Ware, Bjorner & Kosinski, 1999). Aggregated case data can be analyzed to yield information about cost, quality, effectiveness and user-friendliness of services provided various population groups (see for example: Quality Metric, February 28, 2000; also The Mental Health Net, http://www.cmhc.com).

DATA IS POLITICAL AND NOT ALL PLAYERS ARE EQUAL

In a market-driven health system the primary customer is the purchaser of services, not the client who uses the system. In this context the interests of purchasers and clients may not be the same. The main goal of purchasers as a group is cost containment. Quality is a concern but purchasing decisions are driven mainly by costs (Hibbard and Jewett, 1997). Clients, on the other hand, are generally focused on getting the best quality care that is available. Cost is an issue of secondary importance. For the insured the strength of its importance tends to bear an inverse relationship to the individual's state of health (Tumlinson, 1997). The current system for financing health services and especially behavioral health services, tends to favor the concerns of purchasers over client's (Buck et al., 1999; Goldman, McCulloch & Sturm, 1998; Zarin, West, Pincus & Taniellan, 1999). This imbalance is fostered by purchaser confusion about quality and the lack of adequate information about the client's experience with the delivery system (Milbank Memorial Fund, 2000; Their & Gelijns, 1998). Social workers and others concerned about the adequacy and quality of behavioral health services, would do well to advocate for information technologies that place client evaluations of their experience at the center of the information system, thus making the delivery system more accountable to its users.

MODEL OF AN INTEGRATED CLINICAL INFORMATION SYSTEM FOR BEHAVIORAL HEALTH OUTPATIENT SERVICES

The model information system (ICIS) presented here demonstrates how such a system might be conceptualized in the delivery of behavioral health services. Refer to Figure 1 below for a diagrammatic presentation of this model.

Inputs. These include client presentation of problems and symptoms, clinician assessments, diagnostic and/or problem formulation, analysis of strengths and resources and the intervention plan. The inputs include clinical decision software (periodically updated by CD or available in real-time from the Internet) that makes use of combinatorial logic that relates client-presented problems and symptoms to the full range of possible diagnoses, treatment interventions and management paths). The software offers a range of screening, diagnostic and management interventions from current, empirically validated, best practices for a

FIGURE 1. Model of a Clinical Information System for Behavioral Health Outpatient Services

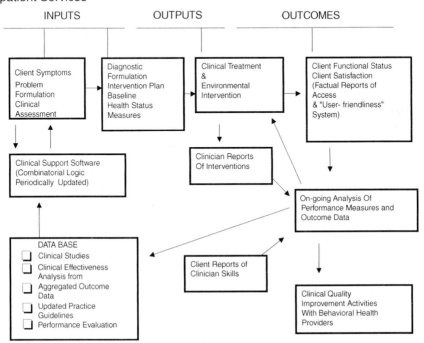

number of behavioral health conditions. Such a software has been developed by the PKC Corporation (PKC Corporation, 1994). Also available in this ICIS model, as an input to the decision process, are proposed clinical effectiveness studies, and feedback on efficacy of best practices as determined by outcomes analysis from local practice experience.

Outputs. Included here are the various aspects of the intervention plan which may be limited to clinical treatment only or include such important environmental services as housing, income maintenance, child care, transportation, etc., and permits coordination and tracking of services delivered by other providers. Also included in outputs are clinician reports of all services provided in a given episode of care as well as client reports of clinician skills (Wasko, 1998). The latter scale asks clients factual questions about specific clinician skills as well as client evaluation of own functional improvement.

Outcomes. These include client reports of changes in health status, improvements in environmental supports and client satisfaction with access, service quality and responsiveness of the delivery system. Also included as outcomes are real-time, individual-level feedback of client functioning after specified interventions. This feedback permits adjustment of the individual intervention plan. Additional outcomes include periodic feedback to individual clinicians of severity-adjusted findings (based on aggregated individual case data) on the efficacy of particular intervention strategies for specific client groups.

Analysis of aggregated outcomes data are also fed back to the database where they provide information to all clinicians participating in the system on the efficacy of particular intervention strategies in the local practice environment. Over time finding that suggest significant difference between effectiveness studies and clinical efficacy could be integrated into the combinatorial software that contributes inputs to the clinical decision process. Because clinicians have long noted the difference between results obtained in clinical trials and in the actual practice setting, this systematic process of data collection, analysis and feedback should eventually provide another evaluative perspective on recommended best practices (Ankuta & Abeles, 1993; Lohr et al., 1998). Analysis of aggregated data could also be used to track variation in clinical practice that correlates with less favorable client outcomes and become the topic of clinical quality improvement activities.

Dissemination of Relevant Findings. Current technology offers a variety of ways to disseminate quality improvement findings. These include individual clinician feedback via e-mail, as well as grant-funded web-casts of major report findings and creation and dissemination of

CD's for student training and continuing education. With the spread of wide-band DVD technology inter-active video conferencing could be used for case and program consultation.

CASE EXAMPLE OF SOCIAL WORK PRACTICE USING AN INTEGRATED CLINICAL INFORMATION SYSTEM

A case example will illustrate how such an information system might function. Suppose Mrs. Jones, a client of David Smith, seeks an appointment. She complains she is depressed. Smith is a clinical social worker and a member of a practice group in a rural area that provides outpatient behavioral health services to residents of a local community by contract with a regional community mental health center. The practice group to which Social Worker Smith belongs has recently agreed to participate in a demonstration project to develop an ICIS.

To protect client confidentiality and privacy a variety of safeguards are structured into ICIS processes. For example, all personal identifiers will be removed and the case given an encrypted identification number. Client confidentiality and informed consent protocols require the social worker to explain to the client how the information system works and describe the safeguards to ensure that no personally identifiable information will be electronically transferred. Clients will be given written descriptions of their rights of confidentiality and informed consent. This document will also include a data release form for the client's signature. This document specifies the conditions under which information about the client may be released and for what purposes.

Computerized Data Collection. Following the project protocol, Social Worker Smith interviews Mrs. Jones and uses a computerized questionnaire to gather information about her symptoms. The initial questions inquire about her physical as well as mental functioning and are designed to rule-out underlying physiological conditions (for example, a malfunctioning thyroid) that might be responsible for the depression.

Coordination of Physical and Mental Health Assessments. Should Mrs. Jones' responses suggest the strong possibility of an underlying, causal, physiological condition, and Social Worker Smith finds no indications of other, psycho-social factors that might be responsible for her depression, ICIS protocol recommends referral to Mrs. Jones' primary care physician. However, if exploration suggests psycho-social factors may be contributing to the depression, Social Worker Smith develops a diagnostic formulation and adds counseling services to the treatment plan. The protocol will encourage coordination and tracking of both the medical and the counseling interventions.

Collection of Baseline Data. During the initial session Mrs. Jones completes a brief health status scale and perhaps a condition-specific depression measure as well. This may be done alone or with the help of Social Worker Smith using a computer in the clinician's office. Her responses will provide baseline data on her level of functioning. The social worker will also inquire about other services that she may be accessing that relate to her capacity to cope effectively. The data is then entered in the client file.

Data Storage and Electronic Transmission. Individually identifiable patient data is retained in the practice group computer system. Confidentiality is protected through use of a series of need-to-know levels of system access. Encrypted, personally non-identifiable data is transferred by e-mail from the practice system to the data analysis firm that holds the contract to perform analytic services for the system. This agreement could be written among various parties, for example, between the data firm and the practice group, or the state community mental health system, or the state Medicaid agency that funds mental health services. A number of businesses currently perform many of the functions described here (see, for example, The Mental Health Net at http://www.cmhc.com).

To protect confidentiality the system would use case numbers rather than names, birth dates or social security numbers, and one of the more recent encryption software that makes use of a complex key–128 bits recommended (Patterson, 2000). The e-mail systems of both the clinical group and the data contractor would use a stand-alone encryption software to ensure the security of the data transactions (for example, PGP for Personal Privacy).

Coordination of Physical and Mental Health Services. Social Worker Smith then reviews Mrs. Jones' specific responses about her depression using a combinatorial logic software that associates her particular symptoms with diagnostic probabilities that her depression reflects a particular etiology, and presents treatment options based on current effectiveness studies. ICIS analysis suggests that Mrs. Jones' depression appears likely to be associated with the hormonal changes of menopause as well as her pronounced tendency to negative, self-deprecatory evaluations. Based on this assessment, the social worker consults with Mrs. Jones and her physician about obtaining a hormonal assessment and, if the blood tests confirm the ICIS diagnostic assessment, a prescription for anti-depressant medications. He then undertakes 4 to 6 sessions of brief, cognitive-affective therapy to help Mrs. Jones develop more positive self-messages and better ways of coping on bad days.

The Information System Is Not a Substitute for Clinician Judgment. It should be noted that the information system is designed to augment the social worker's knowledge. It does not serve as a substitute for clinical skill and experience. Protocol suggestions are subject to clinical judgment and client willingness. Mrs. Jones may have very strong resistance to anti-depressant medication. The information system will provide Social Worker Smith with the best available knowledge about the effectiveness of such medications to relieve depressions associated with menopause. Mrs. Jones has a right to know this information. She also has the right to reject it. Social Worker Smith is obligated to assist Mrs. Jones in reaching the decision that is correct for her.

Recording Interventions. At some point early in the service process, Social Worker Smith completes a brief intervention tracking form in which he records the various interventions Mrs. Jones has received. In the event she is also receiving services from another provider (perhaps a support group), Social Worker Smith will note this information. The presumption is that the social worker will inquire about other service providers and secure Mrs. Jones' permission to communicate with them. In this way the record of resources correlated with service outcomes will be accurate. This data will also be transmitted by e-mail to the data analysis contractor.

Collection of Quality and Outcome Data. At the end of her counseling therapy Mrs. Jones is asked to complete an evaluation scale that asks about Social Worker Smith's clinical skills, the symptomatic outcomes of her treatment and her satisfaction with the service she received. She will also be asked to complete a second set of health status forms that will measure changes in her functional condition. If the sponsors of the information system are also interested in various aspects of service quality, such as ease or difficulty of access to health services, or responsiveness of Mrs. Jones' insurance plan or managed care company in processing claims or providing consumer information, Mrs. Jones may be asked to complete additional questions. Overall, the total number of items collected is kept small in an effort to reduce the burden and cost of data collection and analysis.

Options for Data Collection and Clinical Feedback. The outcome data may be collected by computer in Social Worker Smith's practice office (*not* administered by Social Worker Smith) either by software resident on a practice office machine or directly linked to the analysis firm's web-site. If collected on a practice site computer, the data file may be transmitted via e-mail to the contractor. Strict security protocols are followed for maintaining confidentiality of client identity and her responses. Social Worker Smith will not have access to client identifiable data on his performance. Both he and Mrs. Jones will have access to the results of the health status and outcomes analysis. Feedback on the health status measures could be used to help her mark therapeutic progress or the lack of it. The use of periodic feedback of health status measures as a therapeutic tool with longer term clients is also an option of this system.

Aggregate Data Management, Analysis and Application. All outcomes data will be stripped of personally identifiable information, aggregated and analyzed. Analysis of aggregated case data could then be used to improve quality of service delivery. For example, changes in client functioning measured by severity adjusted outcome data for the population group that received cognitive-affective therapy for depression could be compared to changes in outcomes expected from results obtained in clinical effectiveness trials. Over time it might be that a subset of this population, women who are menopausal, and exhibiting symptoms of depression, are identified as showing most significant improvement when counseling is combined with prescription of anti-depressant medications and Hormone Replacement Therapy. This information could be used for clinical quality improvement purposes and fed-back into the information system via inclusion in the combinatorial software used in the clinical decision process. Social Worker Smith might find, over the course of several years, that his clinical experience with clients similar to Mrs. Jones, and the knowledge gained of the clinical efficacy of combined counseling and pharmacological therapy, lead him to become the peer leader of quality improvement presentations to encourage colleagues to incorporate this approach in their practice.

HOW THE DATA COULD BE USED

Individual Case Data Is Practical for Clinicians. Clinical support systems require data that is reliable at the level of the individual case. They do not require large data sets to yield useful information for treatment purposes although large pools of aggregated data are required to enhance knowledge about clinical quality and the effectiveness and efficacy of treatments provided to population groups. Feedback on individual cases could improve the quality and efficiency of care given to individuals. Periodic reports of quality and service effectiveness drawn from data aggregated from multiple providers in their local area could be useful in guiding practitioners toward treatments of proven effectiveness. The main effect of case feedback and aggregated case analysis would be to enhance learning about what works.

Reliable Case Data Can Be Collected to Evaluate Provider Performance and Client Outcomes. Internet assisted data collection provides an easy way to capture data on individual provider performance. The ease of web-based, consumer self-administered, report scales and Internet transfer of data files by e-mail, and removes much of the burden of data collection.

Having the means to secure data on individual clients and clinician functioning is the next step in monitoring quality of service delivery. It is the current goal of large purchaser and accreditation organizations such as the National Committee for Quality Assurance (Thompson, 1998). Current data from the Health Employers Data Information Set (HEDIS) and the Consumer Assessment of Health Plan Services (CAHPS) measures have yielded information useful for comparing the performance of health plans' *service quality* (access, plan responsiveness to client complaints, information needs, etc.) but provide little that informs purchasers or consumers about the quality of services offered by *individual clinicians* (NCQA, 2000). Consumer groups as well as employers argue that it is the quality of services provided by their local provider that is of greatest interest to patients and clients. This is especially true in rural areas where plans may come and go but the only provider in town tends to stay.

PRACTICAL EFFECTS OF IMPLEMENTING ICIS FOR BEHAVIORAL HEALTH SERVICES

A major problem of behavioral health professionals is staying current with a rapidly proliferating knowledge base. A model such as the one described here could systematize inputs and bring the best currently available information about treatment effectiveness and efficacy to bear in real time when it is most useful. Careful selection of data elements would permit relatively inexpensive monitoring of quality of clinician skills and client outcomes and satisfaction. The information system as a whole creates the potential for organized learning about what works best for various client groups having different levels of problem severity and receiving service from different providers. Given a data set of sufficient size, patterns of variation in treatment intervention that are significant for client outcomes could be identified and made the object of quality improvement activity.

Impact on Individual Clinicians. Since the model presented here would create a continuous flow of information, complete with feedback loops, it will impact all participants in the system. Effects would be both positive and negative. For example, individual behavioral health practitioners currently use a wide variety of treatment models in their work with clients. Many of these models have not been empirically validated (that is, they may or may not be effective) but practitioners have, nonetheless, invested a high level of belief in their efficacy. The implementation of ICIS would likely create practitioner discomfort on at least two levels: the individual's customary pattern of work would be disrupted by the requirement to incorporate computerized data collection into the practice process. Moreover, individual case level and/or aggregated data analysis may show that specific practice models may not be effective with some clients. To the extent that workers fear learning that their work is ineffective they may resist data-based practice systems.

They may also resist for a whole host of other reasons as well. One frequently voiced concern is whether or not electronic data systems violate ethical standards of practice because they pose an inherent threat to privacy and confidentiality that cannot be overcome. This is a major concern raised by the most negative critics of data systems. The counter argument is that ethical principals of practice are the same whether the exchange between client and clinician takes place electronically or face-to-face. Ethical concerns about confidentiality, for example, are salient to the extent that technical inadequacy causes the ethical standard to be violated. When the technology is adequate to protect and promote ethical practice, the choice not to use it is made on other grounds, usually economic, political or personal. Goldsmith describes the barriers to using Internet technology to improve the productivity and quality of health practice and notes that the greatest barrier to realizing technical potential is lack of trust. The historical experience of practitioners is that data systems have been imposed upon them and that all such systems will be used to "gather information about their practice, and discipline them or deprive them of income" (Goldsmith, 2000, p. 151).

On the other hand, it seems inevitable that such systems will evolve as the technical capacity grows, costs decrease and a new generation of technologically savvy practitioners arrives on the scene. Social workers and other professionals who cannot adapt to these systems will be left behind. On the positive side, practitioners who approach data based practice with the desire to critically evaluate their work and to learn additional technical and clinical skills will find that ICIS provides the opportunity to make clinical practice a continuous learning experience.

Effect on Organizational Structure and Function. Perhaps the greatest impacts of ICIS would be on organizational function and structure of the agencies themselves. Many public agencies suffer from additive reporting requirements. That is, data collection and paper demands tend to increase, but are seldom reduced. An integrated information system would require the organization to rethink the functionality of many of its information collecting processes and to streamline as many as possible. A second effect of ICIS would be to flatten the organizational authority structure and reduce the number of middle managers and supervisors. This is so because ICIS places primary system accountability at the point of information exchange between the worker, the client and ICIS itself. Front-line workers will require two kinds of expertise: technical ability to use the data system (and understand its limitations) and skill in interacting with clients such that the client feels understood, the clinician secures accurate information and, in indeterminate situations (which constitute most of practice) client and worker are able to develop the best individualized plan from among several courses of action suggested by the system.

The nature of this process will require more rather than less skill on the part of the clinician. A related effect will be that, because availability of information tends to democratize decision processes, clients (and their advocates) will likely tend to see themselves as partners with the clinician in working out the best treatment plan for the individual client.

The organizations that are initially best suited to implement ICIS are managed care organizations. Their structure and emphasis on tracking utilization and costs make it relatively easy to evolve an ICIS. However, as conceptualized here, ICIS could tend to decentralize clinical decision-making since information would be available to develop norms of cost-effective practice for given clinical conditions. The culture of the organization could conceivably use this information to vest greater decision-making discretion with clinicians who would have a range of numerical norms against which to rate their own performance.

FACTORS AFFECTING DEVELOPMENT AND USE OF INTEGRATED INFORMATION SYSTEMS

The case scenario described above could be implemented now, although not all the data collection instruments described above are fully developed. Well-tested, standardized instruments exist for measuring both generic and condition-specific health status (Ware, 1997; Quality Metric, 2000). The scale designed to measure client evaluation of behavioral health clinician skills is in the initial stages of development (Wasko, 1998). Sophisticated knowledge coupling software exists (such as the Problem Knowledge Coupler marketed by PKC Corporation) and has been applied in a number of different healthcare settings (Kozak, 1998; PKC Corporation, 2000b; Yee, 1994). Web-based scale administration, scoring and analysis of health status measures have been initiated by at least one firm this year (Quality Metric, 2000; Ware, Bjorner, Kosinski, 1999).

Breakthrough in Psychometric Applications. Technical innovations by Ware and colleagues (1999) in psychometric analysis have made brief, precise, individually reliable measures of health status available, thus opening the way for low-cost, low-burden measures. The psychometric innovation can be applied to other measures as well and suggests that a major cost barrier has been breached. This should create increased interest in the development of integrated information systems.

The Pursuit of Disease Management. The holy grail of health service delivery in recent years has been the pursuit of disease management technologies. Payers and managed care companies alike are interested in strategies that permit tracking of treatment provided persons with complex, chronic and high-cost conditions to determine the most cost-effective ways to deliver the health services they require. Clinical information systems that provide reliable data on treatment effectiveness at the case level have been stymied by lack of precise measures as well as technical difficulties in obtaining real-time analysis and feedback of case data. Internet-based, real-time analysis of newly developing measures promises a solution to this problem. Both public and private purchasers of health care services are sure to be interested in the further development of information systems that make use of this technology.

Costs. License restrictions and the cost of these web-based technologies and analytic services, as they are currently marketed, place them beyond the range of most small organizations. Quality Metric, for example, requires a $2,500 annual fee and a 30 cents charge per individual assessment from web-based users of the SF 36 and SF 12 health assessment tools (Quality Metric, 2000). However, the standardized health status scales themselves, as well as their scoring kits, are available at free or minimal cost for non-commercial use. Quality Metric also operates a data analysis service that charges $99 per data file and 50 cents per individual assessment, placing the use of these technologies within the reach of smaller organizations so long as they do not wish to use web-based systems to assess client health status (Quality Metric, 2000).

Internet marketing of input technology has not yet reached the same level of development as that of the outcomes products. Costs are likely to be beyond the pocketbook of small providers but within the reach of larger entities. PKC Corporation, for example, charges $2,880 for its license fee plus an annual maintenance fee of $960 for its mental/behavioral health tool set. This problem-knowledge-coupler uses the individual client symptom list to assess the probability of various diagnostic conditions and the related empirically validated treatment interventions. The full coupler set (physical as well as mental/behavioral health) costs $3,600 for the license fee and $1,200 for the annual maintenance fee (PKC, 2000a).

The cost of data collection and transfer is relatively insignificant. The major cost barriers to the development of ICIS for small providers are the required on-going investment in software upgrades, technical assistance and the cost of data analysis. Small providers, especially those in rural areas will not be able to support such costs by themselves. Because ICIS represents a major step forward in system development and service delivery, the only equitable way to finance the operation of the system is to include it as an allowable administrative cost in purchase of service contracts. The benefit from this added cost would occur in demonstrable gains in increased productivity, quality and cost effectiveness of service delivery.

The Role of Advocacy Groups. Client advocacy groups such as Foundation for Accountability (FACCT) and Families USA are a force promoting client relevant measures of health status, quality and outcomes of care. Behavioral health advocates, in particular those representing persons with severe mental illness such as the National Association of the Mentally Ill (NAMI) have long complained that much of what is relevant to clients is ignored by clinicians. The development of precise measures that inquire about the client's experience of behavioral health services and their incorporation into information systems that will impact what services will and will not be provided, is sure to attract the attention of these organizations. To the extent that public purchasers of behavioral health services sponsor integrated information systems such as that modeled here, client advocacy groups will want a say in the process that defines what data will be collected and how it will be used.

Their influence will serve to promote the collection of consumer relevant data.

The Response of Social Workers. Social workers and other direct service professionals may be a force for development of clinical data systems and also a barrier to innovation. There is a wide range of variability in computer literacy among social workers. Some clinicians and some clients view computer decision support and data collection as an impediment to getting down to the issues that brought the client to counseling. Moreover, the profession has been divided for some time over the feasibility and the desirability of efforts to measure practice process and service outcomes. Resistance to quantitative measures has ranged from the epistemological–"You can't measure practice; it's an art!"–to skepticism about the level of conceptual sophistication and the ethics of practice underlying scale development and data analysis. The economic and political realities of the profession's relationship with managed care organizations have done little to ease suspicions about how these entities would use data collected in models such as that outlined above.

In the long run a more positive social work response to data-based practice depends on individual practitioners achieving comfort with computerized data systems and recognizing that such systems demand more rather than less knowledge, art and skill. As clients become increasingly familiar with negotiating a wired, high-tech world, they will demand that social workers and other behavioral health practitioners deliver the same level of convenience and accountability that clients expect when they purchase other goods and services. Sooner or later integrated information systems will be developed. In the short run social workers who wish to ensure that the technical data systems accurately reflect the complexity and the humanity of truly accountable practice will grapple with the multiple issues of this new practice environment and seek to master it.

WHO WILL USE WEB-BASED TECHNOLOGY TO DEVELOP INTEGRATED CLINICAL INFORMATION SYSTEMS FOR BEHAVIORAL HEALTH SERVICES?

Having the capability does not guarantee the development and use of these systems. Barriers exist at the level of the individual clinician as well as within the service bureaucracies. Nonetheless, the trend toward more flexible, user-friendly and cheaper technology offers the possibility that technical feasibility in combination with market forces may foster a greater level of political acceptance among stakeholder groups.

Managed Behavioral Health Organizations May Find Promotion of These Technologies in Their Future Interest. Reliance on market strategies to organize and deliver health services has tended to reinforce uneven private sector provision of behavioral health services (Zarin et al., 1999). Generally, Managed Behavioral Health Organizations (MBHOs) have lagged managed care organizations in the general health sector in the development of quality assessment and outcome technologies. There have been few indications so far that these companies wish to collect and disseminate information on the client's experience of their services beyond generic satisfaction data. The major thrust of MBHOs has been cost containment, not quality and effectiveness of clinical care (Buck, 1997; Burnam & Escarce, 1999; Goldman, McCulloch & Sturm, 1998). However, tighter accreditation standards (NCQA, 2000) and diminishing capacity to wring cost savings from their provider networks suggest that MBHOs may become interested in technologies that will promote disease management and assessment of the efficacy of practitioner interventions. To the extent that quality assessment technology can produce more cost-effective service delivery, technological development may foster structural change in the delivery system. This shift in emphasis would necessarily entail a change in the relationship between the MBHOs and their provider networks because quality improvement requires a high level of collegial coordination at the point of service delivery and an organizational willingness to decentralize clinical decision-making.

Public Agencies May Not Be First to Innovate. Public sector agencies, on the other hand, are frequently overwhelmed with mandates to collect more and more data. The data that is collected is all too often of uncertain quality and accumulates, unanalyzed, contributing to public social worker cynicism about the usefulness of efforts to produce valid and reliable data on the quality of behavioral health services. However, because all data collection, once initiated, serves some systemic function, efforts to prune data requirements are difficult to achieve. Efforts to add new data collection on top of existing requirements tend to be resisted. Although public agencies are frequently innovators in service delivery and evaluation, many are not. Nonetheless, rising health care costs may motivate the states to use integrated information systems as a means of promoting cost-effective service delivery.

Provider and Consumer Directed Service Organizations. While there does not appear to be immediate motivation for the private and public sector bureaucracies to establish clinical information systems of the kind modeled here, the rise of provider sponsored organizations (provider owned corporate entities that contract directly with purchasers to provide health services) suggest these entities may become a potential home for the development of integrated clinical information systems for behavioral (and other) health services. Market competition and the desire of providers, and some consumer-run service delivery organizations, to exert greater control over behavioral health services is are spurring growth of these new entities. To the extent that these organizations contract with purchasers of health services–private employers and state agencies–to provide behavioral health services, and are entrepreneurial in their use of data to demonstrate the quality and cost-effectiveness of their work, they may promote the growth of relatively low-cost information technologies.

The Role of the States. States, through state level policy initiatives, may also facilitate adoption of these technologies and mount demonstration projects that require successful contractors to use empirically validated "best practices" and produce client-oriented outcome data. West Virginia offers an example of one state that has recently undertaken a demonstration project to test combinatorial logic software systems in the provision of health services to seniors. Community service workers use computerized functional assessment tools to develop service plans to provide home-based services to elders and disabled individuals. Assessment data is electronically communicated among care providers and statewide aggregated case data is analyzed for outcome studies, resource management and strategic planning (PKC Corporation, 2000b; West Virginia Office of the Governor, 2000).

CONCLUSIONS

The political feasibility of integrated data systems appears to be growing because technological innovation, driven by market competition is achieving acceptance that was not possible through political deliberation. The new technologies will likely be used. They provide the means for containing costs as well as improving quality by more precisely regulating the amount and kind of services that will be purchased. Large profits await the successful marketing of disease management information systems. Whether these systems are user friendly and sensitive to the needs of those they treat depends in large part on the extent to which data is collected on consumer-defined concerns.

To date, the history of the development of quality measures suggests that large purchasers (employers and state and federal governmental entities) will determine what specific technologies will be used to construct the data systems that finally emerge to become the standardized infrastructure of the information system. The political feasibility of integrated clinical data systems increases in direct proportion to the agreement among purchasers of behavioral health services on the kinds of accountability measures they will require from their contracting providers. In an era of incremental reform and technical solutions, political feasibility increases when information systems are selected by funding entities, first for demonstration purposes, and then underwritten as administrative costs of mandated data collection and service evaluation. When the purse drives systemic innovation providers soon follow.

In the politics of technology development the package with the best psychometric record that wins the race to be adopted in both the private and public sectors becomes the instrument system of choice. Inclusion of factual information about the client's actual experience of the process and outcomes of service delivery offers the best hope of making the delivery system accountable to its users. While the developmental politics are playing out, social workers and other advocates who are concerned about the quality of the services their clients receive, should weigh-in on the side of data systems that place client evaluations of the behavioral health services they actually got at the center of the information system.

In order to undertake such practical advocacy, however, social work as a profession needs to come to terms with the gap between the practice reality of the marketplace and practitioner understanding of the ways that accountability is changing in a high tech world. This would suggest, at a minimum, that the profession and its educational institutions need to move toward producing social workers who are conceptually and practically able to connect client empowerment with practitioner accountability and empirically validated practice. Only then will social workers move to actively incorporate the client's experience as the centerpiece of service information systems.

REFERENCES

Ankuta, G. & Abeles, N. (1993). Client satisfaction, clinical significance, and meaningful change in psychotherapy. *Professional Psychology Research and Practice*, *24*, 70-74.

Buck, J., et al. (1999, March/April). Behavioral health benefits in employer-sponsored health plans, 1997. *Health Affairs, 18*, 67-78.

Burnam, A. & Escarce, J. (1999, September/October). Equity in managed care for mental disorders: benefit parity is not sufficient to ensure equity. *Health Affairs, 18*, 22-31.

Debating health care reform: A primer. (1993). *Health Affairs*, Special Issue, 264 pp [On-line]. Available: http://www.projhope.org//HA/archive.htm

Eddy, D. (1998, July/August). Performance measurement: Problems and solutions. *Health Affairs, 17*, 7-25.

Gold, M., Burnbauer, L.& Chu, K. (1995/1996 Winter). How adequate are state data to support health reform or monitor health system change? *Inquiry, 32*, 468-475.

Goldman, W., McCulloch, J. & Sturm, R. (1998, March/April). Costs and use of mental health services before and after managed care. *Health Affairs, 17*, 40-52.

Goldsmith, J. (2000, January/February). How will the Internet change our health system? *Health Affairs, 19*, 148-156.

Hibbard, J. & Jewett, J. (1997, May). Will Quality Report Cards Help Consumers? *Health Affairs, 16*, 218-228.

John A. Hartford Foundation, Inc. (1997). Health care cost and quality-community health management information systems (CHMIS) [On-line]. Available: http://www.jhartfound.org/Programs/Qualcost/chmis.html Retrieved August 6, 2000.

Kozak, A. (1998?). Knowledge coupling: Implementing outcomes measurement through the disciplined and routine control of inputs (Unpublished paper). PKC Corporation, One Mill Street, Box A8, Burlington, VT 05401, 802-658-5351.

Leichter, H. (1993, Summer). Health care reform in Vermont: A work in progress. *Health Affairs, 12*, 71-81.

Leichter, H. (1994, Winter). Health care reform in Vermont, the next chapter. *Health Affairs, 13*, 78-103.

Lohr, K., et al. (1998). Health policy issues and applications for evidence-based medicine and clinical practice guidelines. *Health Policy, 46*, 1-19.

Mathematica Policy Research, Inc. (1994, August 29). Half empty and half full: The capacity of state data to support health reform (Report submitted to The Robert Wood Johnson Foundation). Washington, DC: M. Gold, L. Burnbauer & K. Chu.

Mathematica Policy Research, Inc. (1996, April). Comparative analysis of five initiatives to improve the quality and use of data (Report submitted to The Robert Wood Johnson Foundation). Washington, DC: K. Chu & S. Sweetland.

Mathematica Policy Research, Inc. (1996, July). Enhancing information for state health policy: illustrative state efforts (Report submitted to The Robert Wood Johnson Foundation). Washington, DC: K. Chu, A. Cherlow, & M. Gold.

Millbank Memorial Fund. (2000, July). Better information, better outcomes the use of health technology assessment and clinical effectiveness data in health care purchasing decisions in the United Kingdom and the United States [On-line]. Available: http://www.milbank.org/000726purchasing.html

National Committee for Quality Assurance. (2000). 1999 state of managed care quality report [On-line]. Available: http://www.ncqa.org/indexsm.htm

Oliver, T. & Dowell, E. (1994, Spring). Interest groups and health reform: lessons from California. *Health Affairs, 13*, 123-141.

Patterson, D. (2000). *Personal computer applications in the social services.* Boston: Allyn and Bacon.

PGP for Personal Privacy (software) [On-line]. Available: http://www.nai.com

PKC Corporation. (2000). Complete coupler set [On-line]. Available: http://www.pkc. com/products/complete_couplers.html

PKC Corporation. (2000a). Mental/behavioral health tool set [On-line]. Available: http://www.pkc.com/products/mental.html

PKC Corporation. (2000b). West Virginia Health Care Authority PKC senior assessment coupler pilot project (Unpublished description of project). PKC Corporation, One Mill Street, Box A 8, Burlington, VT 05401, 802-658-5351.

PKC Corporation. (1994). Working with problem knowledge couplers [On-line]. Available: http://www.mhv.net/~wyee/working.html

Quality Metric. (1999). Dynamic health assessment tools-the DynHA™System [On-line]. Available: http://www.qmetric.com/products/dynha/Retrieved July 5, 2000.

Quality Metric. (2000). Products and services [On-line]. Available: http://www. qmetric.com/prod cuts/Retrieved July 15, 2000.

Quality Metric. (2000, February 28). Today Quality Metric, Inc. announced the launch of a new generation of health survey tools (News Release). [On-line]. Available: http://www.qmetric.com/news/releasehumana.php3 Retrieved July 15, 2000.

Their, S. & Gelijns, A. (1998, July/August). Improving health: the reason performance measurement matters (Perspective). *Health Affairs, 17*, 26-28.

Thompson, J., et al. (1998, January/February). The NCQA's quality compass: evaluating managed care in the United States (Health Tracking). *Health Affairs, 17*, 152-158.

Tumlinson, A. et al. (1997, May). *Health Affairs, 16*, 229-238.

Ware, J. (1997). The SF-36survey [On-line]. Available: http://www.sf36.com/ general/sf36.html

Ware, J., Bjorner, J & Kosinski, M. (1999). Dynamic health assessment (Original article prepared for publication in MAPI Research Institute's Quality of Life Newsletter) [On-line]. Available: http://www.qmetric.com/products/dynha/articles/MAPI-article.php3 Retrieved July 15, 2000.

Wasko, N. (1998). The development of a battery of brief self report instruments to assess client experience and satisfaction with outpatient behavioral health counseling services (Doctoral dissertation). Albany, NY: State University of New York at Albany, School of Social Welfare.

Weir, M. (1995, Spring). Institutional and political obstacles to reform (Perspective). *Health Affairs, 14*, 102-104.

West Virginia Office of the Governor. (2000, June 28). Governor Cecil H. Underwood today joined members of the WV Health Care Authority and PKC Corporation to announce plans for a health care pilot project targeted at improving the quality of life for seniors (Press release) [On-line]. Available: http://www.state.wv.us/scripts/ governor/detail.cfm?Page=pr&ID=1389&Start=1 Retrieved July 14, 2000.

Yee, W. (1994, December). Knowledge coupling: Support for psychiatric decision-making [On-line]. Available: http://www.mhv.net/~wyee/pkcpsy.html

Zarin, D., West, J., Pincus, H. & Taniellan, T. (1999, September). Characteristics of health plans that treat psychiatric patients: psychiatrists report that patient care is affected by financial considerations more often under managed care plans. *Health Affairs, 18*, 226-236.

Evaluation of Distance Education Programs in Social Work

Jane A. Macy
Ronald H. Rooney
C. David Hollister
Paul P. Freddolino

SUMMARY. Social work courses and programs delivered with distance technologies continue to increase in number. This article reports on current social work education research on distance courses and pro-

Jane A. Macy, PhD, is Assistant Professor, Social Work Program, University of Washington Tacoma, 1900 Commerce St., Tacoma, WA 98402-3100 (E-mail: jmacy@u.washington.edu).

Ronald H. Rooney, PhD, is Professor, University of Minnesota School of Social Work, 105 Peters Hall, 1404 Gortner Ave., St. Paul, MN 55108 (E-mail: rrooney@che.umn.edu).

C. David Hollister, PhD, is Professor, University of Minnesota School of Social Work, 105 Peters Hall, 1404 Gortner Ave., St. Paul, MN 55108 (E-mail: dhollister@che.umn.edu).

Paul P. Freddolino, PhD, is Professor and Coordinator of Distance Education, School of Social Work, Michigan State University, 254 Baker Hall, East Lansing, MI 48824 (E-mail: freddoli@pilot.msu.edu).

[Haworth co-indexing entry note]: "Evaluation of Distance Education Programs in Social Work." Macy, Jane A., Ronald H. Rooney, C. David Hollister, and Paul P. Freddolino. Co-published simultaneously in *Journal of Technology in Human Services* (The Haworth Press, Inc.) Vol. 18, No. 3/4, 2001, pp. 63-84; and: *New Advances in Technology for Social Work Education and Practice* (ed: Julie Miller-Cribbs) The Haworth Press, Inc., 2001, pp. 63-84. Single or multiple copies of this article are available for a fee from The Haworth Document Delivery Service [1-800-342-9678, 9:00 a.m. - 5:00 p.m. (EST). E-mail address: getinfo@haworthpressinc.com].

grams, and makes recommendations for future distance education research. Distance education research in other fields is described to give context for social work efforts. *[Article copies available for a fee from The Haworth Document Delivery Service: 1-800-342-9678. E-mail address: <getinfo@haworthpressinc.com> Website: <http://www.HaworthPress.com> © 2001 by The Haworth Press, Inc. All rights reserved.]*

KEYWORDS. Distance education, interactive television, web-based, social work education

Distance education has been defined as formal teacher-learner arrangements in which the teacher and learner are geographically separated most or all of the time and the communication between them is through a technology medium such as audiocassette, telephone, radio, television, computers, interactive videodisk and print (Coe & Gandy, 1998). Social work programs utilizing distance technologies continue to steadily grow in number, now including 20% of programs and representing an increase of 6% in the past five years (Siegel, Jennings, Conklin, & Flynn, 2000). Social work courses utilizing Web and internet technology are also increasing in number, though the frequency of that usage is not clear. While proponents claim benefits to students to students from technology use, critics raise questions about the quality of the education delivered (Krueger & Stretch, 2000; Thyer, Artelt, Markward & Dozier, 1997). We suggest that social work education is not well served at this point by calls to halt distance education or to embrace it without reservations. Rather, information is needed about the strengths and weaknesses of social work distance education programs for reaching educational objectives. We begin by putting social work's experience with distance education into the larger context of distance education research in higher education. Next, we describe the nature and range of studies of distance education in social work. Third, we present tentative conclusions based on the results of a review of available evaluation data. Finally, we present implications and suggest areas for future study. As is the case with on-campus social work education, there are more questions than answers in distance education concerning the specific linkages between various technological systems (e.g., picturetel, codec ITV, fiber-optic systems, etc.), specific educational processes (group discussions, amount of lecture time, specific problem-focused in-class exercises, etc.) and specific educational outcomes.

We hope to contribute to the current debate and to help set pragmatic goals for developing new knowledge.

OVERVIEW OF DISTANCE EDUCATION LITERATURE OUTSIDE SOCIAL WORK

Research on distance education varies considerably, given the uneven adoption of distance education and the numerous combinations of technological systems being utilized. Despite the unevenness between fields, there is substantial evidence that distance education brings about learning that is as good as or better than that in traditional classrooms (Biner, Dean, & Mellinger, 1994; Ritchie & Newby, 1989; Zirkin & Sumler, 1995). Zirkin and Sumler's (1995) review of research found that "evaluations of the use of technology in distance education at the post-secondary level have generally been favorable with regard to levels of student achievement and retention. In general, researchers have found that the various distance education instructional formats have been found to be as effective, if not more effective, than traditional face-to-face instruction in the classroom. The formats evaluated ranged from computer conferencing to interactive video and videodisc instructional modes" (p. 99).

Learner-Related Research

Much of distance education research that has been done to date examines either learner-related or faculty-related issues. Interactivity is a critical concept in the distance education learner research literature. Moore's conceptualization of educational interaction includes three kinds of interaction: learner with content, learner with instructor, and learner with learner (as cited in Ritchie, 1991). Most studies of student/learner success find that interactivity is a common element to student achievement (Zirkin & Sumler, 1995).

One overarching question regarding distance learning is whether it is different from the learning that occurs in traditional face-to-face classrooms. Is effective learning at a distance primarily an effect of variations in the behaviors of teaching institutions, a function of learner characteristics, or is it a function of an interaction between the two? What learner characteristics are of particular significance and in what ways can institutions respond to them? These questions, and multiple variations upon them, continue to be the focus of much of the research on learners. Social work educators and researchers can derive research questions that are a subset of broader distance education concerns and which reflect the unique needs and challenges of social work education.

Gibson's (1991) review of distance education literature regarding learners and learning noted the need for further research in distance education to encourage theory building and to gain a "deeper appreciation of the contribution of the socio-cultural context" (p. 40). She also calls for greater use of qualitative methodologies to understand the experiences of distance education learners.

Faculty-Related Research

Studies of faculty have generally been concerned with faculty attitudes towards distance education, including studies examining faculty skepticism about distance education (Black, 1992), faculty receptivity to college credit distance education (Clark, 1993), faculty motivations for participating in distance education (Burnham, 1988), analysis of the relationship between personal job satisfaction and attitudes towards teaching in a distance program (Taylor & White, 1991), and faculty resistance to instructional technology (Gunawardena, 1990; McNeil, 1990). A recent study conducted by the National Education Association (NEA) found that there was enthusiasm among its college faculty members for distance education teaching. Respondents also noted several concerns as well, citing preparation time, workload and salary issues (Carr, 2000). These findings are similar to others from the last decade. Black found that faculty support for distance education was "largely determined by the perceived compatibility of distance education with their beliefs and values about university education in general" (Black, 1992, p. 15). Black goes on to report "Most faculty who supported distance education emphasized accessibility values, while those who opposed distance education viewed quality as the priority" (p. 17). The research indicates that faculty attitudes towards distance education are complex (Clark, 1993; Dillon and Walsh, 1992).

The most recent NEA study reported by Carr (2000) echoed findings from Dillon and Walsh (1992), who concluded after conducting a comprehensive literature review on faculty in distance education that, "In general, these studies indicate that faculty who teach at a distance are positive toward distance teaching and that faculty attitudes improve as experience with distance education increases and faculty become more familiar with the technology and logistics" (p. 9). They also found that in general, "the data indicate that faculty who deliver education at a distance are well-educated, full-time veteran instructors who represent all sectors of higher education and who come from all ranks and a wide variety of disciplines" (p. 16).

Interactive Television

Interactive television (ITV) is currently a popular choice for social work distance education programs. A strong body of research on interactive television and teleconferencing exists. An extensive review of the literature regarding the educational merit of instructional television resulted in several findings. Comparative studies indicate that "students taking courses via television achieve, in most cases, as well as students taking courses via traditional methods" and that "Findings of equivalent student achievement hold even when rigorous methodological research standards are applied" (Whittington, 1987, p. 54). Since the time of that review, a number of studies have confirmed these findings. Outcomes for students have been found to be as good, if not better, for distance students than for traditional classroom students (Dillon, Gunawardena, & Parker, 1992; Zirkin & Sumler, 1995).

Interactive television has been institutionalized to the point that many institutions offer credit courses or full degree programs via ITV. For many of these programs, synchronous learning (learning in which the learner and teacher interact in real time) has been supplemented with asynchronous learning modes such as e-mail, discussion groups on-line, and electronic bulletin boards. The focus of much of the interactive television research has been the same as that of distance education in general. Additionally, ITV research has been concerned with interaction (Bischoff, Bisconer, Kooker, & Woods, 1996; Fulford & Zhang, 1993; MacKinnon, Walshe, Cummings, & Velonis, 1995; Ritchie & Newby, 1989) and student satisfaction and affective responses to interactive television (Biner, Bink, Huffman, & Dean, 1995; Biner, Dean, & Mellinger, 1994; Wilkes & Burnham, 1991).

The research on learners in distance education, and ITV in particular, has been concerned primarily with student outcomes, performance, or satisfaction (Wilkes & Burnham, 1991; Biner, Dean, & Mellinger, 1994). While a strong body of research on ITV exists, the primary goal of this research has been to demonstrate comparability in student outcomes between traditional methods of teaching and use of ITV. There is relatively little literature within distance education in the United States in general, and within social work education, that provides in-depth, detailed descriptions of distance education experiences from a student point of view.

Much of the other ITV research has focused on the role of interaction between participants utilizing ITV (Bischoff, Bisconer, Kooker, & Woods, 1996; Fulford & Zhang, 1993; MacKinnon, Walshe, Cummings, & Velonis, 1995; Ritchie & Newby, 1989). Typically only one aspect of student experience is investigated (e.g., interaction between class members or satisfaction with the sound and video quality) rather than the entire experience of the student. Research conducted at Ball State has included studies of student satisfaction with telecourses (Biner, Dean, & Mellinger, 1994), predictors of student performance (Bink, Biner, Huffman, Geer, & Dean, 1995) and personality characteristics that help predict successful telecourse performance (Biner, Bink, Huffman, & Dean, 1995). These large-scale research studies used rigorous quantitative methods that increase our confidence in generalizing the results due to strong external validity. In addition they help us understand what learners bring to distance education via ITV.

These studies have indicated that remote site group size may predict satisfaction with all facets of courses taken as well as relative performance (Biner, Welsh, Barone, Summers, & Dean, 1997); that prior academic GPA, year in college, and promptness of material delivery contribute to prediction of final course grades while demographic variables were not significant in predicting course performance (Bink, Biner, Huffman, Geer, & Dean, 1995); that students enrolled in telecourses had unique personality profiles and that certain traits predicted success for telecourse students (Biner, Bink, Huffman, & Dean (1995); and that there are identifiable dimensions to student satisfaction with interactive television college courses (Biner, Dean, & Mellinger, 1994).

In an interesting and useful early study, McCleary and Egan (1989) studied a three-course sequence of classes taught to students off-campus via ITV and on campus (by the same instructor) in a conventional fashion in a studio classroom. Their design allowed them to use distinctive experimental conditions in each of the three courses. Of particular concern to the researchers were variables associated with learner performance, retention of students, instructor effectiveness, learner receptivity, and course design features associated with distance learning. Specific variables included the role of on-site facilitators, student evaluation procedures, provision of learning materials, instructor visits to sites, feedback to students in distance sites, and use of visual material and media. McCleary and Egan highlight certain course design elements as critical to the success of instruction using two-way interactive television. These elements included the role of the on-site facilitator, the use of a course manual, and the use of visual material and media. Interestingly, they did not find any evidence that instructor site visits were of particular impact, though they urge further examinations of this feature.

MacKinnon, Walshe, Cummings, and Velonis (1995) were interested in investigating pedagogical styles and interaction patterns possible utilizing ITV in educational settings. Their thoughtful discussion of these experiences provides a number of suggestions for educators using an ITV system. "The nature of interactive television technology invites educators to think about teaching and learning in a different manner . . . the main assumption is that students must be actively involved in learning processes. Although lecturing can be as engaging as any other method of teaching in a conventional classroom, we have found the most effective uses of interactive television to be those designed to sustain the interaction of participants in dialogue" (p. 91). They go on to add "We believe that interactive television supports learning in a number of social contexts and types of interaction" (p. 91). Also noted are the various roles a moderator can play and the importance of technical decisions (microphone placement, seating, control of camera, views). Of interest to social work educators may be their observation that they found that they could structure the interaction to heighten tensions due to differences or they could use it to encourage tolerance and understanding in order to have students collaboratively negotiate solutions to problems.

Bischoff, Bisconer, Kooker, and Woods (1996) found that ITV showed parity on measures of structure and transactional distance when compared with traditional learning classrooms. Bischoff et al. (1996) concluded that "interactive television, as a course delivery format, did not appear to have a negative effect on dialogue, structure, or transactional distance. Data suggest that concurrent access to e-mail may have an influence on the findings. Interactive television may be equivalent to face-to-face instruction for delivering educational content and process to remote learners who prefer this type of learning environment" (p. 16). They go on to suggest that they believe that a seminar and discussion format can be effectively implemented in an interactive television setting.

Web-Based and Web-Assisted Instruction

If ITV has raised the question of whether learners need to receive education in on-campus classrooms, web-based instruction asks whether they need to leave their own homes. New models of education focus on the life-long learner, rather than the learner who takes two or four years out to complete education at a residential college or university (Rowley, Lujan, & Dolence, 1998). Courses delivered through the web offer asynchronous learning, completed at a time and place selected by the learner (Schmidt, 2000). Learning with the web also presents special demands on the learner to participate actively rather than receive education passively as the recipient of "seat time" in an in-person lecture (Gumport & Chun, 1999; Forsyth, 1998). This can be demanding for students accustomed to teacher-centered education (Hobbs, (1990). As with ITV research, initial studies have compared student learning in the form of grades to that achieved through in-person instruction (Hantula, 1998). As with other distance and ITV education, there is concern regarding the ways in which learning can be made to be more interactive as well as active (Aberson, Berger, Emerson, & Romero, 1997; Morrison, Ross, Gopalarishnan, & Casey, 1995). While web-based educational efforts are increasing exponentially, the research documenting its effectiveness lags behind. There are many examples of courses that are either supplemented by web resources or courses that are fully on-line, in all areas of higher education.

OVERVIEW OF SOCIAL WORK DISTANCE EDUCATION EVALUATIONS

As distance education technologies have become more widely utilized in social work education, the number of studies evaluating their use has also increased. These evaluative studies are, however, somewhat limited in the scope of the variables considered. Quite typical are studies that compare social work students' satisfaction with distance courses to students' satisfaction with traditional classroom courses (Coe & Gandy, 1998; Freddolino & Sutherland, 2000; Hollister & Kim, 1999; Macy, 1999; Schoech, 2000; Thyer, Artelt, Markward & Dozier, 1998; Thyer, Polk & Gaudin, 1997). Some also utilize measures of students' learning, principally students' course grades and/or performance on class assignments (Hollister & McGee, 2000; Petracchi & Morgenbesser, 1995; Petracchi & Patchner, 2000). The individual courses evaluated encompass a range of social work courses, such as social policy (Huff, 2000); substance abuse (Hollister & McGee, 2000; Petracchi & Morgenbesser, 1995); research methods (Pettrachi & Patchner, 2000); statistics (Harrington, 1999; Henley & Dunlap, 1998; Wong & Law, 1998); child welfare (Thyer, Polk & Gaudin, 1997), human behavior and the social environment (Barnett-Queen, 1998; Barnett-Queen & Zhu, 1999; Haslet, Lehmann, & McLaughlin, 1998;), human diversity (Huff, 1999), social welfare history (Faux & Black-Hughes, 2000), social welfare law (Sarnoff, 1999), practice methods (Coe & Elliot, 1999; Cummins, 1998; Hagan, 1998; Oullette, Sells, & Rittner, 1999; Sells & Rittner, 1998): and field instruction (Burke & Macy, 1998; Cohen & Black, 1998; McFall & Freddolino, 2000b). The evaluative studies have focused initially on courses delivered by television-based modalities, including satellite transmission with two-way audio (Brown & Stanley, 1998; Rooney & Bibus, 1995), one-way closed circuit television (Raymond, 1996), and by ITV (two-way video and two-way audio). More recently studies have appeared which evaluate the use of the WorldWideWeb either to enhance traditional instruction (Faux and Black-Hughes, 2000; Galambos & Neal, 1998; Gonzalez & Huff, 1998; Lancaster, Stokes, & Summary, 1998; Ouellette, 1998; Schoech, 2000; Wernet & Olliges, 1998; Wernet, Olliges & Dellicath, 2000) or to provide entire courses on line (Barnett-Queen, 1998; Kolbo & Washington, 1998; Sarnoff, 1999; Stocks and Freddolino, 2000). There is also growing exploration of the use of CD-ROM along with other media (Cummins, 1998).

Evaluations of social work degree programs that are delivered entirely or primarily through distance education are still quite rare, although comprehensive conceptual frameworks that could lead to such studies are being developed (Forster & Washington, 2000; Haagenstad & Kraft, 1998; Heitkamp & Henly, 1998; Kalke, Macy, Rooney, & Burke, 1998). Potts and Hagen (2000) have conducted a comprehensive empirical evaluation of a distance MSW program. An evaluation by Haga and Heitkamp (2000) of a baccalaureate social work program included a seven-year follow-up study of alumni. In general, however, more evaluations are needed that focus not only on social work student satisfaction and learning outcomes, but also include dimensions such as social work faculty satisfaction (Freddolino, 1997a; Kalke, Rooney, & Macy, 1998; Raymond, 1996), degree of institutional fit with distance programming, cost and resource analyses (Forster & Washington, 2000), and career paths of graduates.

OBSERVATIONS AND CONCLUSIONS ABOUT SOCIAL WORK DISTANCE EDUCATION EVALUATIONS

Studies of distance learning in social work now encompass web-based as well as television modalities. There has been a considerable increase in the last two years in published studies of distance education evaluations in social work with *Research in Social Work Practice* and the *Journal of Technology in Human Services* devoting complete issues and the *Journal of Social Work Education* incorporating special sections on distance education and technology in two issues. Conclusions are complicated by the fact that technologies employed vary enormously across programs; hence the independent variable often differs across studies. Also, outcome variables utilized are also often distinct to the program.

Despite those differences in both independent and dependent variables, course and program outcomes achieved in social work distance education courses and programs are comparable to those achieved in traditional face-to-face programs. As well, distance education formats present particular strengths and challenges for social work education. In one of the early reports of distance education instruction, Weinbach, Gandy and Tartaglia (1984) reported that 77% of distance students rated the quality of instruction comparable in quality to traditional courses and 78% felt it met their learning needs. Meanwhile, 75% of faculty approached distance education instruction with some trepidation. That nervousness dissipated and ultimately all were convinced it was effective. Thyer, Polk, and Gaudin (1997) found live teaching was evaluated significantly more positively than two-way interactive television teaching. While students in a child and adolescent psychopathology assessment course did not differ significantly in their appraisals between in-person and interactive instruction, students in a course on treatment of substance abuse favored live instruction (Thyer, Artelt, Markward, & Dozier, 1998). Coe and Elliott (1999) report a study of a single direct practice course comparing students receiving instruction via ITV and students receiving in-person instruction. Among the variables studied were classroom socialization, perception of the instructor; consultation with the instructor; advisement; access to library and identification with the school of social work. Students in the distant site reported higher socialization scores, perhaps because many worked together and completed assignments cooperatively. There were no differences on perception of and consultation with the instructor though distance learners rated advisement and access to library lower than on campus learners and reported less identification with the school of social work and more identification with the institution where classes were taken. Seventy-five percent of the distance students reported that they would prefer on-site instruction near home. Meanwhile 66% of distance learners said that their 2nd and 3rd choices were a combination of satellite and in-person instruction or having all courses delivered via satellite to a site near their homes. There were no significant differences in outcome measures, but on-campus students tended to have higher scores (Coe & Elliott, 1999). Wilson (1999) has suggested that " . . . too many early evaluations accepted student self-assessments as evidence of actual learning, and comparison of grade point averages may not reliably measure actual learning and skill development" (p. 328). Addressing this point, Huff (2000) compared the learning of critical thinking skills with ITV and in-person classes, finding that both groups significantly improved and there were not significant differences between them. In addition, Johnson and Huff (2000) found that distance students were significantly more likely to utilize to utilize email to communicate with the instructor and other students than students in the home site, perhaps by increasing interaction to reduce a sense of isolation.

In addition to reports comparing individual courses, evaluations of distance education programs have also emerged. In a series of studies conducted at Michigan State University, learning environments in traditional and ITV classrooms have been compared. Using the ACES (Adult Classroom Environment Scale) classroom environments in Marquette, Gaylord and the main campus were perceived by the students in the sites as essentially equivalent on most of the dimensions measured by the instrument (Freddolino & Sutherland, 2000). Student perceptions of the field environment were comparable between students in the two distance sites and the main campus sites while there was a tendency for distance students to rate agency climate and local resources more favorably (McFall & Freddolino, 2000a). Meanwhile, a survey of distance education agencies providing field instruction found that the connection to a distance program student permitted those agencies to provide more services, enhanced their access to learning new knowledge about interventions and exposed them to use of technology by students (McFall & Freddolino, 2000b). Potts and Hagen (2000) reported in a multi-year evaluation that course outcomes and satisfaction levels have been comparable between home-site and distance students with higher reported cross-cultural sensitivity among distance students. In a study comparing the experiences of traditional in-person students and those receiving classes via ITV in Mississippi, Forster (1997) reported that there were no significant differences on grades, assignments and exams between students in the two formats. Faculty and facilitators did notice differences in sustaining attention among students in distant sites and developing rapport with them (Forster & Washington, 2000). In a seven year follow-up of students who received their BSW degrees entirely through ITV instruction, Haga and Heitkamp (2000) report that all distance graduates were licensed to practice and 92% were practicing social work with 92% working in communities with populations under 1700, the target group for the distance program. Finally, qualitative studies of the subjective experience of distance learners are beginning to emerge in social work (Macy, 1999). Areas for improvement noted across studies have been the need for improved access to library resources; delineation of faculty rewards for participation in distance education; the challenge of developing relationships with distant learners; advising; and identification of distance students with the main campus program.

Web-based instruction, a more recent development in social work education, also presents comparable outcomes with in-person instruction in terms of course outcomes. Students, including non-traditional students, have reported satisfaction with web-based learning. Wernet, Olliges and Delicath (2000) report that non-traditional, working students were more likely to use the web site in courses taught with a web-based platform than traditional students. Barnett-Queen and Zhu (2000) found that students in a web-based course and those in the traditional in-person format learned well in both formats with no significant differences for learning styles. As with ITV, others have reported learner preference for in-person instruction and that learners scored better with that instruction. For example, students with lower undergraduate grade point averages did less well with a programmed instruction format than the in-person format (Harrington, 1999). Faux and Black-Hughes (2000) found that students in an undergraduate history course preferred contact with an instructor to internet instruction and performed better when taught with traditional lectures. Schoech (2000), in a report of an internet doctoral course, reported that while course satisfaction was as high as in face-to-face offerings, mechanisms needed to be built in to augment informal learning. A second iteration of an internet-based graduate social work research methods course added opportunities for interaction through self-tests, automated feedback discussion questions and links to an internet discussion list. Students in the second iteration participated more in class list discussions than those in the first and rated their experiences more positively. Increasing opportunities for interactivity made it easier for an active learning environment to be created (Stocks & Freddolino, 2000).

IMPLICATIONS AND AREAS FOR FUTURE RESEARCH

Huff (2000) has suggested that "numerous studies have supported equal acquisition of content when a comparison is made between distance education students and on-site students. Perhaps it is time for the comparisons to stop. Rather than continuing efforts to prove that distance education is as good as traditional education, future research should simply focus on how to improve distance education courses by making them even more effective learning experiences for students" (p. 413). There is a role for advancing our knowledge of student learning across programs and sites. If we are successful in crafting or agreeing upon common instruments, it will be possible to move beyond the current single course or single program studies to cross-program evaluations.

In addition to assessments, which focus on comparability to traditional programs, we need to explore more carefully the particular merits or strengths of particular formats on their own terms. For example, the fact that distance learning groups appear to become relatively cohesive and supportive raise models for us to consider so that such strengths might be imported into our residential/on-campus programs.

Just as our use and understanding of technology in social work education has increased, so too has the number of research questions we might explore. We echo Ouellette, Sells, and Rittner (1999): "Instead of comparing technology-supported instructional mediums to conventional classroom learning environments, the time has come to begin assessing which instructional medium is i) best suited for what type of student; ii) which best accomplishes what specific learning outcome; iii) which pedagogical principle is best operationalized by a particular medium" (CD-ROM). We need research focused on a number of areas, research that explores the use of specific technologies; learner characteristics; faculty concerns and characteristics; pedagogy and content area; and administrative and broader community/stakeholder issues. While there is much overlap between the categories, possible research questions and variables in each of these areas are described in the following sections.

Technology

The technology itself, as noted elsewhere, poses challenges for researchers. We need careful consideration of the types of technology that support effective and successful professional training and education.

Models of technology use that examine the impact of combinations of technologies are becoming increasingly common and need to be investigated. For example, can learning be enhanced when web-based materials and on-line discussion groups supplement an ITV course?

The types and kinds of technology (e.g., ITV systems, web-based software) vary enormously across programs and institutions. What role does technical competence play (on the part of both students and instructors)? What influence do technical difficulties have on outcomes? We also need studies that examine the impact and success of certain kinds of technology across institutions and settings in order to more accurately understand what works and what does not for large numbers of social work students. While we have primarily concerned ourselves with ITV and web-based instruction in this article, other technologies are being used and must also be evaluated (e.g., individual videoconferencing, streaming video).

Learner Characteristics

There are a host of variables that might be explored in regards to learners. Recent contributions from adult learning research have helped us recognize important differences between learners. Studies that take into account age, sex, ethnicity, culture, professional experience, learning style, motivation, to name a few, may help us become much better able to meet the individual learning needs of students. For example, does distance education work better for students who already have substantial experience in the social services (versus those who have little or no experience)? One could hypothesize that more experienced students already have a set of experiences to which to relate social work concepts and may not need as much face-to-face instruction as those less experienced. It could also be that those who work full-time are more appreciative of the convenience of distance education than those who work part-time or less, and that this may engender greater motivation to succeed within distance education formats.

It is particularly important to study more deeply the experiences of students in varied instructional formats to track both the strengths and difficulties of those formats. Such study might lead us into greater appreciation of the role of learning style in utilizing educational formats. Research on learners stands to benefit all of social work education, not just those efforts focused on distance education.

Within social work education circles we need to continue our work on defining success and competence and the measures of those concepts. As described earlier, comparability between distance and on-campus programs has been a central focus of much of the research. As in on campus, face-to-face programs, there is a need to go beyond course grades as we work to compare formats. Specific social work skills and knowledge, such as critical thinking, would be helpful to assess and compare.

Faculty Concerns and Characteristics

More research is also needed about instructional style and instructor characteristics that seem to be associated with successful ITV and web-based classes. Just as we work to understand the interplay of learner variables, we would benefit from a better understanding of the match between instructor variables and technologies. Is every instructor able to be successful at ITV instruction, for example? Pedagogical responsibilities change with the technologies employed, with instructor time and rewards a critical issue. Acquiring a new set of pedagogical skills requires time and effort, as well as physical resources. How are these best taught or provided?

Pedagogy and Content Areas

As we add studies of web-based instruction to those of ITV, more information is needed about appropriate technologies according to subject matter. Is each technology equally effective for teaching different content areas such as HBSE, policy, research, and practice? What characteristics of teaching style, pedagogy, are associated with success in different formats of instruction? We need to also ask what characteristics of teaching style are associated with success across formats (if any).

As studies across the distance education field emphasize active learning, methods for increasing such learning across all technologies are needed. An assumption has been that practice skills need to be taught through in-person, face-to-face instruction. This assumption needs to be examined, with studies of skills outcomes obtained through the use of the various formats.

Administrative/Broader Community Issues

Over time, we need to broaden the scope of our evaluations to include consideration of how stakeholders assess the benefits of such programs. For example, how are those benefits assessed by the professional communities that graduates of distance programs join, community members, taxpayers, legislators and university officials? McFall and Freddolino's (2000a) study of the impact on field practicum agencies suggests some benefits not typically considered in assessing educational outcomes.

From an administrative perspective, several issues could benefit from increased attention and investigation. Faculty willingness to use technology, workload, incentives, support, and material and/or course ownership are being discussed to some degree in most academic institutions today.

While we have sorted by broad categories crucial areas for additional research, it is clear that work must be done to understand the interplay between and among all of these. What is an effective match between a technology, the subject matter and a particular student? How do an instructor's learning style, pedagogy, specific technology employed, and prior experience with that technology come together to influence educational outcomes?

Evaluation of distance education programs is helping us to reexamine our assumptions about education in all delivery formats. Answering the questions we have posed will likely help us improve our efforts to teach students in more traditional formats as well. It would behoove us in social work education to think "big picture" and to ask the same questions of our on-campus education efforts as we are doing with our distance programs. For example, what evidence do we have that professional socialization occurs through our in-person instruction? Such questions then lead us to ask questions of our entire educational programs, not just the distance programs. We agree with Quam's (1999) proposal, in an editorial for a volume of the *Journal of Social Work Education* with a special section on use of technology in education, that the appropriate focus is not on technology as a whole for social work education but rather on how faculty can use technology to its fullest extent to improve the way education is delivered to all students, whether in on-campus classrooms, distance site classrooms, or in their own homes.

REFERENCES

Aberson, C. L. Berger, D. E., Emerson, E. P. & Romero, V. O. (1997). WISE: web interface for statistics education. *Behavior Research Methods, Instruments and Computers, 29*(2), 217-221

Barnett-Queen, T. (1998,August). *HBSE on the Web: Demonstration of an interactive HBSE distance education course utilizing the WWW as the primary delivery method.* Paper presented at the conference on Information Technologies for Social Work Education and Practice, Charleston, SC.

Barnett-Queen, T. & Zhu, E.(1999). Distance Education: Analysis of learning preferences in two sections of an undergraduate HBSE-Like Human Growth and Development Course: Face-to-face and web-based distance learning. [CD Rom] *3rd Annual Technology Conference for Social Work Education and Practice, Conference Proceedings.* Columbus: University of South Carolina College of Social Work.

Biner, P. M., Bink, M. L., Huffman, M. L., & Dean, R. S. (1995). Personality characteristics differentiating and predicting the achievement of televised-course students and traditional-course students. *American Journal of Distance Education, 9* (2), 46-60.

Biner, P. M., Dean, R. S., & Mellinger, A. E. (1994). Factors underlying distance learner satisfaction with televised college-level courses. *American Journal of Distance Education 8* (1), 60-71.

Biner, P. M., Welsh, K. D., Barone, N. M., Summers, M. & Dean, R.S. (1997). The impact of remote-site group size on student satisfaction and relative performance in interactive telecourses. *The American Journal of Distance Education, 11*(1), 23-33.

Bink, M. L., Biner, P. M., Huffman, M. L., Geer, B. L., & Dean, R. S. (1995, Spring). Attitudinal, college/course-related, and demographic predictors of performance in televised continuing education courses. *The Journal of Continuing Higher Education.* 14-20.

Bischoff, W. R., Bisconer, S. W., Kooker, B. M., & Woods, L. C. (1996). Transactional distance and interactive television in the distance education of health care professionals. *American Journal of Distance Education, 10* (3), 4-19.

Black, E. J. (1992). Faculty support for university distance education. *Journal of Distance Education, 7*(2), 5-29.

Brown, N. K. & Stanley, R. M. (1998, August). *Maximizing student participation in a one-way medium.* Paper presented at the conference on Information Technologies for Social Work Education and Practice, Charleston, SC.

Burke, K. & Macy, J. A. (1998, August). *Opportunities and challenges in distance education.* Paper presented at the conference on Information Technologies for Social Work Education and Practice, Charleston, SC.

Carr, S. (2000, July 7). Many professors are optimistic on distance learning, survey finds. *Chronicle of Higher Education,* p. A35.

Clark, T. (1993). Attitudes of higher education faculty toward distance education: A national survey. *American Journal of Distance Education, 7* (2), 19-33.

Coe, J. R. & Elliott, D. (1999). An evaluation of teaching direct practice courses in a distance education program for rural settings. *Journal of Social Work Education, 35* (3), 353-366.

Coe, J. R. & Gandy, J. T. (1998). Perspectives from consumers (students) in a distance education program. *2nd Annual Technology Conference for Social Work Education and Practice, Conference Proceedings* (pp. 91-98).Columbus: University of South Carolina College of Social Work.

Cohen, B. & Black, J. (1998). From a distance: The partnership between field education and distance education MSW program offerings. *2nd Annual Technology
Conference for Social Work Education and Practice, Conference Proceedings*
(pp. 99-108). Columbus: University of South Carolina College of Social Work.

Cummins, L. K. (1998, August). *Social work skills demonstrated: Beginning direct
practice.* Paper presented at the conference on Information Technologies for Social
Work Education and Practice, Charleston, SC.

Dillon, C. L., & Walsh, S. (1992). Faculty: The neglected resource in distance education. *American Journal of Distance Education, 6* (3), 5-2 1.

Faux, T.L. & Black-Hughes, C. (2000). A comparison of using the internet versus lectures to teach social work history. *Research on Social Work Practice, 10* (4),
454-466.

Forster, M. (1997, September). *Evaluating a part-time graduate social work distance
education program at the University of Southern Mississippi.* Paper presented at the
Information Technologies for Social Work Education Conference. Charleston, SC.

Forster, M. & Washington, E. (2000). A model for developing and managing distance
education programs using interactive video technology. *Journal of Social Work Education, 36* (1), 147-160.

Forsyth, I. (1998). *Teaching and learning materials on the Internet.* (2nd Ed.). London:
Kogan Page

Freddolino, P. (1997a, September). *Building on experience: Lessons from a distance
education MSW program.* Paper presented at Information Technologies for Social
Work Education. Charleston, SC.

Freddolino, P.P. (1997b). The importance of relationships for a quality learning environment in interactive TV classrooms. *Journal of Education for Business, 71* (4),
205-208.

Freddolino, P.P. & Sutherland, C (2000). Assessing the comparability of classroom environments in graduate social work education delivered via interactive instructional
television. *Journal of Social Work Education, 36* (1), 115-129.

Fulford, C., & Zhang, S. (1993). Perceptions of interaction: The critical predictor in
distance education. *American Journal of Distance Education, 7* (3), 8-20.

Galambos, C. & Neal, C. (1998). Untangling the net: Using policy resources in the
classroom. *2nd Annual Technology Conference for Social Work Education and
Practice, Conference Proceedings* (pp. 143-151). Columbus: University of South
Carolina College of Social Work.

Gibson, C. C. (1991). *Changing perceptions of learners and learning at a distance: A
review of selected recent research.* (Research Monograph No. 8). University Park,
PA: The Penn State University, American Center for the Study of Distance Education.

Gonzalez, J. E. & Huff, D. (1998). Assessing the impact of instructional technology:
The case of the cyber-history of social work. *2nd Annual Technology Conference
for Social Work Education and Practice, Conference Proceedings* (pp. 179-184).
Columbus: University of South Carolina College of Social Work.

Gumport, P. & Chun, M. (1999). Technology and higher education: Opportunities and
challenges for the new era. In P.G. Altbach, R. Berdahl, & P. Gumport (Eds.),

American higher education in the twenty-first century. (pp. 370-395). Baltimore: Johns Hopkins Press.

Gunawardena, C. N. (1990). Integrating telecommunication systems to reach distance learners. *American Journal of Distance Education, 4* (3), 38-46.

Haagenstad, S. & Kraft, S. (1998). Outcome measures comparing classroom education to distance education. *2nd Annual Technology Conference for Social Work Education and Practice, Conference Proceedings* (pp. 185-188). Columbus: University of South Carolina College of Social Work.

Haga, M. & Heitkamp, T. (2000). Bringing social work education to the prairie. *Journal of Social Work Education, 36* (2), 309-324.

Hagan, C. B. (1998, August). *Distance education: Teaching practice methods using ITV.* Paper presented at the conference on Information Technologies for Social Work Education and Practice, Charleston, SC.

Hantula, D. A. (1998). The virtual industrial/organizational psychology class: Learning and teaching in cyberspace in three iterations. *Behavior Research Methods, Instruments and Computers. 30,* 205-216.

Harrington, D. (1999). Teaching statistics: A comparison of traditional classroom and programmed instruction/distance learning approaches. *Journal of Social Work Education, 35* (3), 343-352.

Haslet, D., Lehmann, B., & McLaughlin, C. (1998, August). *Easing onto the information superhighway: Affordable classroom applications from rural America.* Paper presented at the conference on Information Technologies for Social Work Education and Practice, Charleston, SC.

Heitkamp, T.L. & Henly, G.A. (1998). A conceptual model for evaluating a social work distance education program. *2nd Annual Technology Conference for Social Work Education and Practice, Conference Proceedings* (pp.189-195). Columbus: University of South Carolina College of Social Work.

Henley, H. C.,& Dunlap, K. M. (1998, August). *Traditional and distance learning: Can they be compatible?* Paper presented at the conference on Information Technologies for Social Work Education and Practice, Charleston, SC.

Hobbs, V. (1990) Distance learning in North Dakota: A cross-technology study of the schools, administrators, coordinators, instructors, and students. Two-way interactive television, audiographic tele-learning, and instruction by satellite. (ERIC Document Reproduction Service No. ED 328 225)

Hollister, D., & Kim, Y. (1999). Evaluating ITV-Based MSW Programs: A Comparison of ITV and Traditional Graduates' Perceptions of MSW Program Qualities. [CD Rom] *3rd Annual Technology Conference for Social Work Education and Practice, Conference Proceedings.* Charleston, SC. Columbus: University of South Carolina College of Social Work.

Hollister, C. D., & McGee, G. (2000). Delivering substance abuse and child welfare content through interactive television. *Research on Social Work Practice, 10* (4), 417-427.

Holmberg, B. (1987). The development of distance education research. *American Journal of Distance Education, 1*(3), 16-23.

Huff, M. (2000). A comparison study of live instruction versus interactive television for teaching MSW students critical thinking skills. *Research on Social Work Practice, 10* (4), 400-416.

Johnson, M. M., & Huff, M. T. (2000). Students' use of computer-mediated communication in a distance education course. *Research on Social Work Practice, 10* (4), 519-532.

Kalke, N. L., Rooney, R., & Macy, J. A.(1998, March). *Providing effective education in distance education.* Paper presented at the Annual Program Meeting of the Council on Social Work Education, Orlando, FL.

Kalke, N., Macy, J.A., Rooney, R.H., & Burke, K. (1998, August). *Key questions and critical components: Design, delivery, and evaluation of social work distance education programs.* Paper presented at the conference on Information Technologies for Social Work Education and Practice, Charleston, SC.

Kolbo, J. R., & Washington, E.M. (1998). Internet-based instruction as an interactive approach to managing prerequisite curriculum content in a graduate social work program. *2nd Annual Technology Conference for Social Work Education and Practice, Conference Proceedings* (pp. 212-220). Columbus: University of South Carolina College of Social Work.

Krueger, L. W., & Stretch, J. J. (2000). How hypermodern technology in social work education bites back. *Journal of Social Work Education, 36* (1), 103-114.

Lancaster, K., Stokes, J., & Summary, L.(1998). The use of WebBoard conferencing in social work education. *2nd Annual Technology Conference for Social Work Education and Practice, Conference Proceedings* (pp. 221-227). Columbus: University of South Carolina College of Social Work.

MacKinnon, A., Walshe, B., Cummings, M., & Velonis, U. (1995). An inventory of pedagogical considerations for interactive television. *Journal of Distance Education, 10* (1), 75-94.

Macy, J. A. (1999). A Making the Difference: Reports from Distance MSW Graduates Regarding Essential Supports. [CD Rom] *3rd Annual Technology Conference for Social Work Education and Practice, Conference Proceedings.* Columbus: University of South Carolina College of Social Work.

McCleary, I. D., & Egan, M. W. (1989). Program design and evaluation: Two-way interactive television. *American Journal of Distance Education, 3* (1), 50-60.

McFall, J. P., & Freddolino, P. P. (2000a). The impact of distance education programs on community agencies. *Research on Social Work Practice,10* (4) 438-454.

McFall, J. P., & Freddolino, P. P. (2000b). Quality and comparability in distance field education: lessons learned from comparing three program sites. *Journal of Social Work Education, 36* (2), 293-307.

McNeil, D.R. (1990). *Wiring the ivory tower: A round table on technology in higher education.* Washington D.C.: Academy for Educational Development.

Morrison, G. R., Ross, S. M., Gopalarishnan, M. & Casey, J.(1995). The effects of feedback and incentives on achievement in computer-based instruction. *Contemporary Educational Psychology, 20*(1), 32-50.

Ouellette, P. M. (1998). Moving toward computer-supported instruction in social work practice: The "virtual classroom." *2nd Annual Technology Conference for Social*

Work Education and Practice, Conference Proceedings (pp. 242-248). Columbus: University of South Carolina College of Social Work.

Ouellette P., Sells, S.,& Rittner, B. (1999). Combining teleconferencing with Web-base instruction to teach an advanced Social Work practice course for working with difficult children, adolescents and families: A journey in collaborative teaching and learning. [CD Rom] *3rd Annual Technology Conference for Social Work Education and Practice, Conference Proceedings*. Columbus: University of South Carolina College of Social Work.

Petracchi, H. E., & Morgenbesser, M. (1995). The use of video and one-way broadcast technology to deliver continuing social work education: A comparative assessment of student learning. *Journal of Continuing Social Work Education, 6* (3),18-22.

Petracchi, H. E., & Patchner, M. A. (2000). Social work students and their learning environment: a comparison of interactive television, face-to-face instruction, and the traditional classroom. *Journal of Social Work Education, 36* (2), 335-346.

Potts, M. K., & Hagen, C. B. (2000). Going the distance: using systems theory to design, implement, and evaluate a distance education program. *Journal of Social Work Education, 36* (1), 131-146.

Quam, J. Q. (1999). Technology and teaching: searching for the middle ground. *Journal of Social Work Education, 35* (3), 322-326.

Raymond, F. B. (1996). Delivering the MSW curriculum to non-traditional students through interactive television. In E.T. Reck (Ed). *Modes of Professional Education II: The Electronic Social Work Curriculum in the Twenty-First Century*. Tulane Studies in Social Welfare, 20. New Orleans, LA: Tulane University.

Ritchie, H., & Newby, T. J. (1989). Classroom lecture/discussion vs. live televised instruction: A comparison of effects on student performance, attitude, and interaction. *American Journal of Distance Education, 3* (3), 36-45.

Ritchie, H. (1991). *Interactive televised instruction: What is its potential for interaction?* (Research Monograph No. 8). University Park, PA: The Penn State University, American Center for the Study of Distance Education.

Rooney, R. H., & Bibus, A. A. (1995). Distance learning for child welfare work with involuntary clients: Process and evaluation. *Journal of Continuing Social Work Education, 6* (3), 23-28.

Rowley, D., Lujan, H., & Dolence, M. (1998). *Strategic choices for the academy: How demand for lifelong learning will re-create higher education*. San Francisco: Jossey-Bass.

Schmidt, S. (2000). Distance education 2010: A virtual space odyssey. In Lloyd (Ed.). *Teaching with technology: rethinking tradition* (pp. 75-90). Medford, NJ: Information Today, Inc.

Schoech, D. (2000). Teaching over the internet: Results of one doctoral course. *Research on Social Work Practice, 10* (4),467-486.

Sells, S. P., & Rittner, B. (1998, August). *Teaching across Georgia: A dual campus course*. Paper presented at the conference on Information Technologies for Social Work Education and Practice, Charleston, SC.

Siegel, E., Conklin, J., Jennings, J., & Flynn, S. (2000, February). *The present status of distance learning in social work education: an update*. Paper presented at the Annual Program Meeting of the Council on Social Work Education, New York, NY.

Stocks, J. T., & Freddolino, P. P. (2000). Enhancing computer-mediated teaching through interactivity: the second iteration of a world wide web-based graduate social work course. *Research on Social Work Practice, 10* (4), 505-518.

Taylor, J. C., & White, V. J. (1991, July). Faculty attitudes towards teaching In the distant education mode: An exploratory investigation. *Research in Distance Education*, 7-11.

Thyer, B. A., Polk, G., & Gaudin, J.G. (1997). Distance learning in social work education: a preliminary evaluation. *Journal of Social Work Education, 33* (2), 363-367.

Thyer, B. A., Artelt, T., Markward, M. K., & Dozier, C. D.(1998). Evaluating distance learning in social work education: A replication study. *Journal of Social Work Education, 34* (2), 291-295.

Weinbach, R. W., Gandy, J. T., & Tartaglia, L.J. (1984). Addressing the need of the part-time student through interactive closed-circuit television: an evaluation. *Arete. 9* (2), 12-20.

Wernet, S. P., & Olliges, R. (1998). The application of WebCT (web course tools) in social work education. *2nd Annual Technology Conference for Social Work Education and Practice, Conference Proceedings* (pp. 304-310). Columbus: University of South Carolina College of Social Work.

Wernet, S. P., Olliges, R. H. & Delicath, T. A. (2000). Postcourse evaluations of Web CT (Web Course Tools) classes by social work students. *Research on Social Work Practice, 10* (4), 487-504.

Whittington, N. (1987). Is instructional television educationally effective? A research review. *American Journal of Distance Education, 1*(1), 47-57.

Wilkes, C. W., & Burnham, B. R. (1991). Adult learner motivations and electronic distance education. *American Journal of Distance Education, 5* (1), 43-51.

Wilson, S. (1999). Invited commentary: Distance education and accreditation. *Journal of Social Work Education, 35* (3), 326-330.

Wong, Y. C., & Law, C. K. (1998, August). *Learning IT skills through an introductory statistics course for BSW students.* Paper presented at the conference on Information Technologies for Social Work Education and Practice, Charleston, SC.

Zirkin, B. G., & Sumler, D. E. (1995). Interactive or non-interactive? That is the question!!! An annotated bibliography. *Journal of Distance Education, 10* (1), 95-112.

Distance Education Alumni:
How Far Have They Gone?

Marilyn K. Potts
Christine Hagan Kleinpeter

SUMMARY. This evaluation compared 34 distance education (DE) and 38 on-campus alumni regarding employment-related outcomes; professional activities; satisfaction with MSW program components; and development of knowledge, skills, and values. Findings showed equivalent outcomes in most respects. DE alumni were generally positive about the extent to which the program enabled them to develop professionally. *[Article copies available for a fee from The Haworth Document Delivery Service: 1-800-342-9678. E-mail address: <getinfo@haworthpressinc.com> Website: <http://www.HaworthPress.com> © 2001 by The Haworth Press, Inc. All rights reserved.]*

Marilyn K. Potts, PhD, is Professor of Social Work, California State University, Long Beach.

Christine Hagan Kleinpeter, PsyD, is Assistant Professor of Social Work, California State University, Long Beach.

Correspondence should be addressed to: Department of Social Work, California State University, Long Beach, 1250 Bellflower Blvd., Long Beach, California, 90840-0902. E-mail should be addressed to mpotts@csulb.edu or crshagan@csulb.edu.

The authors thank Jim Kelly for initiating this program; Ginger Wilson, Gary Bess, and Donna Wheeler for their commitment to its success; John Oliver for his many ongoing contributions; and Catherine Goodman for development of the instrument used in this study. We express our admiration for the students who participated in this pioneering venture and welcome them as colleagues. Financial support was provided by the California State University Commission on the Extended University and by the California Social Work Education Center (CalSWEC). An earlier version of this article was presented at the 4th Annual Technology Conference for Social Work Education and Practice, Charleston, South Carolina, August 27-30, 2000.

[Haworth co-indexing entry note]: "Distance Education Alumni: How Far Have They Gone?" Potts, Marilyn K., and Christine Hagan Kleinpeter. Co-published simultaneously in *Journal of Technology in Human Services* (The Haworth Press, Inc.) Vol. 18, No. 3/4, 2001, pp. 85-99; and: *New Advances in Technology for Social Work Education and Practice* (ed: Julie Miller-Cribbs) The Haworth Press, Inc., 2001, pp. 85-99. Single or multiple copies of this article are available for a fee from The Haworth Document Delivery Service [1-800-342-9678, 9:00 a.m. - 5:00 p.m. (EST). E-mail address: getinfo@haworthpressinc.com].

85

KEYWORDS. Alumni, distance education, social work education, educational outcomes

Empirical data suggest that the educational achievement and satisfaction levels of distance learners are at least comparable to those of traditional students (e.g., Coe & Elliott, 1999; Freddolino & Sutherland, 2000; Kikuchi & Sorensen, 1997; Petracchi & Patchner, 1998; Rooney, Freddolino, Hollister, & Macy, 1999). Using a systems theory model, these factors are considered proximal outcomes (Moore & Kearsley, 1996). Far fewer distance education (DE) evaluations have examined more distal outcomes among alumni (Hollister & Kim, 1999; Macy, 2000).

This article describes the evaluation of the first MSW graduates (class of 1998) of a CSWE accredited DE program. Data are presented for 34 DE and 38 on-campus (OC) alumni. This part-time MSW program was based on an urban campus in southern California (California State University, Long Beach) and offered in two rural locations in the central and northern parts of the state (California State University, Chico, and Humboldt State University, respectively). The DE program model consisted of coursework over three academic years and an intensive 14-week field placement during both interim summers. Courses were provided through a combination of in-person delivery and interactive two-way audio-video technology. Behavior, policy, and research courses were taught in "real time" using the interactive technology. Instructors for these courses traveled to each DE site at least twice during each semester, broadcasting from there to the other DE site. Most practice courses, as well as a course on computers in social work, were taught in-person by local faculty. A sequence of two courses, known as Community Projects, was taught in-person and via technology by faculty from the host institution who traveled to each DE site on an alternating weekly basis. Local field placements were arranged, and concurrent field seminars were facilitated by faculty from the local practice community. Each student was assigned a thesis advisor from the Long Beach campus who visited at least three times during the final academic year. Two local site coordinators were engaged to provide logistical support, attend classes to monitor classroom activity, and serve as assistant instructors for experiential exercises. Further description of the DE program can be found in Potts and Hagan (2000).

METHODS

In the Spring of 2000, self-administered questionnaires were mailed to approximately 900 alumni of the classes of 1994 through 1999. After one initial and one follow-up mailing, 231 (25.7%) OC alumni responded. After one initial and two follow-up mailings, 34 (89.5%) DE alumni responded. All DE alumni had been part-time students in the Children, Youth, and Families Concentration. Thus, their responses were compared to OC alumni in the same program model and concentration. In order to obtain a sufficient number of OC alumni, graduates from years 1995 through 1998 were included in the present analyses.

The questionnaire was designed to ascertain the following:

1. Demographic information, prior social work experience, and licensure status.
2. Employment-related characteristics (e.g., employment status, length of job search after graduation, annual salary, type of agency, principal job function, and funding auspices).
3. Professional activities (e.g., NASW membership, enrollment in degree program, professional presentations, publications, grants, and attendance at alumni functions).
4. Changes resulting from earning degree. Items included: changed role in same agency, received promotion, received pay raise, and increased job responsibilities.
5. Satisfaction with MSW program components. This scale contained 7 items: faculty, curriculum, administration, advising, coursework, field practicum, and student organizations. DE alumni were asked also to rate their satisfaction with their site coordinator. Response categories ranged from 1 (not at all satisfied) to 5 (extremely satisfied).
6. Extent to which the program helped in the development of knowledge, skills, and values. This scale contained 20 items derived from departmental objectives and consistent with CSWE standards. Items included: commitment to social action, commitment to values and ethics, sensitivity to needs of oppressed groups, knowledge and skills in direct service, ability to implement community interventions, ability to conduct research, analytic skills necessary for responsible practice, and self-awareness necessary for responsible practice. Response categories ranged from 1 (not at all) to 9 (a great deal).

RESULTS

Demographics

As is typical of DE cohorts, DE alumni were older ($t = 6.56$, $df = 69$, $p < .001$) and had more social work experience ($t = 2.46$, $df = 70$, $p < .05$) than OC alumni (see Table 1). Both groups consisted of over 80% females. DE alumni were more likely than OC alumni to be non-Hispanic white (94.1% and 60.5%, respectively, $X^2 = 11.23$, $df = 1$, $p < .001$).

Employment-Related Characteristics and Licensure

Employment outcomes were similar between OC and DE alumni (see Table 2). One hundred percent and 90.9%, respectively, were employed either full-or part-time. However, more OC alumni (86.8%) than DE alumni (69.7%) were employed full-time ($X^2 = 4.73$, $df = 2$, $p < .05$). Of those currently employed, 100.0% of OC and 90.0% of DE alumni held social work positions. Although the length of their job search did not differ significantly, 73.3% of DE alumni compared to 50.0% of OC alumni experienced a job search length of 0 months (i.e., they were employed prior to or immediately after graduation). Annual salaries were higher among OC alumni ($t = 3.15$, $df = 59$, $p < .01$), which is perhaps attributable to urban/rural salary differentials. More DE alumni (50.0%) than OC alumni (29.7%) indicated that they were *not* working toward licensure ($X^2 = 5.81$, $df = 2$, $p < .05$). (To become a Licensed Clinical Social Worker [LCSW] in California, individuals must earn an MSW or equivalent, practice for two years under the supervision of an LCSW, and pass both written and oral examinations.)

As shown in Table 3, the most frequently reported types of agencies among both groups were child welfare and outpatient mental health. Of DE alumni, 44.4% worked in child welfare, compared to 36.8% of OC alumni. Of DE alumni, 22.2% worked in outpatient mental health, compared to 18.4%% of OC alumni. A majority of both groups held primarily direct service positions (65.8% of OC alumni and 77.8% of DE alumni). They were nearly identical in terms of the proportion holding primarily administrative positions (10.5% of OC alumni and 11.1% of DE alumni), although more OC alumni (18.4%) than DE alumni (7.4%) held positions involving an equal mix of direct service and administration. DE alumni were significantly more likely than OC alumni to work in the public sector (74.1% and 45.9%, respectively, $X^2 = 7.36$, $df = 2$,

TABLE 1. Demographic Characteristics and Social Work Experience

Characteristic	On-Campus (n = 38) Number (Percent)	Distance Education (n = 34) Number (Percent)
Age[b]		
< 30	11 (28.9)	0 (0.0)
30-39	19 (50.0)	7 (21.2)
40-49	5 (13.2)	15 (45.5)
≥ 50	3 (7.9)	11 (33.3)
Gender		
Female	31 (81.6)	29 (85.3)
Male	7 (18.4)	5 (14.7)
Ethnicity[b]		
African American	6 (15.8)	0 (0.0)
Asian American	1 (2.6)	1 (2.9)
Hispanic/Latino(a)	5 (13.2)	0 (0.0)
Non-Hispanic White	23 (60.5)	32 (94.1)
Other	3 (7.9)	1 (2.9)
Social Work Experience Prior to MSW Program[a]		
None	2 (5.3)	3 (8.8)
Less than 1 year	6 (15.8)	1 (2.9)
1-3 years	13 (34.2)	6 (17.6)
4-6 years	9 (23.7)	7 (20.6)
7-9 years	4 (10.5)	5 (14.7)
10 or more years	4 (10.5)	12 (35.3)

Note: Some variables contain missing data.
[a] $p < .05$
[b] $p < .001$

$p < .05$). In contrast, OC alumni were more likely than DE alumni to work for private non-profit organizations (51.4% and 18.5%, respectively).

Professional Activities

The groups were equivalent regarding the extent to which they had engaged in most of the professional activities included in the questionnaire (see Table 4). These included employment by field placement

TABLE 2. Employment-Related Characteristics and Licensure

Characteristic	On-Campus (n = 38) Number (Percent)	Distance Education (n = 34) Number (Percent)
Currently Employed[a]		
Yes, full-time	33 (86.8)	23 (69.7)
Yes, part-time	5 (13.2)	7 (21.2)
No	0 (0.0)	3 (9.1)
Employed in Social Work		
Yes	38 (100.0)	27 (90.0)
No	0 (0.0)	3 (10.0)
Length of Job Search (Months)		
0 months	18 (50.0)	22 (73.3)
1-2 months	9 (25.0)	2 (6.7)
3-4 months	4 (11.1)	3 (10.0)
5 or more months	5 (13.9)	3 (10.0)
Annual Salary (Based on Full-Time)[b]		
< $20,000	0 (0.0)	0 (0.0)
$20,000-$29,999	2 (5.4)	6 (25.0)
$30,000-$39,999	15 (40.5)	12 (50.0)
$40,000-$49,999	11 (29.7)	5 (20.8)
$50,000-$59,999	8 (21.6)	1 (4.2)
$\geq$ $60,000	1 (2.7)	0 (0.0)
Licensure[a]		
Not working toward	11 (29.7)	17 (50.0)
Working toward	22 (59.5)	17 (50.0)
Licensed	4 (10.8)	0 (0.0)

Note: Employment in social work, length of job search, and annual salary asked only of those employed full-time or part-time. Some variables contain missing data.
[a]$p < .05$
[b]$p < .01$

agency, involvement in volunteer work, NASW membership, enrollment in college course, presentation of paper at professional conference, receipt of grant, collaboration with former student colleagues, and provision of training with former student colleagues. However, OC alumni were more likely than DE alumni to have published an article or a chapter (13.2% and 0.0%, respectively, $X^2 = 4.67$, $df = 1$, $p < .05$). In

TABLE 3. Aspects of Current Employment

Aspect of Employment	On-Campus (n = 38) Number (Percent)	Distance Education (n = 30) Number (Percent)
Type of Agency		
Child welfare	14 (36.8)	12 (44.4)
Outpatient facility	7 (18.4)	6 (22.2)
Medical hospital	3 (7.9)	1 (3.7)
School	3 (7.9)	4 (14.8)
Psychiatric hospital	2 (5.3)	0 (0.0)
Private practice	1 (2.6)	1 (3.7)
Nursing home/hospice	0 (0.0)	1 (3.7)
Public assistance	0 (0.0)	1 (3.7)
Other	8 (21.1)	1 (3.7)
Principal Job Function		
Primary Direct Service	25 (65.8)	21 (77.8)
Primary Administration	4 (10.5)	3 (11.1)
Equal Mix	7 (18.4)	2 (7.4)
Policy Analysis	1 (2.6)	0 (0.0)
Academic/Teaching	0 (0.0)	1 (3.7)
Other	1 (2.6)	0 (0.0)
Funding Auspices[a]		
Public	17 (45.9)	20 (74.1)
Private, Nonprofit	19 (51.4)	5 (18.5)
Private, Profit	1 (2.7)	2 (7.4)

Note: Asked only of those employed full-time or part-time. Some variables contain missing data.
[a] $p < .05$

contrast, DE alumni were more likely than OC alumni to have socialized with former student colleagues (81.8% and 50.0%, respectively, $X^2 = 7.84$, $df = 1$, $p < .01$) and to have attended alumni functions (24.2% and 7.9%, respectively, $X^2 = 3.61$, $df = 1$, $p < .05$).

Changes Resulting from Earning MSW

OC and DE alumni groups were similar in terms of the changes they had experienced since graduation (see Table 5). Roughly one-third of

TABLE 4. Professional Activities

Activity	On-Campus (n = 38) Number (Percent)	Distance Education (n = 33) Number (Percent)
Employed where did field placement	11 (28.9)	9 (27.3)
Involved in volunteer work	9 (23.7)	8 (24.2)
Member of NASW	15 (39.5)	13 (39.4)
Attended college course	6 (15.8)	3 (9.1)
Enrolled in degree program	1 (2.6)	3 (9.1)
Presented paper at professional conference	2 (5.3)	1 (3.0)
Published article or chapter[a]	5 (13.2)	0 (0.0)
Received grant for training, research, etc.	1 (2.6)	3 (9.1)
Collaborated with former student colleagues	3 (7.9)	5 (15.2)
Socialized with former student colleagues[b]	19 (50.0)	27 (81.8)
Provided training with former student colleagues	6 (15.8)	3 (9.1)
Joined alumni association	5 (13.2)	3 (9.1)
Attended alumni function[a]	3 (7.9)	8 (24.2)

Note: N = 33 for distance education group since one respondent failed to complete this section of the questionnaire.
[a] $p < .05$
[b] $p < .01$

each group had changed their role within the same agency, received a pay raise, and/or increased their job responsibilities. One-fifth of each group had been promoted.

TABLE 5. Changes Resulting from Earning MSW

Change	On-Campus (n = 24) Number (Percent)	Distance Education (n = 24) Number (Percent)
Changed role in same agency	7 (29.2)	8 (33.3)
Received promotion	5 (20.8)	5 (20.8)
Received pay raise	8 (33.3)	7 (29.2)
Increased job responsibilities	7 (29.2)	8 (33.3)
Other	11 (45.8)	6 (25.0)

Note: Asked only of those employed in social service agency prior to graduation

Satisfaction with MSW Program Components

Levels of satisfaction with MSW program components are depicted in Table 6. On a 5-point scale, satisfaction levels among OC alumni ranged from 2.90 (student organizations) to 4.00 (field practicum). Satisfaction levels among DE alumni ranged from 2.46 (student organizations) to 4.52 (site coordinator). Compared to OC alumni, DE alumni were more satisfied with faculty ($t = 1.98$, $df = 70$, $p < .05$) and less satisfied with administration ($t = 3.30$, $df = 70$, $p < .01$). Overall mean scores were similar (OC = 3.59, DE = 3.68).

Development of Knowledge, Skills, and Values

Responses regarding the extent to which the MSW program had enabled alumni to develop knowledge, skills, and values are shown in Table 7. On a 9-point scale, ratings among OC alumni ranged from 5.89 (awareness of determinants of collective behavior) to 7.61 (commit-

TABLE 6. Satisfaction with MSW Program Components

Component	On-Campus (n = 38) Mean	Distance Education (n = 34) Mean
Faculty[a]	3.76	4.15
Curriculum	3.55	3.50
Administration[b]	3.58	2.76
Advising	3.68	3.61
Coursework	3.59	3.62
Field Practicum	4.00	4.15
Student Organizations	2.90	2.46
Site Coordinator	NA	4.52
Overall Score	3.59	3.68

Note: Possible range was 1 (not at all satisfied) to 5 (extremely satisfied). Overall score includes responses regarding site coordinator for distance education group only. Excluding responses regarding site coordinator, the mean overall score for the distance education group was 3.49.
[a]$p<.05$
[b]$p<.01$

ment to values and ethics and self-awareness for responsible practice). Ratings among DE alumni ranged from 5.59 (capacity to use computers) to 7.50 (understanding of policies and practices). DE alumni had higher ratings than OC alumni regarding the extent to which the program had enhanced their understanding of policies and practices ($t = 2.00$, $df = 70$, $p < .05$) and their ability to conduct research ($t = 2.69$, $df = 70$, $p < .01$). Conversely, OC alumni had higher ratings than DE alumni regarding the extent to which the program had enhanced their capacity to use computers ($t = 2.48$, $df = 70$, $p < .05$). Overall mean scores were nearly identical (OC = 6.72, DE = 6.71).

DISCUSSION

These results suggest that DE alumni are satisfied with most aspects of their educational experience and positive about the extent to which the MSW program enabled them to develop as professionals. As noted above, there is a large body of information documenting the comparability of OC and DE programs, based on the perspectives of current stu-

TABLE 7. Extent to Which MSW Program Helped in Development of Knowledge, Skills, and Values

Item	On-Campus (n = 38) Mean	Distance Education (n = 34) Mean
Commitment to social action	6.63	6.71
Understanding of policies and practices[a]	6.74	7.50
Commitment to values and ethics	7.61	7.47
Sensitivity to needs of oppressed groups	7.24	6.97
Capacity to intervene with diverse cultures	7.37	6.65
Commitment to equitable provision of services	7.53	6.91
Knowledge and skills in direct service	6.74	6.53
Ability to analyze community problems	6.34	6.35
Ability to implement community interventions	6.13	6.32
Ability to apply research to practice	6.34	7.06
Ability to conduct research[b]	5.97	7.15
Ability to analyze social problems	6.71	6.94
Ability to formulate social policy	6.03	6.44
Awareness of determinants of collective behavior	5.89	5.79
Awareness of determinants of individual behavior	6.53	6.53
Analytic skills for responsible practice	7.29	6.82
Self-awareness for responsible practice	7.61	7.41
Capacity to function effectively in agency	7.13	7.03
Capacity to translate knowledge into action	7.21	7.09
Capacity to understand and use computer technology[a]	6.05	5.59
Overall Score	6.72	6.71

Note: Possible range was 1 (not at all) to 9 (a great deal).
[a]$p < .05$
[b]$p < .01$

dents and on proximal outcome measures. The present study found a similar level of comparability, based on the perspectives of alumni and on more distal outcome measures.

A number of limitations should be recognized. First, the response rate for OC students was low. If those OC alumni who honored the request for information were more satisfied with the program than other OC alumni, this could have biased the results in favor of the OC group. Second, the sample size was rather small, precluding the possibility of controlling for demographic differences between groups. However, previous comparisons of these OC and DE students have shown no effects of demographic characteristics on pre-graduation evaluations (Potts & Hagan, 2000). Third, the instrument used was a self-administered, quantitative questionnaire and thus afforded no opportunity to clarify, probe, or obtain contextual information. Some questions may have been misleading and some answers may have taken out of context. For example, the employment status question did not ascertain whether the respondents *wanted* to be employed. The questions concerning employment role changes and increased responsibilities were particularly open to interpretation. Finally, the generalizability of these results is limited since other programs in other areas vary widely in terms of student characteristics, mode of delivery, use of site coordinators, etc.

Nevertheless, it appears from these data that nearly all alumni were successfully employed and that DE alumni, in particular, had succeeded in finding employment prior to or immediately after graduation (i.e., nearly three-fourths of DE alumni experienced a job search lasting 0 months). Consistent with the MSW program's emphasis on public social services, nearly three-fourths of DE alumni (compared to nearly one-half of OC alumni) held jobs in the public sector. Nearly one-half of DE and over one-third of OC alumni were working in the field of child welfare, although this is perhaps a function of the high proportion of students in both groups who had received a stipend stipulating a period of post-graduation employment in a public child welfare setting.

However, a surprisingly low proportion of alumni in both groups indicated that they had received a pay raise, increased their job responsibilities, and/or been promoted. These findings may be attributable to the phrasing of these questions (i.e., they were to be answered only by those who were employed in social services prior to graduation, but may have been misunderstood). Yet, more in-depth studies of the actual job responsibilities of MSW alumni are warranted, along with further examination of the extent to MSW degrees are rewarded by employers in both urban and rural areas. Given the low proportion of DE alumni working toward licensure, the relevance of this in the rural communities involved should be explored, along with possible curriculum changes (i.e., less emphasis on content included in the state's licensing examination).

OC and DE groups were generally equivalent in terms of their participation in professional activities. Although few OC alumni had published, it was notable that *no* DE alumni had done so. An independently conducted research project is required for the MSW thesis and thesis advisors frequently encourage their students to publish their results. These results suggest that the on-campus thesis advisors of DE students may need to try harder to remain in touch after graduation, encouraging publication and supporting DE alumni through the publication process.

For two professional activities (socializing with former student colleagues and attending alumni functions), DE alumni exceeded OC alumni. While no alumni events are held at DE sites by the institution's official alumni association, events for current DE students, alumni, and the practice community are frequently organized to coincide with faculty visits during the second cycle of the program in both areas. These events may provide a ready-made structure for enhancing official alumni association involvement in these rural areas, to the possible advantage of the alumni, the larger professional community, and the host institution as it recruits future MSW cohorts.

Regarding their perceptions of MSW program components, both OC and DE alumni were relatively dissatisfied with student organizations, indicating that more meaningful activities should be promoted, perhaps directed specifically toward students in various part-time program models. It was gratifying to note that DE alumni were highly satisfied with their faculty, field practicum experience, and site coordinator. On the other hand, it is clear that DE students' perceptions of the administration deserve further exploration. Steps should be taken to ascertain the target of their concerns (i.e., departmental and/or university administration) and to investigate ways to facilitate more positive interactions.

Finally, there was a notable absence of differences between OC and DE alumni in terms of their perceptions regarding the development of knowledge, skills, and values. Areas for possible improvement noted among both groups included several aspects of macro practice. In addition, DE alumni were less positive than OC alumni regarding their capacity to use computer technology. Since the department's required course on computers in social work was taught in-person by local faculty, this finding suggests the need for more extensive monitoring of instructional quality by the host institution.

In conclusion, DE in social work has clearly moved beyond its infancy. Given the vast amount of information concerning the equivalency of OC and DE programs, first among students and more and more among alumni as programs mature, few today can argue validly against DE as a concept. However, much work needs to be done to examine (1) outcomes across the many different DE models, (2) competency-based outcomes among students, (3) the effects of DE programs on client well-being and agency functioning, and (4) the effects of DE programs on the social work communities of which they are a part. Such studies should move beyond a deficit model (i.e., the need to document equivalency with "traditional" social work education) toward a focus on maximizing the unique strengths of various DE approaches (Coe & Gandy, 1998).

REFERENCES

Coe, J.R., & Elliott, D. (1999). An evaluation of teaching direct practice courses in a distance education program for rural settings. *Journal of Social Work Education, 35,* 353-365.

Coe, J.R., & Gandy, J.T. (1998, August). Perspectives from consumers (students) in a distance education program. Paper presented at the Conference on Information Technologies for Social Work Education and Practice, Charleston, SC.

Freddolino, P.P., & Sutherland, C.A. (2000). Assessing the comparability of classroom environments in graduate social work education delivered via interactive instructional television. *Journal of Social Work Education, 36,* 115-129.

Hollister, C.D., & Kim, Y. (1999, September). Evaluating ITV-based MSW programs: A comparison of ITV and traditional graduates' perceptions of MSW program qualities. Paper presented at the Conference on Information Technologies for Social Work Education and Practice, Charleston, SC.

Kikuchi, S.L., & Sorensen, S.R. (1997, September). Reach out and touch someone: Experiences of the rural off-campus MSW program, Graduate School of Social Work, University of Utah. Paper presented at the Conference on Information Technologies for Social Work: Using to Teach, Teaching to Use, Charleston, SC.

Macy, J.A., (2000, March). Social work distance education student experiences: A view from the other side. Paper presented at the Annual Program Meeting of the Council on Social Work Education, San Francisco, CA.

Moore, M.G., & Kearsley, G. (1996). *Distance education: A systems view.* Belmont, CA: Wadsworth.

Petracchi, H.E., & Patchner, M.A. (1998, August). ITV versus face-to-face instruction: Outcomes of a two-year study. Paper presented at the Conference on Information Technologies for Social Work Education and Practice, Charleston, SC.

Potts, M.K, & Hagan, C.B. (2000). Going the distance: Using systems theory to design, implement, and evaluate a distance education program. *Journal of Social Work Education, 36*, 131-145.

Rooney, R., Freddolino, P., Hollister, C., & Macy, J. (1999, March). Evaluating distance programs in social work: What does it all mean? Paper presented at the Annual Program Meeting of the Council on Social Work Education, San Francisco, CA.

Distance Education:
A Multidimensional Evaluation

Bruce Dalton

SUMMARY. The empirical evaluation of distance education is social work has lagged behind that of other fields. This research compares classes taught in person and via interactive television on the dimensions of student satisfaction (course evaluations), and educational outcomes (pre-test, post test, and follow up design). The research design and controlling for the instructor variable (the same instructor taught both courses) adds methodological rigor not present in prior evaluations. Outcome differences between the instructional mediums were explained by the demographic and other differences brought by the students. This research joins the bulk of such research that finds the effectiveness of the mediums comparable. *[Article copies available for a fee from The Haworth Document Delivery Service: 1-800-342-9678. E-mail address: <getinfo@haworthpressinc.com> Website: <http://www.HaworthPress.com> © 2001 by The Haworth Press, Inc. All rights reserved.]*

KEYWORDS. Distance education, distance learning, student outcomes

Distance education has been opening the door to higher education for over a century (Price, 1993). During this time, distance education programs have allowed many thousands, and perhaps millions of students to overcome the hurdle of distance to pursue college or other degrees.

Bruce Dalton is Assistant Professor at the College of Social Work, University of South Carolina, Columbia, SC 29208.

[Haworth co-indexing entry note]: "Distance Education: A Multidimensional Evaluation." Dalton. Bruce. Co-published simultaneously in *Journal of Technology in Human Services* (The Haworth Press, Inc.) Vol. 18, No. 3/4, 2001. pp. 101-115; and: *New Advances in Technology for Social Work Education and Practice* (ed: Julie Miller-Cribbs) The Haworth Press, Inc., 2001, pp. 101-115. Single or multiple copies of this article are available for a fee from The Haworth Document Delivery Service [1-800-342-9678, 9:00 a.m. - 5:00 p.m. (EST). E-mail address: getinfo@haworthpressinc.com].

101

The nature of the distance education medium has evolved along with advances in technology from postal correspondence courses to that of video, interactive television, and web-based courses (Klesius, Homan, & Thompson, 1997; Raymond & Pike, 1997). Social work has embraced distance education with increasing commitment of resources to the expensive technologies it now requires (Thyer et al., 1998). Recent surveys of social work programs indicate that about 16% to 17% offer distance education and that this proportion is growing (Coe & Elliot, 1999).

This changing and growing educational medium has been extensively evaluated in many different educational fields. Russell (1999) has reviewed 355 mostly empirical reports, summaries, and papers comparing distance education to in-person education in a wide variety of disciplines, and found the overwhelming majority of these to show no significant difference between the two mediums. Of those that did find a difference, the benefit was often on the side of distance.

Russell's (1999) review includes evaluations of distance education in a variety of domains, including student satisfaction, perceptions, and educational outcome. Convenience is also of value to the students (Klesius et al., 1997), and this factor is of course the primary historical consideration for the development of distance education programs. While convenience is a driving force behind distance education, preference for the in-person medium works against distance education. Ratings of the learning environment, classroom interaction, access to libraries, and overall enjoyment of the educational process and setting generally favor in-person instruction over distance mediums (Coe & Elliot, 1999; Thyer et al., 1998). Students are generally willing to endure a distance medium to benefit from the convenience (Klesius et al., 1997).

Medium preference may also be an issue with instructors, with faculty often being resistant to distance education (Russell, 1999; Waltz, 1998). The resistance may merely be lack of familiarity with the medium and accompanying equipment, which can be overcome with a good training program (Dasher-Alston & Patton, 1998) and perhaps mentoring through the first few sessions. Waltz (1998) however states that distance learning classrooms are limiting in ways which are enduring, and not just a factor of familiarity. Waltz contends that distance learning classrooms usurp the pedagogical choices of the instructor, forcing the instructor to teach in the limited ways allowed by the technology. This view seems supported by the findings of Freddolino (1998) who notes that faculty teaching via interactive television have had to adapt to the medium in various ways, such as using more written material as handouts, using presentation software to produce computer-generated graphics and outlines (which can be time consuming, an inconvenience factor for faculty), and reworking lectures.

Medium preference is also an issue for administrators. While distance education programs appear to altruistically make education available to students who would otherwise lack the opportunity, they also appeal to administrators by adding to the status of their institutions, as well as increasing market share. There is also the potential for reaching more students at a lower cost per student. The costs would of course vary by whether the distance education is facilitated by postal correspondence, or a more technologically expensive medium. Computer systems and interactive television have high start up costs that may take many years to recover through increased enrollment and the increased efficiency of larger classes. Whether there is financial appeal to any particular institution or department offering distance education courses would depend on the particular circumstances and funding mechanisms (Dasher-Alston & Patton, 1998). It is possible that for administrators the presence of financial or prestige incentives could compete with considerations of the educational merit of the program.

Compared to empirical evaluation of distance education in other fields, empirical evaluation of social work distance education has lagged behind, and that which has been done more often examines attitudes or other "feel good" variables, seldom whether the students in distance classes acquire as much knowledge of the course content (Thyer et al., 1998). Thyer et al. state that only three published empirical outcome studies evaluating televised instruction in social work education have appeared. Of those three, only one considers a learning effectiveness measure (grades) and that found the students taught by way of televised videotapes did better than those receiving live instruction. Since the review by Thyer et al. three more articles have been published that compared grades in distance education classes to in-person classes (Harrington, 1999; Forster & Rehner, 1998; Coe & Elliot, 1999). These three articles must be added to those collected by Russell that find no significant difference between the mediums.

The preceding discussion shows that there are many perspectives from which to evaluate distance education. While the attitudes and preferences of the various actors in distance education are important and relevant, the primary concern must be the effectiveness of the distance medium in imparting knowledge. Making education convenient to the students, presenting it to them via a medium that is pleasant, cost effectiveness, and other administrative concerns are important and need to be considered. However, we must not allow ourselves to use a medium that is not proven effective.

> Of greatest concern to us is the absence of well-crafted compari- son articles that examine not simply student attitudes toward dis- tance learning, but the actual knowledge and skills that students acquire from televised teaching . . . This can best be accomplished by using pre-and post-test designs with objective assessments of student knowledge and skills at the beginning and end of the courses. Ideally, this demonstration could involve the same in- structor teaching two sections of the same class during the same school term, one exclusively by live instruction and the other only by distance learning. (Thyer, Polk, & Gaudin, 1997:367)

This study contributes to the social work distance education literature by providing a comprehensive comparison of two social work research classes taught in person and another social work research class taught via interactive television, all by the same instructor. Using a quasi-ex- perimental pretest, posttest, follow-up comparison group design, stu- dent knowledge of the course material was measured three times during the semester in three different class sections. This allowed students' rel- ative gains to be compared between those who attend on-site and those who view via interactive television. This is a methodological improve- ment over simple end of the semester grade comparison, which is equiv- alent to a non-experimental posttest only design (Campbell & Stanley, 1963).

METHOD

Sample

The sample consisted of 121 students enrolled in three research methods courses in the spring of 1999. Two of these courses were tradi- tional on-campus courses with primarily full time students (N = 12 and N = 29) taught on a weekday afternoon. The third course was an interac- tive televised distance education course with 80 students, 22 of whom attended in the studio, five of whom watched in an overflow room down the hall from the studio, and 53 who attended at a variety of viewing sites around the state. The distance education course was taken primarily by part-time students and met on Monday evenings. These 80 students were also required to attend in person on the main campus on Saturday afternoons at the beginning, middle, and end of the semester for course orientation and testing.

Procedure

The author was assigned to teach three sections of Social Work Research Methods in the spring of 1999, one of which was a distance course taught via interactive television. This afforded an opportunity for methodological control not previously reported in the social work distance education literature as the instructor variable is held constant. This means not just the intangibles of instructor personality and style, but also whether the same content is covered as " . . . instructors can introduce tremendous variation into seemingly standardized course formats" (Shavelson, 1986:52).

With permission from the publisher, the pretest/posttest/follow-up questionnaire contained 20 questions taken from the test manual for the course text[1] (Rubin & Babbie, 1997). This assured the questionnaire reflected the material in the course, which was closely structured around the text, and also that the questions were of adequate quality as they had been written by the text authors to reflect and measure the content of such a course. The questionnaire also contained demographic items. All three sections were administered the pretest at the first class meeting, the post test immediately before the midterm, and the follow up immediately before the final. The factual material on the questionnaire was covered during the first half of the course and all sections proceeded through the material at the same pace. The post test measures how well the students learned the material and performed on the post test questionnaire, given the same day as the midterm exam. The final exam was not cumulative, so after the midterm there was no grade incentive to continue studying the earlier material. The follow up thus became a test of long term retention of the material (Dalton & Kuhn, 1998). It is possible that questionnaire scores could drop from post test to follow up.

Not previously reported in the social work distance education literature is the use of teaching evaluations to compare on site and distance courses. This will be a valuable addition to previous student opinion research. The teaching evaluation is a process the students are familiar and comfortable with, thus removing some of the artificiality of the research situation.

Course grades will also be compared between the groups. Grades measure a broader range of student performance than the questionnaire as they include written assignments. A drawback to using grades as an outcome measure is that they limit this part of the research to a posttest only design. A benefit is that there are no missing cases since all students are assigned grades.

An informed consent form was distributed to all students on the first day of class. The instructor left the room during questionnaire administration to ensure anonymity and to remove any appearance of coercion. Students used their birthdays as an identification number on the questionnaire to allow for matching of the three questionnaire administrations.

The distance section gave students two separate experiences, both of which differed from an on-site class. Students viewing at the distance sites and the local studio overflow room watched the class on a monitor and had to call in questions or comments on a telephone that was provided at each site. These calls were connected to a speaker in the studio so the instructor and all students heard the question or comment simultaneously. Students in the studio saw the instructor in person and could ask questions or make comments spontaneously or by raising their hand. Microphones in the room allowed these questions or comments to be broadcast to all sites. The studio students' experience differed from the experience of students' in the on-site classes in three ways. First, the class was receiving phone calls from students not present in the room. Second, there were television cameras present in the room, which could have inhibited students from asking questions or making comments. Third, the instructor's mobility was limited due to having to stay seated at a desk in order to stay on camera. There were four test groups in this research: (1) Group 1 was taught live on-site with a lecture/discussion method, (2) Group 2 was taught live on-site with a cooperative learning method, (3) Group 3s was the studio audience for the distance course, and (4) Group 3d was the 12 viewing sites for the distance course and the overflow room.

RESULTS

Demographic Variables

The pretest was completed by 99 students, the posttest at midsemester by 92 students, and the follow up on the last class meeting by 83 students. The highest attrition occurred in the on-site lecture/discussion class, though the author is unable to explain why. Because of missing data on individual variables the number useable varies by analysis. Table 1 shows mean values and ANOVA results for demographic variables by test group. These results show that the test groups varied on several measures, with students in the two on site courses resembling each other (Groups 1 and 2), and the students in the distance course resembling each other whether they attended in the studio or at a distance site (Groups 3s and 3d). Students who attended the on site courses were more likely to be younger, better off financially, to have taken more previous research courses, to have fewer employment hours, and fewer hours of housework or other care obligations.

Table 2 shows chi-square results for demographic variables by test group. Because of the size of the cross tabulation there were more cells with an expected count of less than five than the chi-square statistic allows (20%). This violates an assumption of the test and makes the results of the tests suspect. A visual examination of the data shows that the on site courses were almost exclusively full time students while the distance course was almost exclusively part time students. That part-time students generally take the distance course would be expected, and the late afternoon meeting time would account for part-time students being in the studio audience even if they were local. Visual examination of the data also shows a higher percentage of African American students in the studio than elsewhere.

Questionnaire Results

The questionnaire was administered at the beginning, middle, and end of the course. Table 3 shows the questionnaire results represented as percent correct of the 20 items at the three different test administrations. Campbell and Stanley (1963) suggest that the best way to analyze data of this nature is to compare the groups on the amount of change that takes place over time, and to use the pretest score as a covariate in the analysis to control for pre test variance. For this purpose two new variables were computed, that of the change in scores from pretest to post test, and that of the change in scores from pretest to follow up. A further benefit of this is that it accounts for attrition, a problem especially present in Group 1 in Table 3. For a respondent to be included in the new variables they must have completed the questionnaire at two administrations. Also included are selected demographic variables as suggested by Cheng (1991). The demographic variables are those which were found to differ significantly between groups; age, income, number of previous research courses, hours worked for money, hours per week on

TABLE 1. ANOVA Results for Demographic Variables by Group

Test Group	1	2	3s	3d	
Variable		Mean (n)			ANOVA
Age	25 (25)	28 (13)	34 (15)	31 (39)	F = 5.2, p = .002
Household income (in thousands)	47 (18)	100 (10)*	30 (12)	43 (38)	F = 8.5, p < .001
Undergrad GPA	3.34 (24)	3.24 (12)	3.08 (14)	3.21 (39)	Not significant
Years of human service experience	4.0 (22)	4.6 (13)	5.8 (14)	6.8 (37)	Not significant
Previous social work courses	5.5 (24)	6.8 (13)	2.8 (14)	5.2 (38)	Not significant
Previous research courses	1.7 (24)	1.4 (12)	.57 (14)	.94 (38)	F = 6.1, p = .001
Hours employed per week	9.4 (12)	7.0 (10)	37 (16)	38 (40)	F = 18.5, p < .001
Hours of housework or other care per week	11 (12)	10 (10)	18 (15)	29 (38)	F = 3.1, p = .033

The group are defined as follows (1) Group 1 was taught live on-site with a lecture/discussion method, (2) Group 2 was taught live on-site with a cooperative learning method, (3) Group 3s was the studio audience for the distance course, and (4) Group 3d, which were the 12 viewing sites for the distance course and the overflow room.
* Of the five students reporting household incomes of six figures or more, three were in this section, including the two highest (200,000 and 250,000).

TABLE 2. Chi-Square Results for Demographic Variables by Group

Test Group	1	2	3s	3d	
Variable			n (%)		Chi-Square
Gender					
Male	6 (30)	2 (6)	1 (5)	5 (31)	
Female	14 (70)	34 (94)	19 (95)	11 (69)	Not significant
Race					
African American	5 (22)	2 (15)	8 (57)	5 (16)	
European American	19 (78)	11(85)	6 (43)	33 (84)	χ^2=12, p=.008*
Enrollment Status					
Part-time	1 (7)	0 (0)	16 (94)	38 (95)	
Full-time	13 (93)	12 (100)	1 (6)	2 (5)	χ^2=66, p<.001*

The groups are defined as follows 1) Group 1 was taught live on-site with a lecture/discussion method, 2) Group 2 was taught live on-site with a cooperative learning method, 3) Group 3s was the studio audience for the distance course, and 4) Group 3d, which were the 12 viewing sites for the distance course and the overflow room.
* Two cells (25%) had an expected count of less than five which violates an assumption of the test, thus results must be accepted with caution.

housework or other care, and race. Part- or full-time enrollment status was not used as that too closely mirrors the test group variable. Using a process analogous to a backward regression, variables are removed from the equation one by one in order of least significance until the removal of any further would no longer control for the effect of the group variable upon change score. Backward regression would generally con-

TABLE 3. Average Test Scores as Percent Correct by Group and Time

Test Group	1	2	3s	3d
Variable		Percent Correct (n)		
Pretest	64 (23)	65 (13)	66 (15)	65 (39)
Post test	81 (19)	77 (12)	69 (18)	77 (41)
Follow up	79 (14)	82 (12)	68 (17)	76 (39)

The groups are defined as follows 1) Group 1 was taught live on-site with a lecture/discussion method, 2) Group 2 was taught live on-site with a cooperative learning method, 3) Group 3s was the studio audience for the distance course, and 4) Group 3d, which were the 12 viewing sites for the distance course and the overflow room.

tinue until all nonsignificant variables were removed from the equation. However, in this case the purpose is merely to account for the effect of group membership upon the dependent variable with as few control variables as possible.

Table 4 shows the results of ANCOVA for pretest to posttest change scores with the model reduced in this way. The effect of the test group upon pretest to post test gain scores is effectively accounted for by the student's original pretest score, income, and the number of hours they are employed each week. Removal of any further variables would have allowed the test group variable to become a significant factor in the equation.

Table 5 shows the ANCOVA results for the pretest to follow up change scores. In this case only one demographic variable could be removed and the test group variable still be accounted for, that is, still a nonsignificant factor in the equation. Thus, the significance of the effect of group membership upon pretest to follow up change scores is effectively explained by the student's original pretest score and the external variables of race, income, the number of hours they are employed each week, and the number of hours they are responsible for housework and other care. Removal of any further variables would have allowed the test group variable to become a significant factor in the equation. In this model race was a significant factor influencing the pretest to follow up change scores. When the covariates were controlled for (held constant), African Americans had a mean change in score of 5 while European Americans had a mean change score of 15. T-tests were conducted on the available data to explore the nature of the differences between African Americans and European Americans in the sample. As shown in Table 6, significant differences exist between the races on the variables of pretest scores, income, number of previous research courses, and hours employed per week. These variables had been included in the

TABLE 4. ANCOVA: Dependent Variable is Posttest Change in Questionnaire Score (Posttest Score Minus Pretest Score)

Source	Degrees of Freedom	Mean Square	F	Sig.
Intercept	1	.422	51.3	.000
Pretest	1	.288	35	.000
Test Group	3	.013	1.6	.194
Income	1	.026	3.2	.081
Hours Employed	1	.025	3.1	.085
Model	6	.059	7.2	.000
Error	49	.082		

Adjusted R^2 = .402

TABLE 5. ANCOVA: Dependent Variable is Follow Up Change in Questionnaire Score (Follow Up Score Minus Pretest Score)

Source	Degrees of Freedom	Mean Square	F	Sig.
Intercept	1	.369	57	.000
Pretest	1	.275	42.5	.000
Test Group	3	.009	1.5	.228
Race	1	.056	8.7	.005
Income	1	.019	3.0	.088
Hours Employed	1	.001	0.1	.759
Hours Housework and Other Care	1	.001	0.1	.728
Model	9	.044	6.8	.000
Error	42	.006		

Adjusted R^2 = .507

original model however, and race still was a significant effect upon the pretest to follow up gain scores.

Due to its influence upon which test group, or class, a student enrolled in, the effect of part-time or full-time status was also examined (Table 7). Part-time and full-time students differed significantly on the demographic variables of age, income, number of previous research courses, hours employed per week, hours of housework or other care per week, and also the outcome variables. While they did not differ on

TABLE 6. T-Test Analysis of Variables by Race

Variable	Af. Amer. Mean (n)	Euro. Amer. Mean (n)	t	df	p
Age	30.4 (22)	30.2 (72)	−.08	92	.930
Income	30,218 (18)	56,069 (63)	2.54	79	.013
Undergrad GPA	3.27 (20)	3.23 (72)	−.39	90	.698
Years of Human Service Experience	5.26 (21)	5.73 (66)	.34	85	.735
Number of Previous Soc. Work Courses	4.71 (19)	4.81 (70)	.10	89	.921
Number of Previous Research Courses	.68 (19)	1.25 (71)	3.50	64*	.001
Hours Employed (week)	39.1 (14)	26.1 (54)	−2.22	21*	.038
Hours Housework or Other Care (week)	22.96 (14)	19.14 (51)	−.55	63	.584
Pretest Scores (%)	60 (22)	66 (72)	2.28	92	.025
Posttest Scores (%)	62 (16)	79 (63)	3.76	19*	.001
Follow Up Scores (%)	62 (16)	80 (57)	5.42	71	.000
Change Pretest to Posttest (%)	4.8 (15)	13.4 (62)	2.51	75	.014
Change Pretest to Follow Up (%)	2.4 (16)	11.8 (57)	2.76	71	.007

* For these variables Levene's test revealed unequal variance between groups. This required a different method of computing the t-test which also changed the manner in which degrees of freedom were calculated.

TABLE 7. T-Test Analysis of Variables by Enrollment Status

Variable	Part-Time Mean (n)	Full-Time Mean (n)	t	df	p
Age	32.3 (49)	25.5 (26)	4.03	64*	.000
Income	40,234 (45)	73,275 (20)	−2.41	21*	.025
Undergrad GPA	3.18 (48)	3.29 (25)	−1.24	71	.219
Years of Human Service Experience	6.46 (47)	3.90 (24)	1.93	69	.058
Number of Previous Soc. Work Courses	4.68 (47)	6.32 (26)	−1.35	71	.182
Number of Previous Research Courses	.83 (47)	1.52 (25)	13.34	70	.001
Hours Employed (week)	39.4 (53)	8.77 (26)	9.18	77	.000
Hours Housework or Other Care (week)	27.2 (51)	10.14 (25)	3.37	63*	.001
Pretest Scores (%)	65 (49)	67 (26)	8.61	73	.392
Posttest Scores (%)	74 (47)	80 (28)	−1.77	73	.082
Follow Up Scores (%)	72 (54)	82 (29)	−3.04	81	.003
Change Pretest to Posttest (%)	9.5 (43)	11.6 (26)	−.72	67	.477
Change Pretest to Follow Up (%)	7.7 (49)	14.3 (26)	−2.42	66*	.018

* For these variables Levene's test revealed unequal variance between groups. This required a different method of computing the t-test which also changed the manner in which degrees of freedom were calculated.

the pretest scores they differed on questionnaire scores both more substantially and more significantly as the semester went on. The full-time students continued to improve as the semester went on as shown by their gaining from posttest to follow up while the part-time students regressed slightly.

Grade Comparisons

Grades were also compared between the test groups. All students were assigned grades so there are no missing cases, and the location of all students was know to the instructor, thus five test groups could be constructed: (1) Group 1 was taught in person with a lecture/discussion method; (2) Group 2 was taught in person with a cooperative learning method; (3) Group 3s was the studio audience for the distance course; (4) Group 3d, which were the 12 viewing sites for the distance course; and (5) Group 3o, the students who regularly attended in the overflow room down the hall from the studio. ANOVA showed the course grade did not vary significantly between groups ($F = .875$, $p = .181$). When the test was repeated combining the overflow room with the rest of the distance sites (as was the case with the questionnaire data) the results were still not significant ($F = 1.03$, $p = .390$). In both tests all pairwise comparisons were also not significant.

Teacher Evaluations

Course evaluations were administered on the last day of class in all three sections. As they were anonymous it was not possible to separate the distance students who attended in the studio from the distance students who attended via television, thus there were only three test groups at this point, the two day time on-site sections, and the distance section (studio, overflow room, and distance sites combined). The means did not differ significantly between sections ($F = 1.67$, $p = .193$).

DISCUSSION

Effectively evaluating educational outcomes requires considering as many different measures as possible, as well as controlling for influences upon the student. Initially the educational medium seemed to impact the questionnaire scores, with the distance students actually losing ground from post test to follow up. The follow up measured long term retention as the earlier material was not repeated after the posttest, and if the statistical analysis had gone no further it might be supposed that the class dynamic or some other aspect of the distance education medium was responsible for the difference in scores. However, by controlling statistically for the student's race, some other demographic and extraneous variables, and the student's pretest scores, it was possible to effectively explain these differences. Grades and course evaluations showed no significant differences between groups even without controlling for other student qualities. Thus it seems that this research must be added to the bulk of such evaluations that find no significant difference between on-site and distance courses.

What was revealed by this data, and what has not been previously reported in the social work education literature, is the information on who the students taking distance courses are. These almost exclusively part-time students are those who may not otherwise have an opportunity to pursue the MSW degree. Having significantly fewer financial resources, and many more hours of responsibility at both work and home, they are under considerably more stress than the full-time students, and as the ANCOVA results show (given that part-time students were almost exclusively distance students, and vice versa), this is what likely accounts for their poorer performance on the follow up questionnaire. In fact the data in Table 7 shows the part-time students to have a mean of 66.6 hours per week committed to employment, housework, and other care, compared to 18.9 hours per week for full-time students. What is surprising is that these part-time students manage to do as well as they do.

Race was also found to be a critical variable in this study. African Americans were both full- and part-time students, but were still as a group at a disadvantage in several areas, including income, number of previous research courses, and hours of work. When these areas were controlled for statistically in the ANCOVA analysis, the African Americans in the study still showed fewer gains on the follow up questionnaire. Given what the author knows about the student body, these African American students were mostly from this and neighboring southern states. There are both past and current discriminations (e.g., primary and secondary school quality in African-American communities) that could account for this difference other than the variables measured in this study.

The results of this study suggest that the provision of a social work research course via interactive television is educationally effective when compared to in-person instruction. Further, it is not merely educationally effective, it is especially necessary in order to expand the availability of social work education in this mostly rural state. It may even be preferable. The part-time students who attend at a distance or at the studio are older, have more responsibility at work and home, and are less privileged economically. It is important to have this type of student enter our profession. These students are sensitized to economic hardship, have struggled to achieve their education while also balancing work and family commitments, and have many other valuable life experiences. If social work is to avoid becoming a profession peopled by the privileged then it is important to continue to use distance education to reach out to these very students. It is apparent the distance education students appreciate the opportunity. On the follow up questionnaire the eight distance students who added written comments about the experience were unanimous in their appreciation for the distance education opportunity.

Distance education has in this study and in the literature reviewed by this and other authors proven to be a valid method of delivering social work courses. During the course of this investigation the initial skepticism of the author regarding distance education has changed to acceptance, and almost enthusiasm. It is hoped that others who are resistant to this medium may also undergo a similar evolution as they are exposed to both the technology and the accumulating evaluative research.

NOTE

1. Permission was granted by Wadsworth Publishing Company, which now owns the rights to this book.

REFERENCES

Campbell, D. T., & Stanley, J. C. (1963). *Experimental and Quasi-experimental Designs for Research*. Boston, MA: Houghton Mifflin Co.

Cheng, H. (1991). Comparison of performance and attitude in traditional and computer conferencing classes. *American Journal of Distance Education, 53*, 51-63.

Coe, J. R., & Elliot, D. (1999). An evaluation of teaching direct practice courses in a distance education program for rural settings. *Journal of Social Work Education, 35*, 353-365

Dalton, B., & Kuhn, A. C. (1998). Researching teaching methodologies in the classroom. *Journal of Teaching in Social Work, 17*, 169-184.

Dasher-Alston, R. M., & Patton, G. W. (1998). Evaluation criteria for distance learning. *Planning for Higher Education, 27*, 11-17.

Foster, M., & Rehner, T. (1998). Part-time M.S.W. distance education: A program evaluation. *Computers in Human Services, 15*, 39-50.

Freddolino, P.P. (1998). Building on experience: Lessons from a distance education M.S.W. program. *Computers in Human Services, 15*, 39-50.

Harrington, D. (1999). Teaching statistics: A comparison of traditional classroom and programmed instruction/distance learning approaches. *Journal of Social Work Education, 35*, 343-352.

Klesius, J. P., Homan, S., & Thompson, T. (1997). Distance education compared to traditional instruction: The students' view. *International Journal of Instructional Media, 24*, 207-220.

Price, M. L. (1993). *Student Satisfaction with Distance Education at the University of South Carolina as it Correlates to Medium of Instruction, Educational level, Gender, Working Status, and Reason for Enrollment.* Unpublished doctoral dissertation, University of South Carolina, Columbia.

Raymond, F. B. III, & Pike, C. (1997). Social work education: Electronic technologies. In *Encyclopedia of Social Work* (19th ed) (Supplement, pp. 281-299). Washington, DC: NASW Press.

Rubin, A., & Babbie, E. (1997). Research Methods for Social Workers (3rd ed). Pacific Grove, CA: Brooks/Cole.

Russell, T. L. (1999). The No Significant Difference Phenomenon. Raleigh, NC: North Carolina State University.

Shavelson, R. J. (1986). *Evaluating Student Outcomes from Telecourse Instruction: A Feasibility Study* (Report No. ISBN-0-8330-0746-7; RAND/R-3422-DPB). Santa Monica, CA: Rand Corporation. (ERIC Document Reproduction Service No. ED 311 867)

Thyer, B. A., Artelt, T, Markward, M. K., & Dozier, C. D. (1998). Evaluating distance learning in social work education: A replication study. *Journal of Social Work Education, 34*, 291-295.

Thyer, B. A., Polk, G., & Gaudin, J. G. (1997). Distance learning in social work education: A preliminary evaluation. *Journal of Social Work Education, 33*, 363-367.

Waltz, S. B. (1998). Distance learning classrooms: A critique. *Bulletin of Science, Technology, and Society, 18*, 204-212.

VIDEO AND WEB-BASED LEARNING AND TRAINING

Using Video Clips as Test Questions: The Development and Use of a Multimedia Exam

Dick Schoech

SUMMARY. Innovations in multimedia provide new formats for delivering and scoring tests and for constructing test items. This article presents a case study of the development of a multimedia exam that assesses child protective services supervisor competence. It describes the need, design, development, validity, standardization, use, status, issues, problems, and lessons learned. While multimedia offers potentials, it also makes modifications, enhancements, and delivery more complicated. By examining this experience, others can avoid mistakes and pitfalls when undertaking future multimedia assessment endeavors. *[Article copies available for a fee from The Haworth Document Delivery Service: 1-800-342-9678. E-mail address: <getinfo@haworthpressinc.com> Website:*

Dick Schoech, PhD, is a Professor at the University of Texas at Arlington School of Social Work. He teaches administration, community practice, and computer applications. Address correspondence to: Dr. Dick Schoech, UTA SSW, Box 19129, Arlington, TX 76019-0129 (E-mail: schoech@uta.edu or http://www.uta.edu/cussn/).

[Haworth co-indexing entry note]: "Using Video Clips as Test Questions: The Development and Use of a Multimedia Exam." Schoech, Dick. Co-published simultaneously in *Journal of Technology in Human Services* (The Haworth Press, Inc.) Vol. 18, No. 3/4, 2001, pp. 117-131; and: *New Advances in Technology for Social Work Education and Practice* (ed: Julie Miller-Cribbs) The Haworth Press, Inc., 2001, pp. 117-131. Single or multiple copies of this article are available for a fee from The Haworth Document Delivery Service [1-800-342-9678, 9:00 a.m. - 5:00 p.m. (EST). E-mail address: getinfo@haworthpressinc.com].

KEYWORDS. Multimedia assessment, multimedia testing, supervisor certification, child protective services

Technology is pervading all aspects of human service delivery, including assessment. A technology enhanced assessment environment allows:

- user self-administration;
- branching or embedded links so users can quickly jump to any part of the assessment;
- customization of assessment items on the fly;
- automatic storing of responses with immediate scoring and automated interpretation;
- new design formats, such as multimedia and virtual reality;
- new assessment strategies, such as interactive games and simulations;
- new delivery techniques, such as CD-ROM and the Internet;
- new delivery tools, such as biofeedback systems and brainwave sensing helmets (Attention.com, 2000).

While calls for assessments designed for digital technology have existed for years (Johnson, Giannetti, & Williams, 1979; Hedlund, 1988; Nurius, 1990) most assessment technology applications are rooted in traditional assessment concepts and based on paper/pencil formats. For example, training development software, such as WebCT, Blackboard, and ToolBook, provide easy construction of traditional multiple choice or fill in the blank test items. To use multimedia with these tools for assessing requires substantial additional work.

Multimedia allows more flexibility in the type of assessment items delivered, for example, the interactive delivery of any combination of pictures, sound, animation, graphics, and video. Databases also are being developed with the capacity to store, query, and work with pictures and video. The Internet can deliver pictures, animation, audio, and video from databases and store user interactions in databases for future analysis. However, the use of multimedia, such as audio, video, and virtual reality, in assessments has largely been experimental.

Internet delivery of video offers great potential for assessment. Internet audio and video can currently be delivered in two forms, (1) download and play and (2) streaming video where files play while they download. Currently, however, web video quality is low and inconsistent without a high speed Internet connection such as provided by dedicated communication lines typical of large organizations. The following techniques are used to accommodate the slow download of large media files.

- Download for several minutes, play the downloaded file, then repeat the download and play process until all the video/audio is played.
- Reduce the video picture to the size of a large postage stamp resulting in a smaller file to download.
- Slow video delivery to several frames per second, rather than the 25-30 frames per second (full motion video) that users expect.
- Use of virtual or animated humans to deliver audio, thus gaining the feel of video along with faster download (Ananova, 2000).
- Use of a downloadable browser plugin that helps manage the multimedia (for example, Shockwave).
- Linking of Internet files to files on a CD-ROM disk on the users computer, for example, text delivered via the Internet while video/audio is delivered via the CD-ROM.

While delivering multimedia over the Internet, especially audio and video, is currently problematic, it will be much more common in the future as can be seen on Internet2. Internet2 is a consortium of governments, industry, and 180+ universities that is accelerating the creation of tomorrow's Internet by developing advanced network applications and technologies (UCAID, 2000). When the Internet can reliably delivery full screen video to people's homes, multimedia assessment development will substantially increase. Currently, human service professionals are primarily experimenting with using the potentials of multimedia for assessment.

Using multimedia for assessment presents technical difficulties and issues other than those involving Internet delivery. For example, high quality video files larger than 30 seconds long can become extremely large and bulky to edit and manipulate using even a fast personal computer. Security of technology-based exams can be more difficult than paper/pencil-based exams, because digital files are easier to capture, copy, and distribute. Many lessons will need to be learned as the power of technology is harnessed in assessment.

This paper presents a case study of a multimedia exam developed to assess supervisor competence. The exam was developed between 1994 and 1997 by the author on a part-time basis with the support of one graduate research assistant. The initial exam is still in use with replacement planned for 2001. The next sections discuss the need, design and development, determining validity, standardization, use and status, issues and problems, and lessons learned. By examining this experience, others can avoid mistakes and pitfalls when undertaking future multimedia assessment endeavors.

THE NEED

The assessment project originated during the development of a voluntary child protective services (CPS) supervisor certification program in Texas. The Protective Services Training Institute (PSTI), a consortium of Texas Schools of Social Work, developed and was using a paper/pencil, multiple-choice exam for supervisor certification for the Texas Department of Protective and Regulatory Services (TDPRS). Since the paper/pencil exam was only a test of knowledge, a more experiential and skills-based exam was desired. Previous skills assessments, such as one in Colorado, relied on multiple observers in simulated situations, and thus were time consuming and costly. The cost to assess one supervisor using observers in the Colorado project was approximately $700 (Stevenson, Leung & Cheung, 1992). This cost was prohibitive given that our budget was small and Texas had 330 supervisors. Technology was seen as potentially providing a less expensive option for assessing supervisory skills.

Based on previous work developing a CPS multimedia training simulation on failure-to-thrive (Satterwhite & Schoech, 1995), PSTI requested the author to develop an exam to assess supervisory skills using multimedia technology. Other criteria specified by the PSTI Certification Committee was that the exam had to:

- complement the written exam which covered policy, theory, and knowledge;
- cover a variety of skills representative of TDPRS's supervisors' job;
- grade itself immediately upon completion;

- be delivered within approximately one hour;
- be secure, because if the exam became public, it could no longer be used;
- be valid and reliable and have the integrity to hold up in court if the department was sued by supervisors who were denied certification due to their low performance on the exam.

DESIGN AND DEVELOPMENT OF THE EXAM

After experimentation, two multimedia formats were selected. The first involved having users rate actual case narratives, performance evaluations, development plans, and corrective plans as to whether they exhibited good or bad practice (see Figure 1). The format required users to click on whether the skills in the exam items (on the right in Figure 1) were or were not exemplified in the narrative (on the left).

FIGURE 1. Screen from the Narrative Part of the Practice Exam

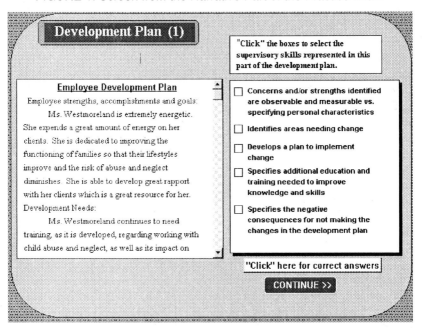

The second format involved having users rate supervision video clips as to whether or not they exhibited desired supervisory skills (see Figure 2). Two hour-long exams were to be developed with each containing the same text and video but with different exam items. During the exam item validation and standardization process, approximately one half of the exam items were expected to be deleted.

Once the design was determined, the next task was to accumulate a master list of supervisory skills from the literature and from TDPRS and PSTI training materials. The master list contained 223 skills organized into 55 skills areas. These skills became exam items (see Table 1).

For the text format section of the exam, TDPRS case narratives, performance evaluations, and corrective plans were obtained and exam items identified for each. Then, TDPRS identified experienced supervisors to review our work. An exam format using ToolBook Instructor was then developed to present the narrative and exam items.

The video format of the exam involved getting video of supervisors in action and identifying exam items that required the user to assess whether the supervisory skills were exhibited in the video. Using actors and scripts in a media studio was considered in order to allow for control and to produce high quality video. However, from viewing training videos, it was concluded that actors often were unable to portray the "look and feel" of CPS. The decision was made to select reality over quality and to video CPS supervisors in their offices during normal supervisory sessions. Our initial idea was to put a video camera in a supervisor's office and tape supervisory activity during a normal workday. Video clips from the supervisor's work would then be selected. However, this method proved too distracting and intimidating. Supervisors were afraid that the video would expose poor work habits or questionable supervisory skills. Therefore, simulated supervisory sessions were taped where supervisors and workers discussed "real or realistic" cases but purposely presented good and bad practices. Thus, no one but the supervisors and workers being videoed would know whether the bad supervisory practices were real or staged.

Our first taping sessions were unusable because workers and supervisors became "actors" and tried to parody the "perfect" supervisor/worker or the "horrible" supervisor/worker. With specific explanation that typical and realistic sessions were desired and more guidance on the type of content desired, for example, confrontation, the needed video was shot. However, the video was not of the quality that most people see on television. Poorly positioned cameras due to cramped offices, hallway noise, and inadequate lighting were common.

FIGURE 2. Screen from the Video Portion of the Practice Exam

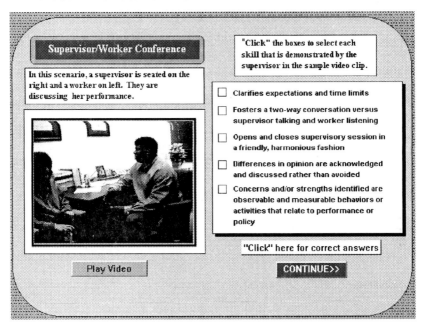

After approximately four hours of video was shot, development staff selected approximately 15 clips that exhibited fruitful interaction for analysis. Experienced TDPRS supervisors were then brought in to review the narrative and video for realism and appropriateness. TDPRS supervisors pointed out that some of the interesting dynamics that were captured could probably not be used. On one video, the supervisors expressed concerns about a worker's performance and the worker was not sure whether the concern was real or role-play. The role-play opened up worker problems that had not been previously discussed. Another interesting dynamic surfaced when a role-play on handling conflict exposed previously unresolved issues. While the interaction was realistic and would have made an excellent test question on confrontation, many supervisors taking the exam would have recognized the "bad blood" the role-play rejuvenated. After this step, 7 narratives and 11 videos remained.

TABLE 1. Several Supervisory Areas That Were Assessed Along with Sample Exam Items

Supervisory area	Skills used as exam item
Manages conflict	Feelings of anger are acknowledged and clarified with workers
Communicates effectively	Clarifies expectations
Attentive listening	Indicates through words, gesture, expressions, posture, tone of voice, or touch an understanding of the emotional content of the topic of conversation
Managing a meeting	Focuses on the task at hand

DETERMINING VALIDITY

One major task was to determine that the exam was valid, that is, that exam items distinguished good supervisory practice as defined by TDPRS rather than as suggested by theory, textbooks, or the developers. To determine validity, a representative statewide focus group of supervisors, program directors, and training experts was convened to examine each narrative/video and all the potential associated exam items. Each item was rated as to:

- difficulty using a scale of easy, medium, or hard;
- relevance using a scale of questionable, acceptable, important, or essential;
- keep item using a scale of 1-5 where yes = 1 and 5 = no.

The focus group examined the 7 narratives and 11 video clips that were associated with 327 exam items. The focus group agreed more on the narratives than on the videos. Participants in the focus group often disagreed on what was good supervisory practice, for example, when a supervisor was supporting rather than "pampering" a worker. Often disagreement concerned differences in rural vs. urban practices. Other disagreements involved philosophies of supervision. Interestingly, video that development staff thought to reveal empathy and patient listening skills were considered by some experienced TDPRS supervisors and administrators to reveal indecisive and inefficient behavior. The disagreement was expected, since focus group members did not have the same supervisory training. The focus group deleted 1 narrative, 3 videos, and 98 exam items.

STANDARDIZATION PROCESS

The standardization process used was that for a criterion-referenced exam as opposed to a norm-referenced exam, because the ultimate aim was to establish a pass/fail criterion for the examination. The standardization process involved determining (1) exam item predictability, (2) exam item difficulty, (3) exam reliability, and (4) pass/fail determination. Standardization was carried out by researchers other than the author and will be discussed only in relation to the focus of this paper.

One problem was obtaining an adequate number of supervisors to standardize the exam. Based on a population of 330 supervisors, a sample of approximately 120 supervisors was needed to take the exam. The multimedia-based nature of the exam made standardization more difficult. Users had to travel to UTA or someone had to travel to users with our multimedia computer. Group administration was not feasible unless a computer lab was available. While Internet delivery was technically feasible, the security of the exam could easily be compromised if someone taking the exam were to capture or copy the exam. After initial attempts to get an adequate number of supervisors to standardize the computer-based exam failed, a videotape/paper/pencil version of the exam was developed for easy group delivery. This version presented the narratives and videos to a group using a videotape and television and collected their response on items printed on paper. The videotape version was used whenever a group of supervisors volunteered to be assessed at any given location or whenever travel to deliver the exam was required.

One hundred and thirty-five items were deleted during the standardization process for the following reasons.

- Some items were too easy or too hard (95% scored the item right or wrong). Exceptions were made to this 95% rule based on expert feedback on the importance of the items as previously determined by the TDPRS focus group.
- Some items did not correlate well (less than .20) with the total score.
- Supervisor's geographic region or ethnicity was significantly correlated with the scores of some items, thus indicating ethnicity or region bias.

After standardization, both exams were combined into a final exam that contained six narratives with 39 exam items along with six videos with 50 exam items.

USE AND CURRENT STATUS

The multimedia exam, along with the written test that focuses on knowledge, has been used as part of the Texas Supervisor Certification Program for the past several years. Certification has changed from a status symbol to a qualification for a salary increase, so the demand for certification has increased. Approximately 280 supervisors have taken the exam or have been involved in its pretest or development. With TDPRS/PSTI funding, UTA personnel travel throughout Texas to administer the exams. The multimedia exam has been pressed on CD-ROM for easy installation on computers at controlled sites throughout the state. It has also been modified to run on a laptop, but the quality of the video suffers on a flat panel display.

ISSUES AND PROBLEMS

Technology issues plagued the exam development and still plagues its use. Due to the size of video files (40-80 MB for a 2-3 minute video), a fast computer was needed to capture and play the video during its development. Initially, the best multimedia computer available, a high end 486, was used. This computer had an enhanced video card, video capture card, 17″ monitor, large hard drive, and fast throughput. Although heavy and bulky, it was taken on many trips to present exam options to the Statewide Certification Committee and to administer the exam. Even with the most powerful PC available, the largest video capable of being played was in a small window 1/4 the size of the screen. Given that the video was not studio quality, it was sometimes difficult to see, especially when later transferred to a laptop computer.

We also struggled with non-technology issues. One issue concerned whether to allow users to play the videos once, twice, or unlimited times while taking the exam. Since the exam was not timed, it was expected that replaying the video would result in higher exam scores. The counter arguments concerned whether user memory, recognition, or both were being assessed. To solve the debate, the exam was programmed to track how many times a user played the video while taking the exam and then to determine whether those who played the video more times made better scores on the exam. We found that replaying the video did not correlate with overall exam score, and therefore, set no limits on playing the videos.

Another issue concerned how much feedback to provide users about their performance. Technology allowed us to provide very specific feedback on items missed along with remedial training. For example, immediately following the exam, users could print out the skills missed under each area. The exam could also provide remedial training in skill areas where the user had the most difficulty. However, the decision was made to not confuse the exam process with training. In the final version, users were only presented with their overall score on the exam.

The major problems with the multimedia exam continue to be the difficulty of administration given the computer requirements, security requirements, and number of people involved. For example, if several people want to take the exam, they have to be scheduled individually using a stand-alone computer or the laptop in a secure examination area.

Another problem concerns technical support. Someone needs to be available to insure that the exam continues to work given hard disks crashes, operating systems changes, and hardware/software upgrades. A similar issue is that the exam is difficult to change. Simple enhancements can require one or several days of work. For example, producing a CD-ROM version required purchasing the latest development software, learning the new software features, converting the old exam into the new software, making any changes, exporting the exam to CD format, and creating the CD. One desired change required many days as the change uncovered a bug in the upgraded software that required a vendor fix. If the exam developers were not available, these changes and additions would be much more difficult.

A revised exam is currently being developed. The revised exam will use the same format of narrative and video with exam items. However, the video will be delivered via videotape and television as was done in the standardization process. A videotape exam will allow for simultaneous administration to one or many users in the same location. Web delivery via streaming video is not an option because of the narrow bandwidth of the TDPRS network and because of the security desired for the exam.

LESSONS LEARNED

Over the six years of developing and using the multimedia exam, several lessons have been learned that others considering similar projects may want to consider. These lessons summarize much of the previous discussion.

Multimedia offers new exam possibilities. Multimedia provides an opportunity to deliver new exam formats, delivery methods, analyses, and feedback to users. These new possibilities have distinct advantages in exams such as the one described in this paper, especially in being more interactive and realistic for users. Using video clips as test questions worked very well in meeting the goal of being realistic and skills based.

Technology increases anxiety. Exams are stressful. Users uncomfortable with computers can become even more anxious about a computer-based exam. To address user anxiety, a widely-available practice exam was developed to allow users to become comfortable with the exam format before they were assessed. Overall, the multimedia format has been accepted by those taking the exam.

Technology poses "hidden" problems. Associated with its increased potential, multimedia presents additional unanticipated problems. The standard advice applies, "prepare to bleed if you are on the cutting edge." While the exam technology was old by today's standards, cutting edge technology is typically fraught with problems. Our high-end multimedia computer had many add-in components and software that did not always work well together. For example, installing new components or software could cause failure in other components or software, such as when a new video capture card deactivates the sound card. The computer often had to be returned to the vendor to fix problems. Selecting a local vendor that provided easy access to support and upgrades was critical. Another hidden problem was that for several years, only one computer could run the exam due to the size of the video files. Size also made file editing and exam copying problematic. However, even with these very large (30-80MB) video files, the largest image produced was 1/4 the size of the screen. Another hidden problem is that of inflexibility. For most of the development cycle, only our customized computer could deliver the video with the speed and resolution desired. This made standardization and delivery problematic. Another hidden problem concerned maintaining and updating the exam. The current paper/pencil exam is much easier to update through a process of developing additional exam items. Producing additional videos involves a more difficult process. Video production and programming skills are not frequently available in human service professionals. Thus, a technician often becomes a key link in the long process of exam conceptualization, development, testing, standardization, and use. With multimedia technicians in demand, it can be difficult to keep the same technician on the project during the long exam development process. If technicians are not used to shoot the video, the videos may lack the quality that users expect. Again, new hardware and software solves some of these problems, but when working on the cutting edge, unanticipated problems will always emerge.

To lessen risk, build on traditional exam formats and processes. It is important to assess the amount of risk one can take with an application such as a multimedia exam. Since our exam needed to be able to be defended in court, we used exam formats that closely paralleled traditional exam formats. This allowed us to base validation and standardization procedures on the techniques used with the paper/pencil exam. Having to develop exam standardization processes for novel exam formats could have been time consuming and problematic. Experimentation with totally new exam formats, for example, virtual reality, is best left with applications that are not critical to an organization's mission.

Multimedia development is a team effort. Producing multimedia involves video, audio, computer, and content area experts. These are rarely found in one person. Therefore, a team needs to be developed to take the exam from conceptualization to implementation. Some members of the team, such as video experts, might be needed for only a short time. Others, such as content area experts, might be needed for a long time. Strong and stable team leadership is needed throughout the long process. To maintain the stability of technical team members with high turnover potential, for example, multimedia developers, consultants rather than paid staff can be used. By budgeting for consultants, one can always hire the same people no matter how many times they change jobs.

Think through the total process before starting. Some of the challenges encountered, such as getting an adequate sample of supervisors to standardize the exam, were not considered at the beginning of the project. Exam development and distribution was not thought out in a step-by-step fashion. If standardization, delivery, and updating would have been thought through from the beginning, the project might have proceeded differently. Developing a plan covering development, use, and updates would have been helpful. While the details of the plan may change as new technology is developed, the process of thinking through the whole project allows one to identify issues and anticipate problems.

Use a prototyping process. Overall planning does not suggest a rigid development process. Once the overall framework has been set, it is helpful to use a very flexible prototyping approach (Schoech, 1999). For example, early on, several quickly developed exam formats were presented to all involved for their evaluation. The preferred options were then refined and developed further, while seeking feedback at each major step. This rapid development, feedback, revision format works well to avoid committing resources in unproductive ways. It also allows developers to quickly change directions as the development team learns about the potentials of multimedia to solve problems. With multimedia, seeing is essential as concepts can be difficult to conceptualize and describe. For example, a quick prototype of how the exam could be used as a training tool was developed and presented to the development team. The team was then able to conceptualize the issue better and make the decision to completely separate training from assessment.

Walk the fine line between current limitations and potentials. Exam development is often a multi-year process, yet technology changes rapidly in several years. Thus, a technology-based exam has the potential to look outdated when it is initially completed. It is difficult to develop projects for technology that will exist 2-3 years in the future. Most technology projects involve constant compromises between potential and current realities. Today, Internet delivery would be considered to avoid many of the delivery issues identified previously. However, other difficult issues, such as security, would surface as new technology is used.

CONCLUSION

Technology is changing assessments. The process of integrating powerful multimedia formats, such as video, audio, and virtual reality into assessment is beginning. When everything works as desired, a technology-based assessment can be very impressive and effective. Our experience shows how difficult the process of using multimedia for assessment can be. For exam developers wanting to develop technology-based exams critical to an organization's mission, little valid and reliable research exists to offer guidance. Consequently, case studies must be relied upon for advice. This project could have saved time and effort if the lessons learned were known before our endeavor began. Hopefully, other exam developers will find the advice applicable and helpful.

REFERENCES

Ananova, Ltd. (2000). About Ananova, the virtual newscaster. Retrieved December 19, 2000 from the World Wide Web: http://www.ananova.com/about/

Attention.com. (2000). The attention trainer system. Retrieved December 19, 2000 from the World Wide Web: http://www.attention.com/start/prod.jsp.

Hedlund, J. (1988). Mental Health Computing in Great Britain. *Computers in Human Services, 3*(3/4) 5-27.

Johnson, J.H., Giannetti, R. A., & Williams, T. A. (1979). The Psychological Systems Questionnaire: An Object Personality Test Designed for On-Line Computer Presentation, scoring, and interpretation. *Behavioral Research Methods & Instrumentation, 11*(2), 257-260.

Nurius, P. S. 91990). A Review of Automated Assessment. *Computers in Human Services, 6*(4), 265-281.

Satterwhite R., & Schoech, D. (1995). Multimedia Training for Child Protective Service Workers: Results of Initial Development and Testing. *Computers in Human Services, 12*(1/2) 81-97.

Schoech, D. (1999). *Human Services Technology: Understanding, Designing, and Implementing Computer and Internet Applications in the Social Services,* New York: The Haworth Press, Inc.

Stevenson, K.M., Leung, P., & Cheung, K.M. (1992) Competency-based Evaluation of Interviewing Skills in Child Sexual Abuse Cases. *Social Work Research & Abstracts, 28*(3), 11-16.

UCAID (University Corporation for Advanced Internet Development), (2000), Retrieved December 19, 2000 from the World Wide Web: http://www.internet2.edu/html/about.html.

A Video Streaming Pilot Project: Applications in Social Work Training and Education

Sandra C. Robin
Richard Reardon
Billie V Strand

SUMMARY. Video streaming or Webcasting is a delivery technology that has potential for enhancing social work education and training. This delivery method moves participation in education and training beyond the barriers of distance and time. This paper discusses a pilot project that used this technology to make a videoconference available to social work colleagues across the country. *[Article copies available for a fee from The Haworth Document Delivery Service: 1-800-342-9678. E-mail address: <getinfo@haworthpressinc.com> Website: <http://www.HaworthPress.com> © 2001 by The Haworth Press, Inc. All rights reserved.]*

Sandra C. Robin, PhD, is Associate Director, Center for Advanced Studies in Child Welfare, School of Social Work, University of Minnesota, 205 Peters Hall, 1401 Gortner Ave., St. Paul, MN 55108 (E-mail:srobin@che.umn.edu).

Richard Reardon, MA, is Media Producer, Distance Education/Media Resources, College of Continuing Education, University of Minnesota, 540 Rarig Center, 330-21st Ave. South, Minneapolis, MN 55455 (E-mail: reardon@tc.umn.edu).

Billie V Strand, MA, is Media Production Supervisor, Distance Education/Media Resources, College of Continuing Education, University of Minnesota, 540 Rarig Center, 330-21st Ave. South, Minneapolis, MN 55455 (E-mail: bstrand@cee.umn.edu).

[Haworth co-indexing entry note]: "A Video Streaming Pilot Project: Applications in Social Work Training and Education." Robin, Sandra C., Richard Reardon, and Billie V Strand. Co-published simultaneously in *Journal of Technology in Human Services* (The Haworth Press, Inc.) Vol. 18, No. 3/4, 2001, pp. 133-143; and: *New Advances in Technology for Social Work Education and Practice* (ed: Julie Miller-Cribbs) The Haworth Press, Inc., 2001, pp. 133-143. Single or multiple copies of this article are available for a fee from The Haworth Document Delivery Service [1-800-342-9678, 9:00 a.m. - 5:00 p.m. (EST). E-mail address: getinfo@haworthpressinc.com].

KEYWORDS. Video streaming/webcasting, online, social work training, social work education

A transformation is occurring in educational institutions and training centers across the country. The vehicle for this transformation is information technology (Harris and DiPaolo, 1996; Horgan, 1998). "The advent of new technologies in education has created unprecedented challenges for academic administrators and faculty to explore several cost-effective technology solutions aimed at improving learning productivity for students, reducing labor intensity, and providing new ways to deliver professional education and better services to students while enhancing the quality of instruction" (Ouellette, 1999, p. 98).

One such new technology is video streaming. Video streaming is a delivery method that combines videoconferencing and the Internet. A live or recorded event can be distributed over the Internet. The audience for the event participates by connecting to the stream, usually via a Web page link. "Streaming technology basically compresses the audio/video signal, breaks that compressed signal into discrete data packets, and sends these packets over the network to a special player which reassembles the packets to simulate a continuous audio/video stream" (Frequently Asked Questions, 2000, p. 2). "Simply stated, streaming refers to the process of delivering audio clips, video clips, or other media presentations in real time to on-line users. A clip can be viewed or heard almost immediately as it downloads from the streaming server; users do not have to wait until it is completely downloaded before playing it back on their computers. Streaming can be live or non-live. Webcasting generally refers to live streaming" (Dupagne, 2000, p. 4). An advantage of using a true streaming file format like Real Video is that the incoming file does not download onto the computer's hard drive as it is being received. Thus there is no data that needs to be stored, or take up local computer hard drive space.

Video streaming or Webcasting as a delivery method allows people across the country and around the world access to an event, if they have the requisite computer equipment. A limitation on the adoption of video streaming as an educational delivery method is the fact that "currently, fewer than three percent of the country has access to the high-speed broadband technologies needed to view streaming video without interruption" (Krebs, 2000). Nonetheless, an increasing number of colleges and universities are considering investing in video streaming technology for use in distance education, as well as for use in other Web-based broadcasts (Dupagne, 2000). A college technology review for 1999-2000 stated that "34% of colleges now offer accredited degree programs online, up from 15% in 1998-99, and by 2002 85% of four year schools will offer online courses" (DiPaolo, 2000). Given this prevalence of online courses, currently heavily print, it is likely that many of these courses will begin incorporating streaming video in the future.

The applicability of video streaming for social work education and training is a question ripe for exploration. Assessing the utility of this primarily unidirectional delivery method for courses or training designed to be bidirectional or multidirectional will be a challenge for social work educators and trainers.

THE VIDEO STREAMING PILOT PROJECT–
UNIVERSITY OF MINNESOTA

In April of 2000 the Center for Advanced Studies in Child Welfare in the School of Social Work, University of Minnesota, offered a satellite videoconference aimed at improving social work practice with children who enter the child welfare system at a very young age. The videoconference, "Working with Children Ages 0-3 and Their Families: A Case Consultation Seminar," was designed to address the concerns of front-line social workers and their colleagues engaged in implementing concurrent planning–Minnesota's response to the federal Adoption and Safe Families Act of 1997.

Implementation of this new federal law has the field of child welfare in a state of flux. The focus of this law is on achieving permanence for children, with specific attention to shortening the length of time that children are in out-of-home care. Of particular concern is the need for attention to the fate of very young children. The live satellite videoconference was designed to speak to this issue. The videoconference consisted of four child protection workers and supervisors presenting, via videotape, representative cases involving children between the ages of 0-3 who are in foster care. A panel of four consultant experts responded live to questions posed by the presenters regarding the service needs of these children and their families. The presenters asked for assistance with particular service and practice issues in the cases, for example, issues related to attachment of a three-year-old child to her mother who suffered from severe mental illness.

The Center made this training opportunity available to all 87 counties in the State of Minnesota by means of the satellite videoconference. All Minnesota counties have satellite capability through their county extension offices. This local accessibility allowed the county social service downlink site coordinator to invite community colleagues who work together on these cases to also attend the videoconference at the local site.

Media production experts from the department of Distance Education/University Media Resources at the University of Minnesota were contacted to provide the production support needed to produce the videoconference. The videoconference originated from the production studio at Rarig Center on the Twin Cities Campus. The Media Resources staff had been researching video streaming and suggested that a concurrent live video stream would be a good opportunity to test the delivery of high-quality audio and video via the Internet. The addition of the video streaming expanded the reach of the satellite videoconference to interested colleagues across the country.

This article is a summary of the video streaming pilot project. It is presented from the perspectives of both the media resources side (the technical aspects) and the social work side (the training/education aspects). Recommendations for using video streaming via the Internet as a delivery option for social work training and education will then be discussed.

PILOT PROJECT RATIONALE

Media Resources. The Distance Education/University Media Resources department was anxious to test the viability of concurrently or synchronously "streaming" a live satellite videoconference. Streaming video on the Internet presents another medium of distribution for clients, and a very economical one. Since resources have already been invested for production and satellite distribution, providing an Internet "stream" of a videoconference event is effective, inexpensive and "value-added." Also, the Social Work videoconference involved minimal screen motion (the content was largely talking heads), which made it ideal for the video compression that is part of Internet streaming.

Social Work. The opportunity to make a satellite videoconference available to colleagues across the nation was made possible through collaborative planning with Media Resources. Although the video streaming was primarily an experiment that the media staff were pursuing, the School of Social Work saw this as an excellent chance to try out a new technology and use it as a vehicle to make the videoconference accessible to a wider audience. Since the Center was interested in receiving feedback on the use of a case consultation training format the opportunity to stream the videoconference live over the Internet was seen as a way to get a response from colleagues nationally on this technique, as well as on video streaming as a delivery method.

PROCESS

Media Resources. To stream video, originating video is encoded into a digital format and then served onto the Internet, via a video server. The video server is software and/or hardware that optimizes the delivery of the video files. One also needs data connections among these devices. University Media Resources provided a video feed, which was produced with streaming in mind, which meant that the video elements were chosen to accommodate low bit rates (no zooms, no pans, etc. were used). The video feed was sent via campus cable to an encoder for analog to digital conversion. The encoder used is a hardware device, which converts video to a particular type of digital video file: Real Video. In the act of generating a Real Video file, the encoder also compresses that file to a size and datarate manageable for distribution over the Internet to computers connecting at a variety of bandwidths–everything from a 28.8 modem to a high-speed local area network. Once encoded, the stream was fed over the campus network backbone to the Real Video Server at the University's Academic and Distributed Computing Center. This server sent the stream off-campus and onto the Internet to anyone who connected to the streams Web address. To provide that connection, a Web page was constructed which identified the event, described the technology needed to receive the stream, set up a test to ensure that client software was working, solicited feedback, and, most importantly, provided a link to the stream. This link was made active about an hour before the event.

Social Work. Online viewers were solicited through nationwide listservs. A month before the videoconference the project director put an e-mail out on one statewide and three national listservs of social work educators, trainers, and deans and directors of schools and departments of social work. These postings announced the upcoming videoconference and invited people to participate, as the videoconference would be streamed live (synchronously) over the Internet. Potential participants were alerted to the type of hardware and software they would need to be able to receive the streamed video. Several days prior to the videoconference a second posting was made to the same listservs advising potential participants of the URL, as well as the 800 number for call-in questions. A request was also made for evaluative feedback on the content and the process of the video streamed conference, and on the technical aspects of the video streaming.

RESULTS

Media Resources. The University of Minnesota Real Server has a sixty-stream license (the software allows sixty users to connect to a stream at once); some 25 users accessed the stream at some point in the two-hour videoconference. Accordingly, anyone who wanted to connect would not have been restricted by license bottlenecks (essentially a busy signal cutoff). While several respondents reported good Internet reception for some of the videoconference they viewed, nearly all reported occurrences of network congestion and its accompanying artifacts. Usually, such congestion results in audio/video mis-synchronization. In these cases the audio would be of good quality but the video would be jerky, or the video would freeze while audio would continue. Some reported having their computer freeze, necessitating a restart (reboot) of the computer. Most reported that the quality varied over the two-hour period of the videoconference. It is impossible to determine if problems were due to the client computer, the local access points (network) or the longer data runs across country. Net congestion and buffering clearly affected many of these users. This is a common problem of national Webcasts, even for those with broadband reception. Often, these problems are localized (e.g., a local campus could experience network congestion that is especially constraining while another campus nearby has no such on-site congestion).

An entire industry has sprung up to service such events. These vendors position several "server farms" across the country as relay "boost" points for national Webcasts relieving congestion in the affected regions. Other strategies that have evolved include originating the Webcast at non-peak server times, avoiding early morning, noon and late afternoon. Providing an audio-only feed (audio rarely experiences congestion, even at low bandwidths) can also alleviate these problems.

Social Work. Approximately 500 people participated in the satellite videoconference across the State of Minnesota and in several counties in Wisconsin. All of these participants completed a form evaluating the videoconference. The total number of people participating via video streaming is unknown. However, feedback on the video streaming was received via 20 e-mails, representing at least 32 (one group of ten) people participating in Arkansas, California, Illinois, Maine, Michigan, Minnesota, Missouri, North Carolina, and Texas. We did not provide a form for these participants to complete. All video stream participant comments e-mailed were free form.

The people participating via video streaming, who identified themselves by e-mail, included: social work educators; trainers; administrators; staff development specialists; researchers; agency based field instructors; tribal social workers; and social work students. Six of these video streaming participants commented that seeing cases that represented child welfare issues from another state helped them, in the words of one respondent, "stay abreast of the issues nationwide, which are driving child welfare." Several also commented on liking the format, and that it was appropriate for the delivery method, "I liked the organization in which the social worker presented the case first and then the consultants responded." As a tool for training and education, one e-mail respondent wrote, "I thought they (the cases) introduced some of the larger service, treatment, and decision-making issues that confront the child welfare field," while another said that it was "a good way to learn about what is happening in child welfare in a different part of the country." In addition, two e-mail respondents said they appreciated the opportunity to participate in a conference in another state while sitting at their own desk. One video streaming participant wrote, "The fact that many people around the nation are able to view and participate in this event–at a reasonable price–is very important for the future of training." Eight of the video streaming participants who emailed feedback saw this as an opportunity to learn about a new delivery option for training and education and a model for distributing information.

RECOMMENDATIONS

Media Resources. It would be best to keep events away from high traffic periods on servers (server loads grow toward noon, and toward 4:00 PM local times). This is admittedly difficult for a national feed because of the different time zones involved. It is also necessary to keep feed data rates low. The "LAN" rate served in this project was 230 kilobits per second. Serving at 150 kilobits may have provided smoother viewing at work sites. Additionally, it may be worth considering an audio-only feed as a choice. Audio feeds are almost trouble free on modern computers and would be recommended for those events having little visualization (until the technology will support video better).

While it is impossible to know the source of the various "reception" problems experienced by some who "tuned in" to the Internet stream, our default video window size of 320 pixels × 240 pixels may have contributed to faulty playback. A video window of this size is approximately one-quarter of some computer screens, and is quite large. In the future, we plan to restrict ourselves to a video window no larger than 240 pixels by 180 pixels. This smaller size could make a significant difference for some networks and computers."

To address the issue of the cost of satellite versus streaming, it might be tempting to imagine foregoing the satellite costs ($2075.00 for the uplink and transponder for the two-hour event), and use the Internet alone for distribution of such a video program. That may not be possible, or economical at the present time. At the University of Minnesota we are fortunate to have a streaming media provider on campus, whose rate of $100 an hour to encode and play the streaming video on the Internet is extremely reasonable.

Although the streaming services market has been estimated to grow into a $2.5 billion industry in a few years, such providers are currently located only in a few major metropolitan areas (Minneapolis has no commercial provider, for example), and their prices vary widely. A recent list of major vendors, and their prices for Webcasting a fictional 20 minute presentation to 1,500 users, indicates that prices vary by thousands of dollars (Petrucha, 2000).

More important than cost, at least for the near future, is the issue of reliability. Satellite broadcasting is an established, proven technology, with reception that does not vary when downlinked correctly. Internet Webcasting is still in its infancy, and while promising, would be nonetheless risky as a sole means of program distribution.

Social Work. Continuing the learning from a video streamed training effort could occur by creating an online chat room or threaded discussion for participants to discuss the ideas presented with others. This type of post videoconference event would allow a national discussion and sharing of ideas focused on the topic of the videoconference.

One limitation identified by two video stream participants who watched the conference together was that viewing the videoconference via video streaming did not allow them to stop the presentation, like they could a videotape, to discuss and process what they were seeing and hearing. In addition there were others who were unable to participate in the videoconference and asked if it was going to be available on videotape. Several social work educators and trainers also indicated a desire to use a videotaped copy for classes and/or for training sessions. As a result, the Center has made videotaped copies of the teleconference available at a reasonable cost ($25). This also speaks to the benefits of saving the video streamed event on a Web server for future access.

Also, due to normal office distractions (phones ringing, people stopping in, etc.) it is best to make arrangements for viewing a video streaming event in an uninterrupted environment (for instance, having phones forwarded to a reception area or wearing headphones, and posting a message on the office door or cubicle entrance that one is unavailable until a specified time, or finding a location that is free from both phones and visitors).

Whether delivered via satellite (synchronous, one way video/audio), interactive television (synchronous, two way video/audio), or video streaming (synchronous or asynchronous one way video/audio) the main programming uses for any technology will continue to be education and training. However, thinking futuristically, video streaming may also be used to do case consulting, client interviewing, client referrals, and client commitments. Anytime it is too disruptive or prohibitive to move people from one site to another video streaming could be an option. (For sensitive cases security could be guaranteed by password protected sites.) As the technology improves, the bandwidth expands, and resources diminish the uses and demand for video streaming will grow.

Media Resources and Social Work. The strengths of video streaming are: the convenience of attending a conference at one's desktop or anywhere there is an Internet connection; the cost savings as uplink/downlink and transponder costs and ISDN (data phone lines) costs rise; and the availability of asynchronous playback anywhere/anytime. The limitations of video streaming are: the current technology limits the frame size and quality of the video picture; the number of people that can participate at one site is limited by computer screen size unless the image is projected or magnified (and such projection could create other difficulties); and the Internet congestion that causes buffering problems.

CONCLUSION

The pilot project discussed in this paper illustrates that video streaming live over the Internet is a viable method for making a local social work training effort available to colleagues across the country, and that colleagues are eager to learn from and about child welfare cases from other states. The video stream participants who provided feedback were primarily social work educators and social work trainers from state social service training offices interested in the concept of case consultation as a training model, as well as in participating in a national video streaming pilot project. The use of video streaming as a training delivery method for frontline social work practitioners and for students will need further consideration.

"Universities are on the cusp of an era of destructive innovation which requires that they confront who they are and how they conduct their business . . . we, like our product, must remain flexible. We must not be fixed on just changing course materials but look at how we deliver them" (Hansen and Vos, 1999, p. 1). The use of Internet technology by way of video streaming or Webcasting is one delivery method that is coming of age. Social work educators and trainers are joining their business, engineering and computer science colleagues in reviewing this new technology which allows expansion of movement beyond the boundaries of time and distance to reach learners, and which, with other advances in information technology, is creating a new educational paradigm.

REFERENCES

DiPaolo, A. Online education: Myth or reality? Keynote presentation to Alliance for Distance Education Summit and the Teaching and Technology Conference. Retrieved on July 20, 2000 from the World Wide Web: *http://scpd.stanford.edu/educa/slide15.html*

Dupagne, M. (2000, March). *How to Set up a Video Streaming Operation: Lessons from a University of Miami Project.* Unpublished manuscript, School of Communication, University of Miami.

Frequently Asked Questions: Microsoft Netshow and Media Player. Retrieved on July 17, 2000 from the World Wide Web: *http://www.liveware5.com/faq.html*

Hansen, D. (1999). "New age teaching": Videostreaming as a teaching and learning tool. *Teleview* (June 24). Retrieved on July 17, 2000 from the World Wide Web: *http://www.tafe.sa.edu.au/video-conf/ata/news/ju199/newage.html*

Harris, D., & DiPaolo, A. (1996). Advancing asynchronous distance education: Using high-speed networks. *IEEE Transactions on Education* (August). Retrieved on June 6, 2000 from the World Wide Web: *http://scpd.stanford.edu/overview/delivery_systems/sol.html*

Harris, D., DiPaolo A., & Goodman, J. (1997, March 4). Final report on Sloan Foundation Grant No. 94-12-7: The virtual classroom and distance education. Retrieved on

June 6, 2000 from the World Wide Web: *http://scpd.stanford.edu/overview/delivery_systems/sol.html*

Hinman, L. (1999). Streaming video: Adding real multimedia to the web. *Syllabus Magazine* (January). Retrieved on June 6, 2000 from the World Wide Web: *http://www.syllabus.com/syllabus* magazine/jan99_magfea.html

Horgan, B. (1998). Transforming higher education using information technology: First steps. *Vision* (January). Retrieved on June 6, 2000 from the World Wide Web: *http://horizon.unc.edu/ts/vision/1998-01.asp*

Krebs, B. (2000). Would-Be Webcasters Clash With Entertainment Industry. *Newsbytes* (June 15) [Infotrac Database].

Meserve, J. (2000). Microsoft touts low-cost streaming media in Windows 2000. *Computerworld* (February 21). Retrieved on June 6, 2000 from the World Wide Web: *http://ww.cnn.com/2000/TECH/computing/02/21/cheap.stream.idg/index.htm*

Ouellette, P. (1999). Moving toward technology-supported instruction in human service practice: The "virtual classroom." *Journal of Technology in Human Services,* *16*(2/3), 97-111.

Petrucha, S. (2000). Houses of a Thousand Streams. *AV Video Multimedia Producer,* (October), 68-76.

Plotnikoff, D. (1999). Streaming audio, video not a true mass medium yet. *San Jose Mercury News* (May 9). [Infotrac Database].

Yap, S. (1999). Videostreaming: jiving or jerking? *TelecomAsia* (January). Retrieved on July 17, 2000 from the World Wide Web: *http:www.telecomasia.net/telecomasia/archive/jan99/video.htm*

Attitudes and Opinions Regarding the Use of the Internet for Continuing Education Among Social Workers

Timothy Barnett-Queen

SUMMARY. Development of continuing education opportunities for social work license renewal requires participant access to the Internet, knowledge of the Internet's use and willingness to enroll in such programs. A survey of a random sample of licensed social workers in New Mexico revealed that 71% of participants (N = 403) have used the Internet while 61% reported no formal training in the use of the Internet and its features. Findings are reported that reveal substantial interest among subjects in the Internet as a medium for continuing education programs for license renewal. *[Article copies available for a fee from The Haworth Document Delivery Service: 1-800-342-9678. E-mail address: <getinfo@haworthpressinc.com> Website: <http://www.HaworthPress.com> © 2001 by The Haworth Press, Inc. All rights reserved.]*

KEYWORDS. Internet and continuing education, technology and continuing education, social work license renewal

Timothy Barnett-Queen, PhD, is affiliated with the School of Social Work MSC 3SW, New Mexico State University, P. O. Box 30001, Las Cruces, NM 88003.

This research was made possible by a grant from the College of Health and Social Services at New Mexico State University.

[Haworth co-indexing entry note]: "Attitudes and Opinions Regarding the Use of the Internet for Continuing Education." Barnett-Queen, Timothy. Co-published simultaneously in *Journal of Technology in Human Services* (The Haworth Press, Inc.) Vol. 18, No. 3/4, 2001, pp. 145-169; and: *New Advances in Technology for Social Work Education and Practice* (ed: Julie Miller-Cribbs) The Haworth Press, Inc., 2001, pp. 145-169. Single or multiple copies of this article are available for a fee from The Haworth Document Delivery Service [1-800-342-9678, 9:00 a.m. - 5:00 p.m. (EST). E-mail address: getinfo@haworth pressinc. com].

For nearly two decades the social work profession has promoted professional continuing education (Petracchi & Morgenbesser, 1995). With the demands of current funding sources, practitioners are finding they need more convenient, economical and efficient access to continuing education required by social work licensure and for personal growth. Concomitant research suggests that social work service and educational institutions have been slow to utilize advances in technology and instructional innovation to provide such continuing education opportunities through distance learning (Burton & Seabury, 1999; Butterfield, 1998; Marson, 1997).

LITERATURE REVIEW

Technology-based distance education has not received great enthusiasm by the majority of social work educators (Siegel & Jennings,1998). The emphasis of interaction and socialization in social work education has also made social work educators cautious when considering distance education (Krueger & Stretch, 2000). However, despite the barriers, distance learning in social work education has grown nearly 5% during a recent two-year period (94-96) (Siegel & Jennings 1998). Now, most social work programs (bachelors and masters) in large and public universities offer distance learning courses. However most distance learning opportunities (both practitioner preparation and continuing education) are synchronous in nature and are conducted utilizing two-way interactive televised transmissions between instructor in one location and students elsewhere (Thyer, Polk & Gaudin, 1997). The general use of technology to deliver social work continuing education opportunities lags behind even that of traditional social work education (Petracchi & Morgenbesser, 1995).

Research on distance learning in social work education is minimal and has focused almost exclusively on social work practitioner preparation (Petracchi & Morgenbesser, 1995). Available literature on continuing education by distance learning has discussed model development rather than empirical efficacy (Jennings, Siegel & Conklin, 1995). What research reports exist from both forms of social work education have predictably concentrated on distance learning via (two-way) interactive television (ITV). Thyer et al. (1997) and Thyer and Artelt (1998) reported that live teaching was evaluated significantly more positively than two-way interactive televised instruction. One limited study has been reported which examined delivery of an undergraduate human services human behavior and course exclusively on the Internet (Barnett-Queen & Zhu, 1999). Student responses to use of computer and Internet technology for distance education were overwhelmingly positive, however the small sample size (N = 17) makes generalization of these findings problematic. Barnett-Queen and Zhu have conducted a replication of their original study with a much larger sample (N = 45) and preliminary findings seem to again support the use of computers and the Internet as a viable method for distance education (1999).

It is acknowledged that ITV does not utilize the unique features of the Internet for distance education (Giffords, 1998). The Internet increases access to professional knowledge as no other current educational methodology (1998). Researchers once envisioned and proposed the Internet as a resource for enrichment, a medium of collaboration, an international platform for expressions, and as a medium for participating active learning (Relan & Gillani, 1997). In real instructional situations, the Internet has been used to engage learners in collaborative and cooperative learning (e.g., Wan and Johnson, 1994; MayaQuest Expedition, 1999). In a web-based learning environment, in addition to learning content, learners may engage in discussion, problem solving, and querying of peers and instructors. The Internet, especially the World Wide Web (WWW), also offers environments for group and team learning. Participants can enjoy greater access to instructors, peers and learning resources. Participants can work cooperatively and collaboratively on projects with team members across the world and learning can go on far beyond the timeframe of the educational offering through the use of e-mail and discussion bulletin boards (Hillman, Willis, & Gunawardena, 1994).

There may be a number of factors affecting use of information technology to acquire continuing education credits. Variables such as social worker's attitudes toward computers, lack of access to computers or the Internet, slow web connection speed, lack of knowledge of web-based resources and the availability of Internet related equipment and software at work may all impact social workers who might have interest in utilizing the Internet for acquisition of continuing education credits (Peters & Romero, 1998).

The significance of this study lies in its potential to develop distance learning continuing education opportunities for New Mexico (NM) social work practitioners as well as other regions of the country, on-going research opportunities to investigate the effectiveness of Internet-based distance learning as an instructional medium for professional continuing education and opportunities for linkages with other educational organizations for collaborative Internet-based social work continuing education development.

METHODS

Subjects and Sample Size

Sample

The mailing list of the NM Board of Social Work Examiners was used by permission from which to draw a random sample. Funding restricted the sample to one-third of NM's licensed social workers (N = 920). A useable response rate of approximately 44% was achieved (N = 403). Data was collected from each level of NM's social work license. NM has three levels of licensure. They include the Licensed Baccalaureate Social Worker (LBSW), Licensed Masters Social Worker (LMSW) and Licensed Independent Social Worker (LISW). The LBSW is licensed to practice generalist social work; the LMSW is licensed to practice advanced generalist, clinical and administrative social work but must be under the direct or indirect supervision of an LISW and the LISW is licensed to practice social work independent of formal social work supervision in all areas of the profession.

Subjects

In addition to the demographic information reported in Table 1, 110 (27%) participants were LBSW's, 131 (33%) were LMSW's and 147 (37%) were LISW's. Fifteen (4%) respondents indicated they held LCSW's from other states but did not indicate which NM license they held. No participants identified her or himself as holding less than a bachelor's degree. One hundred thirty-one (33%) participants reported working in a metropolitan county (150,000 + population), 49 (12%) reported working in an urban county (75,000-149,000 population), 116 (29%) in a small city (30,000-74,900 population) and 100 (25%) work in a rural county.

During the first years of certification and licensure in NM, individuals without a degree in social work could be "grand fathered" into social work licensure. Approximately 18% (N = 73) of participants identified themselves as having either a bachelor's, masters' or doctorate in a field other than social work. All other-bachelor degrees (N = 22; 6%) were

TABLE 1. Demographics (N = 403)

Gender	Female = 310 (77%)			
	Male = 83 (21%)			
Age	Mean = 47 years			
	Range = 24 to 79 years			
Age Groups	24-40 Years = 99 (25%)			
	41-55 Years = 222 (55%)			
	56-79 Years = 77 (19%)			
Ethnicity		Native	African	Latino/
	Asian	American	American	Hispanic
	2 (.5%)	18 (4.5%)	2 (.5%)	103 (26%)
	Pacific Islander	White/ Non/Hispanic	Other	Missing
	1 (.2%)	267 (66%)	8 (2%)	2 (.5%)
Work	Direct Svs	Education	Admin.	Supervision
Duties	263 (65%)	15 (4%)	73 (18%)	25 (6%)

LBSW's; of the other-masters degrees (N = 42; 10%), 29% were licensed as LBSW's (N = 12) and 71% were licensed as LMSW's; of the doctorates in other fields (N = 6; 2%), 78% were licensed as LISW's (n = 7) and two were licensed (from another state) as LCSW (22%). Unfortunately, a shortcoming of the survey made it impossible to know if any of the participants who identified themselves as holding a degree in a field other than social work also held a social work degree.

Design

This research was patterned after a similar study by Peters and Romero (1998). The study utilized a modified version of their questionnaire. The modifications were made with the authors' permission (B. Peters, personal communication, August 28, 1998). The survey was designed to investigate opinions and attitudes regarding the use of computers and the Internet for professional continuing education purposes. The survey also inquired about availability and access to the Internet and the type of computer equipment available to the subject.

The earlier study (1998) used a systematic random sample (N = 981) of Texas licensed social workers (N = 16,000). The authors reported final useable response rate of approximately 41% (N = 358). While Texas social work licensure is somewhat different than NM's, 62% (N = 223) of Peters and Romero's (1998) respondents were licensed at the masters-level. In the present study, 73% (N = 293) reported licensure at the masters-level. Sub-masters license levels were reported in the Texas study as 37% (N = 133) and in NM, 110 reported a LBSW licensure level (27%). Reports of gender of participants were almost identical.

Instrument

The survey consisted of seven sections. The first section requested demographic information in 13 separate categories including standard demographic information (i.e., sex, ethnicity, age, etc.) level of social work license and education, size of county worked in, work setting and duties, access to and training in the use of the Internet, and availability of a computer at home and work. The next three sections of the survey were for computer users only. The second section asked computer users for information on how the participant used the Internet (i.e., e-mail, for supervision, education, seeking resources, etc.). The third section asked for the type and processor speed of the subject's computer at home and work, features of those computers, type of Internet software and Internet connection speed. The fourth section requested information about which Internet features the subject used personally and professionally. All participants were asked to complete the last three sections of the survey. Opinions were sought using a Likert scale regarding subject attitudes toward the use of computers in social work. A similar scale was used to inquire about opinions regarding the use of the Internet for social work continuing education. Additionally subjects were asked to indicate areas of interest of Continuing Education events on the Internet. The final section, using a Likert scale, was to be completed only by non-users of computers. They were asked general opinions and attitudes toward the use of technology in social work and reasons they did not use technology.

The modified survey was field tested among social work undergraduate and graduate students as well as social work faculty. Minor adjustments were recommended and most were made by the author. The original survey was field tested among field instructors in Texas (Peters & Romero, 1998). The survey had no reliability or validity data at the time it was utilized.

Procedure

Data was collected through the use of a mailed survey. Surveys were sent first class along with a cover letter requesting participation and business reply mail (BRM) postage paid return envelope. All materials used New Mexico State University School of Social Work letterhead and logo. Subjects were asked to fill out the survey and return it in the BRM envelope with no identifying information to insure confidentiality. Two weeks from the original mailing date a first class reminder postcard was sent to each potential participant. Address corrections were requested from the postal service. All corrected addresses were re-mailed and a separate reminder postcard sent to them. No efforts were made to use tracking numbers to eliminate duplicate mailings to those who had already responded.

RESULTS

General Internet Usage and Access

All participants (N = 403) responded when asked about access to the Internet. One hundred thirty-one (33%) indicated Internet access at home only, 67 (17%) at work only, 152 both at work and home (38%) and 53 (13%) indicate no Internet access. Approximately 61% (N = 224) of respondents indicated they had no formal training on how to use the Internet while 22% (N = 90) said they had received some type of formal training. Sixteen percent (N = 65) responded that they had never received any training in Internet usage. By comparison, with only 5 participants not responding, 71% (N = 286) reported having used the Internet for personal or professional reasons during the last year, 13% (N = 53) reported they had not used it but planned to during the next year and 15% (N = 59) said they had not used it and had no plan to do so. This usage pattern compares favorably with the Peters and Romero (1998) report. They indicated that approximately 44% (N = 150) of subjects had used the Internet for personal or professional purposes, 25% (N = 85) planned to use it within 1 year and that 32% (N = 110) had not used it and had no plan to do so. Since the Texas report was approximately three years old at the time of this study, much of the difference of the reports of usage are no doubt a result of the general increase of Internet usage among the general population of the United States.

Characteristics of Internet Users

Training and Internet Use. Internet use does not appear to be associated with licensure, academic degree, gender, ethnicity or professional duties. However, several demographic variables were found to be associated with Internet usage among NM's licensed social workers. When the formal-training-in-the-use-of-the-Internet and Internet-use variables were collapsed into dichotomous variables, training was found to be significantly associated with Internet use ($X^2 = 9.88$, $df = 1$, $p < .002$; Phi $= p < .002$). Seventy-eight (20%) respondents who used the Internet reported some type of formal training while 208 (52%) Internet users reported that they had received no such formal training. Conversely, 14 (4%) of those who received formal training reported did not use the Internet while 98 (25%) reported neither receiving training or using the Internet. It is not clear in what particular manner formal training is associated with use of the Internet. Each cell of the contingency table was either over-represented (Training-Used and No Training-No Use) or under-represented (No Training-Used and Training-No Use).

Computers at Home and Work. Two other variables were found to be associated with use of the Internet, whether one owns a computer and whether one's workplace has a computer. Those who own a computer appear to use the Internet at much higher levels than those who do not or those who plan to purchase one this year ($X^2 = 27.26$, $df = 2$, $p < .001$; Cramer's V $p < .001$). Likewise, as one might expect, those whose agencies (work place) have computers appear to use the Internet at much higher levels than those whose agencies do not have computers ($X^2 = 11.34$, $df = 3$, $p < .01$; Cramer's $p < .01$). Worth noting, reports of access (home, work, both) to the Internet were not significantly associated with reports of use of the Internet.

Computer Hardware and Software for Accessing the Internet

When planning web-based continuing education (CE) offerings on the WWW, it is important to take into account computer capacities and connection speeds of potential users. Participants in this research who were either Internet users or who planned to use the Internet during the next year were asked to identify the type of computer equipment, Internet browser software and Internet connection speed they had available to them at home (N = 279) and work (N = 272). Approximately 20% of these respondents reported they did not know the computer equipment at home (16%) or at work (23%). Far fewer were not able to identify browser software at home (6%) and at work (15%). Most of these respondents had Pentium-level equipment at home (61%) or at work (54%). Connection speed at home varied among 14k (3%), 28/33k (15%), 56k (30%) and ISDN/DSL (3%). Approximately 34% reported they did not know their Internet connection speed at home. At work connection speeds varied from 28/33k (6%), 56k (9%) and network connections (14%). Approximately 45% were not able to identify work Internet connection speeds. Similar high rates of lack of knowledge of hardware, software and connection speed were found among Texas social workers (Peters & Romero, 1998).

Specific Use of Internet

Professional Use of Internet

From participants who indicated they either had or planned to access the Internet during the coming year (N = 292), the survey inquired about what professional uses they made, how often they used a specific feature of the Internet for professional purposes or if they projected to use it for that purpose in the coming year. Table 2 summarizes each major category's participant responses. As might be expected, e-mail with professional colleagues (64%), is the work most often done on the Internet. It is worth noting that a slightly lower percentage have used the Internet to seek resources (i.e., for clients, agency and professional growth) and to do research as have used e-mail. Since these tasks require the use of browser software and skills, it appears that a sizeable number of participants may have basic skills necessary to successfully complete the technical aspects of a CE course delivered on the WWW. The same categories of professional usage of the Internet were most used by Texas social workers and at similar levels (Peters & Romero, 1998).

Characteristics of Specific Usage of Internet

Each of the most heavily used professional tasks (i.e., e-mail with colleagues, seeking client services, seeking agency services, and seeking opportunities for professional growth) were analyzed further. While the task of research was reported to be used often by participants, it was not investigated further due to lack of a clear definition of the term. Three variables were found to be associated with each of these tasks (access to Internet, formal training in use of Internet and whether one had experience using the Internet) after the task variables were collapsed into dichotomous variables. Prior to collapsing, no associations were found. Computer ownership at home was not significantly associated, but was more strongly so than other potential associations. It appears that how often one uses the Internet for these tasks is not as

TABLE 2. Professional Usage of Internet (N = 292)

			Frequency/Month (%)				
Type	None	1-5	6-10	11-15	16-20	>21	Plan to
Professional E-mail							
With colleagues	62(23)	71(26)	33(12)	18(7)	12(4)	63(23)	35(13)
With clients	196(71)	32(12)	7(3)	3(1)	3(1)	7(3)	14(5)
Education	214(78)	22(8)	3(1)	1(<1)	1(<1)	2(1)	24(9)
Seek Resources	70(25)	97(35)	39(14)	26(9)	5(2)	20(7)	31(11)
Employment							
For Clients	223(81)	24(9)	2(1)	3(1)	2(1)	2(1)	11(4)
For Self	166(60)	67(24)	9(3)	8(3)	2(1)	7(3)	18(7)
Research	84(30)	77(28)	39(14)	33(12)	8(3)	26(9)	27(10)

important as is whether or not one uses the Internet for these professional tasks. The association of each independent variables with each heavily used task is reported below.

Professional Collaboration on the Internet with Colleagues. (See Table 3.) Access to the Internet was associated with the task of professional collaboration with colleagues (Cramer's V = $p < .001$). It appears that where one has access to the Internet may be associated with this task. Those who reported access at both home and work used the Internet for professional collaboration much more than expected (39%). However, those who had access at home only used it far less than expected (13%). Neither of these findings are surprising.

Whether one had formal training in the use of the Internet is associated with professional collaboration (Phi = $p < .001$). This association was found after training was collapsed into a dichotomous variable. Strong differences in expectations were found in all four cells. Fewer subjects than expected indicated they used the Internet for professional collaboration who had no training (45%). Many more subjects than expected indicated they had no training and did not do this task (29%). Those who had training who reported using the Internet for collaboration were in greater numbers than expected (22%). Yet those who had training in the use of the Internet and did not perform this task were under-represented (4%).

The final independent variable to be associated with professional collaboration with colleagues on the Internet one might expect. Whether or not the subject had experience using the Internet was associated with this task. This independent variable when initially tested had three cate-

TABLE 3. Professional Collaboration on the Internet with Colleagues (N = 292)

Collaboration and Internet Access

		Internet Access			
	Home Only	Work Only	Both	Neither	Total
No collaboration	38	19	25	15	97
Collaboration	48	32	114	3	197

$X^2 = 40.09$, $df = 3$, $p < .001$

Collaboration and Formal Internet Training

	Formal Training		
	Training	No Training	Total
No collaboration	13	84	97
Collaboration	64	132	196

$X^2 = 12.41$, $df = 1$, $p < .001$

Collaboration and Use of Internet

	Have Used the Internet		
	Used Internet	Have not used Internet	Total
No collaboration	64	33	97
Collaboration	188	7	195

$X^2 = 50.74$, $df = 1$, $p < .001$

gories (yes, no and plan to this year). It did not achieve significance. However, when plan-to-this-year was included with the "no" category, significance was achieved (Phi = $p < .001$). Subjects who responded to this question were far more likely than expected (64%), when they had experience using the Internet, to use it for professional collaboration, whereas those who had used the Internet but did not perform the task did so less frequently than expected (22%).

Seeking Resources on the Internet for Client Services. (See Table 4.) Access to the Internet was associated with this activity as well (Cramer's V = $p < 001$.). As with the previous independent variable, those who reported access at both home and work sought resources for client services more often than expected (37%). Those who reported access at home only used it less than expected for this activity (14%).

Formal training in the use of the Internet appears important here as well (Phi = $p < .017$). Strong differences were found in each cell, although not as strong as with professional collaboration. It is possible this weakening of association might be due to e-mail requiring fewer complex Internet skills and being more ubiquitous in the work place.

TABLE 4. Seeking Client Services on the Internet (N = 292)

Seeking Client Services and Internet Access

	Internet access				
	Home Only	Work Only	Both	Neither	Total
Do not seek services	41	16	27	15	99
Seek services	46	38	108	4	196

$X^2 = 36.24$, $df = 3$, $p < .001$

Seeking Client Services and Formal Internet Training

	Formal Training		
	Training	No Training	Total
Do not seek services	18	81	99
Seek services	61	134	195

$X^2 = 5.75$, $df = 1$, $p < .017$

Seeking Client Services and Use of Internet

	Have Used the Internet		
	Used Internet	Have not used Internet	Total
Do not seek services	65	34	99
Seek services	188	6	194

$X^2 = 54.31$, $df = 1$, $p < .001$

As expected, the actual use of the Internet is associated with seeking services for clients on the Internet (Phi = $p < .001$). Subjects who responded to this question were far more likely than expected, when they had used the Internet, to also seek client services using the Internet (64%) whereas those who had used the Internet but did not perform the task did so less frequently than expected (22%).

Seeking Resources for Professional Growth. (See Table 5.) Access to the Internet (Cramer's V = $p < .001$), formal training in the use of the Internet (Phi = $p < .036$) and actual use of the Internet (Phi = $p < .001$) were all associated with seeking resources for professional growth. Again it appears that access at both work and home (18%), having had formal training (21%) and experience in the use of the Internet (69%) are associated with this Internet behavior.

In a separate section of the survey the Internet-users and projected users were asked to identify the rate at which they used specific Internet-related features both personally or professionally. The results of professional feature usage are summarized in Table 6. Use of e-mail varies slightly from that reported in Table 2, with e-mail usage re-

TABLE 5. Seeking Resources for Professional Growth (N = 292)

Seeking Professional Growth Resoucres and Internet Access

	Internet access				
	Home Only	Work Only	Both	Neither	Total
Do not seek resources	34	18	23	12	87
Seek resources	52	33	115	5	205

$X^2 = 29.53$, $df = 3$, $p < .001$

Seeking Professional Growth Resources and Formal Internet Training

	Formal Training		
	Training	No Training	Total
Do not seek resources	16	71	87
Seek resources	62	143	205

$X^2 = 4.38$, $df = 1$, $p < .034$

Seeking Professional Growth Resources and Use of Internet

			Have Used the Internet
	Used Internet	Have not used Internet	Total
Do not seek resources	54	33	87
Seek resources	200	4	204

$X^2 = 71.10$, $df = 1$, $p < .001$

ported here slightly higher. While there is overlap between this section and the previous section, the two vary in at least one manner. The previous section inquired about specific behaviors on the Internet (i.e., use of communication, searching for resources, etc.) without using technological terminology. This sections asks about the frequency of use of specific Internet features, using technological terms. While the previous section yielded several significant associations, this section yielded only one and then only after the two variables were collapsed into dichotomous variables. As in the previous section, it appears that the use of the feature is what is important rather than the frequency of its use.

Characteristics of Internet Features Used

As might be expected, e-mail was reported to be used more frequently and by more participants than any of the other Internet features

TABLE 6. Internet Features Used Professionally (N = 286)

Type	None	1-5	6-10	11-15	16-20	>21	Plan to
			Frequency/Month (%)				
E-mail	44(15)	52(18)	31(11)	11(4)	29(10)	106(37)	26(9)
FTP/Downloads	108(38)	76(27)	28(10)	13(5)	6(2)	11(4)	17(6)
Search Engines	83(29)	71(25)	34(12)	18(6)	19(7)	33(12)	19(7)
WWW Browsing	104(36)	72(25)	25(9)	11(4)	11(4)	30(10)	18(6)
Bulletin Boards	177(62)	49(17)	5(2)	2(1)	0	15(5)	24(8)
Listservs	186(65)	32(11)	13(5)	2(1)	3(1)	15(5)	14(5)
Chatrooms	253(88)	5(2)	1(1)	0	0	1(1)	10(3)

listed. Of the 286 participants responding to this section, approximately 216 (76%) indicated they used the Internet for e-mail. This feature was also reported to be used more often than any of the other features. This is a similar finding as the previous section (i.e., professional collaboration with colleagues). The other heavily used feature was the use of search engines (N = 184; 64%). The other features listed appear to be used much less frequently. When compared to the Texas study (1998), while the use of e-mail is similar, the Texas participants reported heavier and more frequent use of these Internet features.

Professional E-Mail and Internet Training. Formal Internet training was associated with the use (dichotomous) of e-mail for professional purposes (Phi = $p < .001$). No other variables, either professional or personal, achieved a significant association with independent variables. Table 7 summarizes the results of this association. Very few participants (N = 7; 2%) reported having formal Internet training and no use of professional e-mail. Likewise, when trained, many more participants than expected (N = 70; 24%) reported the use of professional e-mail. Based on this and previous results, it seems that training may be an important factor in the professional use of the Internet.

Attitudes Toward Use of Computers in Social Work Practice

All participants (N = 403) were asked their attitudes and opinions about the use of computers in social work professional practice. The findings are what one might expect with the Internet-users generally having a more positive opinion of the usefulness of computers than those planning to use the Internet and Internet non-users. While those planning to use the Internet during the next year reported feeling more

TABLE 7. Professional Use of Internet Features (N = 286)

Professional Use of E-mail and Formal Internet Training

	Formal Training		
	Training	No Training	Total
Do not use e-mail	7	63	70
Use e-mail	70	158	228

$X^2 = 11.97$, $df = 1$, $p < .001$

strongly than the other groups that schools of social work should pro-vide more training in the use of software for computers and the Internet; all groups were neutral regarding the dehumanizing effect of computers on clients. Table 8 summarizes the results of attitudes toward the use of computers in social work practice.

Once again the current results, when inquiry was the same, are quite similar to the study reported by Peters and Romero (1998). The Texas study reported slightly stronger agreement across most similar catego-ries of inquiry. As with NM participants, there did not appear to be great differences among the opinions of participants across the three groups in these categories of inquiry. None of the attitudes reported in either study were negative toward computers and the Internet in social work practice and education (1998). Because the four items reported here are not of central interest to the current analysis, no further results will be reported at this time.

Interest in Social Work Continuing Education on the Internet

All participants (N = 403) were given the opportunity to indicate in-terest in, opinions about and suggestions for topics for CE using the Internet as the instructional medium. While none of the inquiries re-ceived a ringing endorsement, neither were they routinely responded to in a negative fashion. On a 5 point Likert scale, non-users showed a sur-prising interest in the WWW as a medium for obtaining social work CE credits (*M* = 2.2). It is not clear at this time how to interpret this finding. Further inquiry and analysis are required. Also of interest is the consis-tency of positive responses when asked about interest in the Internet as a medium for continuing education units (CEU's). Table 9 summarizes these findings. Table 10 documents all respondents' suggested topics for CEU's on the Internet. None of the items in this section appeared in the Peters and Romero study (1998).

TABLE 8. Attitudes Toward Use of Computers in Social Work Practice (N = 403)

Item	User		Plan-to-Use		Non-User	
	Mean	SD	Mean	SD	Mean	SD
Computers useful direct practice	2.4	1.3	2.6	1.2	2.9	1.3
Computers useful macro services	1.8	1.0	2.0	1.0	2.3	1.2
Computers dehumanize clients	3.7	1.2	3.5	1.3	3.1	1.4
SW schools should provide more computer training	2.1	1.1	1.7	1.0	2.3	1.0

Note: 1 = Strongly Agree; 2 = Agree; 3 = Neutral; 4 = Disagree; 5 = Strongly Disagree

Characteristics Associated with Attitudes and Opinions about the Use of the Internet as Medium for Social Work Continuing Education

Expressed Interest in the Internet as a Means of Getting Required Social Work CE. There are several independent variables which appear associated with interest in the Internet as a means for acquiring required CE hours for social work license renewal. After checking ethnicity for significance, the variable was re-coded in two separate manners for additional analysis. Because of the ethnic make up of this sample, the two largest ethnic groups (White/Non-Hispanic = 267, 66%; Latino/Hispanic = 103, 26%) were analyzed and the other ethnic groups, which made up less than 9% of the sample, were dropped from this analysis. When ethnicity was collapsed into this dichotomous variable, it achieved a significant association with the collapsed interest variable (Agree, Neutral, Disagree). The results are reported in Table 11 (Cramer's V = $p < .009$). More Hispanic participants (21%) expressed interest in the Internet as a medium for CEU's than were expected and fewer White participants (45%) than expected. The opposite applies to disagreement (Hispanic = 3%; White = 16%).

After dropping non-social work degrees from the sample, highest degree achieved a significant relationship with interest in the Internet as a medium for CE (Cramer's V = $p < .01$). The results of this test for significance must be interpreted cautiously as one of the nine cells was empty. Of interest in this association is the relative strong interest in the Internet for CE related to license renewal among bachelor's in social work (BSW) compared with their masters and doctorate in social work colleagues.

After putting participant ages into ranges that approximate the quartiles of the full sample (see Table 1), the age ranges of participants

TABLE 9. Interest in Social Work Continuing Education on the Internet (N = 403)

Item	User Mean	User SD	Plan-to-Use Mean	Plan-to-Use SD	Non-User Mean	Non-User SD
Interested in WWW as medium for obtaining SW CEU's	2.1	1.3	2.4	1.4	2.2	1.3
Interested in WWW as medium for obtaining required SW CEU's	2.0	1.3	2.3	1.3	2.6	1.3
CEU's on WWW good idea	1.9	2.1	1.2	1.2	2.6	1.4
If trained and equipped would enroll In WWW-based CEU	2.1	1.3	2.1	1.3	2.6	1.4

Note: 1 = Strongly Agree; 2 = Agree; 3 = Neutral; 4 = Disagree; 5 = Strongly Disagree

TABLE 10. CE Topics Using WWW as Medium (N = 403)

Suggested Topics	User (n = 266)	Plan-to-Use (n = 48)	Non-User (n = 50)	Totals (Frequencies)
Ethics	162	31	25	218 (54%)
Direct Practice	166	32	29	227 (56%)
Administration	97	16	10	123 (31%)
Supervision	119	20	15	154 (38%)
Human Behavior	173	34	30	237 (59%)
Social Welfare Policy	121	22	18	161 (40%)
Stress Management	131	24	25	180 (45%)
Personal Growth	160	29	23	212 (53%)
Other	47	7	5	59 (15%)

achieved a significant association with this dependent variable (Cramer's $V = p < .031$). Of note is the stronger than expected interest among the lowest age range (i.e., 24-40 years = 19%) as compared to the middle and upper age ranges (41-55 years = 36%; 56-79 = 11%). Level of social work licensure also became significantly associated with this dependent variable when the LCSW category (N = 15; 4%) was dropped from the sample. The justification for dropping LCSW was that NM does not have a LCSW license category and while it might be likely the LCSW's were soon to become LISW's in NM, one could not be sure. The more prudent analysis was to drop them from the sample for this test. Striking about this association (Cramer's $V = p < .038$)

TABLE 11. Characteristics Associated with Attitudes and Opinions About the Use of the Internet as Medium for Social Work Continuing Education (N = 403)

Interest and Ethnicity

	Ethnicity		
	Hispanic	White	Total
Agree	78	163	241
Neutral	12	42	54
Disagree	10	59	69

$X^2 = 9.47$, $df = 2$, $p < .009$

Interest and Highest Degree Earned in Social Work

	Highest Degree Earned			
	Bachelors	Masters	Doctorates	Total
Agree	71	184	8	263
Neutral	12	49	0	61
Disagree	12	53	7	72

$X^2 = 13.22$, $df = 4$, $p < .01$

Interest and Age Range

	Age Range (in years)			
	24 - 40	41 - 55	56 - 79	Total
Agree	76	142	42	260
Neutral	9	36	14	59
Disagree	11	43	18	72

$X^2 = 10.60$, $df = 4$, $p < .03$

Interest and Social Work License

	Social Work License			
	LBSW	LMSW	LISW	Total
Agree	82	88	84	254
Neutral	14	16	28	58
Disagree	13	22	34	69

$X^2 = 10.14$, $df = 4$, $p < .04$

Interest and Actual Use of Internet

	Have Used the Internet		
	Used Internet	Have not used Internet	Total
Agree	198	62	260
Neutral	44	16	60
Disagree	42	29	71

$X^2 = 8.12$, $df = 2$, $p < .02$

is the much higher expression of interest among LBSW's (22%) than expected and the much lower interest among LISW's (22%).

The final independent variable associated with interest in the Internet as a medium for required CE's is whether or not subjects have used the Internet. The "not-now-but-plan-to" category was merged with the "no" category to make the variable dichotomous. As expected, use of the Internet appears to be associated with interest (Cramer's V = $p < .017$).

CE Courses on the Internet for Social Work Licensure is a Good Idea. This variable (good-idea) generated some similar responses and results but also some which were distinctive. Table 12 summarizes the significant findings.

Unlike the interest variable above, highest degree achieved did not reach significance ($p < .11$). The dichotomous ethnicity variable resulted in a significant association (Cramer's V = $p < .031$) with the good idea dependent variable. Hispanics expressed greater agreement (23%) than did their White fellow-respondents (49%). The age-range variable also reached a significant association with good idea (Cramer's V = $p < .043$). The younger group expressed higher than expected agreement with putting CE courses on the Internet for license renewal than did their two older counterparts. Level of social work license was found to be significantly associated with this dependent variable (Cramer's V = $p < .003$). Again LBSW's (30%) expressed stronger agreement than did the LMSW's (25%) and LISW's (24%). Those who reported having experience with use of the Internet were more likely to agree that putting CE courses on the Internet was a good idea than were those who have not used the medium (Cramer's V = $p < .007$).

Finally, the work county in which a participant practiced social work was found to be significantly associated with the good idea variable (Cramer's V = $p < .006$). After collapsing the two less populated work settings, the three category variable (metropolitan, urban and rural) was associated. Those participants who worked in urban (population of 75,000-149,999) and rural (74,999 and under) settings were more likely than expected to agree with using the Internet as a medium for CE than were those in the largest category (population of 150,000+). It is important to note that 2 of the 6 cells in this test had frequencies lower than 5.

With Proper Training and Equipment Subjects Would Enroll In CEU Events on the Internet. Table 13 contains a summary of the enroll variable. Fewer independent variables were found to have significant associations with this final dependent variable. While the collapsed social work licensure ($p < .09$), actual use of the Internet ($p < .10$), and the sub-

TABLE 12. Putting CE Courses on the Internet to Help Meet Required CEU's for Social Work License Renewal is Good Idea (N = 403)

Good idea and Ethnicity

| | Ethnicity | | |
	Hispanic	White	Total
Agree	83	180	263
Neutral	10	40	50
Disagree	9	46	55

$X^2 = 6.96$, $df = 2$, $p < .031$

Good idea and Age Range

| | Age Range (in years) | | | |
	24 - 40	41 - 55	56 - 79	Total
Agree	82	153	48	283
Neutral	7	32	15	54
Disagree	10	36	12	58

$X^2 = 9.87$, $df = 4$, $p < .04$

Good idea and Social Work License

| | Social Work License | | | |
	LBSW	LMSW	LISW	Total
Agree	88	95	93	276
Neutral	13	11	30	54
Disagree	8	24	23	55

$X^2 = 15.71$, df = 4, $p < .003$

Good idea and Actual Use of Internet

| | Have Used the Internet | | |
	Used Internet	Have not used Internet	Total
Agree	215	68	283
Neutral	37	18	55
Disagree	32	25	57

$X^2 = 9.91$, $df = 2$, $p < .007$

Good idea and Work County

| | Work County | | | |
	Metropolitan	Urban	Rural	Total
Agree	82	43	158	283
Neutral	28	2	25	55
Disagree	21	4	30	55

$X^2 = 14.33$, $df = 4$, $p < .006$

TABLE 13. With Proper Training and Equipment Subjects Would Enroll in CEU Events on the Internet (N = 403)

Enroll and Age Range

| | Age Range (in years) | | | |
	24-40	41-55	56-79	Total
Agree	78	146	44	268
Neutral	12	30	13	55
Disagree	9	40	18	67

$X^2 = 9.47$, $df = 4$, $p < .05$

Enroll and Social Work Highest Degree

| | Social Work Highest Degree | | | |
	BSW	MSW	Doctorate	Total
Agree	75	190	7	272
Neutral	10	46	0	56
Disagree	9	50	8	67

$X^2 = 21.41$, $df = 4$, $p < .001$

ject's use of listservs ($p < .06$) were found to have strong relationships, in the analysis of the enroll variable, they did not result in significance.

The age range independent variable was again was significantly associated with interest in enrolling in a social work license renewal CE event on the Internet (Cramer's V = $p < .05$). The younger age range (24-40 years) expressed higher than expected interest while the two older age groups expressed lower. Significance was also found when the three category highest degree earned variable was analyzed (Cramer's V = $p < .001$). BSW degree holders express much higher interest than did their masters and doctoral-level colleagues. It is important to note that one cell in this contingency table had a frequency of zero. As a result, it must be interpreted with caution.

DISCUSSION AND APPLICATION

Independent variables of interest, along with the critical dependent variables associated with interest in the Internet as a medium for acquiring CE for social work license renewal, were put into a logistic regression model to determine if any were predictive. Unfortunately, with a sample of this size, too many low frequency and empty cells prevented meaningful findings.

The vast majority of respondents (N = 350; 87%) reported access to the Internet either at home, work or both. Almost three-fourths (N = 286; 71%) indicated using the Internet at one time or another for personal or professional purposes. Yet, only 39% (N = 179) reported participating in any type of training related to Internet use. Despite low levels of training approximately 76% (N = 216) of Internet users reported using the most popular feature of the Internet (e-mail) for professional purposes. Other features of the Internet had far less usage among respondents. One possible reason might be the lack of training in their use. However the finding of relatively high rates of use of Internet e-mail across the various categories of the sample is important. While not the most ideal pedagogy, on-line continuing education courses could be offered strictly using e-mail.

It is not entirely clear why when asked about professional usage of the Internet to seek resources, that much higher rates of use were reported than when asked about experience with search engines, WWW browsing and other Internet features used when seeking resources on the Internet. One possible explanation is the apparent lack of familiarity with Internet terminology (i.e., search engines, browsing). It does seem however that, as with professional e-mail, training and access to the Internet are important factors in whether or not NM social workers actually use such features.

Awareness of hardware and software appear to be quite low. Such lack of awareness may help explain the lack of training, lack of suitable experience with computers or lack of interest in the details of new technologies. Such lack of awareness may also contribute to the relative infrequent use and narrow selection of Internet features. Most respondents who identified themselves as Internet users appeared to use a very narrow range of communication and Internet-related software (i.e., e-mail and web-browsers). This information is very important when considering the development and pedagogical models for CE events on the Internet for social workers.

Among the associations found in this study, the most important seems to be that young Hispanic LBSW's who practice in small cities and rural areas have the most positive attitudes and greatest interest in the Internet as a medium for CE. While this sub-group's access and use of the Internet is not the most frequent among the groups studied, the frequency with which one uses features of the Internet did not appear associated with interest in the Internet as a CE medium. In NM, young

Hispanics may be over represented among the LBSW level of licensure and conversely under represented among the advanced license groups. NM LBSW's are more likely to practice in either the largest city (i.e., Albuquerque) or in rural communities. Many Hispanic social workers in NM are first generation college graduates. Because they tend to be younger than other ethnic groups it is possible that they encountered computers and the Internet in both public education and during their professional social work training. New Mexico is a large state geographically with a relatively small population and has large distances between many rural locations and larger cities; the Internet could prove to be a great time and money saver for such practitioners. While not directly investigated in this study, there may be a high level of motivation to increase one's level of education and social work licensure among young Hispanic practitioners and the Internet may be perceived as one avenue for such efforts. Regardless, a conclusion of this study is that efforts should be made to train, provide equipment and Internet access to this sub-group to facilitate their Internet-related continuing education efforts.

The results of this survey appear to support the need for Internet-related training and educational opportunities before significant CE development efforts are made. Since most social workers have access, and most have used at least a few of the key features associated with WWW-based education, efforts to train potential users should be made while CE development is occurring. Without such efforts, social work continuing educators would seem to run the risk of continuing a "digital divide" among social work practitioners.

However, there appears to be enough positive interest, Internet expertise and access to the Internet to support the development of "low-end, user-friendly" CE offerings on the WWW. Such offerings, at least initially, should utilize Internet software features familiar to the majority of respondents, such as e-mail, web-browsing, use of search engines and a very simple asynchronous discussion procedure such as that housed within WebCT. Due to the possibility of slow connection speeds, the offerings should not require the frequent downloading of large files. These text-based didactic tools have the added advantage of not requiring high-speed Internet connections to be used successfully in the learning environment.

These preliminary findings seem to support the need for and interest in CE events on the Internet among NM licensed social workers. In addition, given the vastness of the state of NM, such on-line learning opportunities could have the added advantage of saving time and money through the convenience of web-based learning.

RECOMMENDATIONS FOR FUTURE RESEARCH

Future research in this area needs to focus on three major fronts. First, larger samples would significantly increase the validity and importance of findings. Next, similar surveys should be done which include greater diversity among social worker's practice locations. A national survey among licensed social workers should be undertaken. Finally, efforts should be made to increase the validity and reliability of the data collection instrument.

REFERENCES

Barnett-Queen, T. R. & Zhu, E. (1999). Distance Education: Analysis of learning styles and preferences in two sections of undergraduate Human Growth and Development Course: Face-to-Face and Web-Based Distance Learning. Retrieved from Conference Proceedings database (Third Annual Technology Conference for Social Work Education and Practice, CD-ROM, August, 1999).

Burton, D., & Seabury, B. The "virtual" social work course: Promises and pitfalls. *New Technology in the Human Services, 12* (3/4), 55-64.

Butterfield, W. H. (1998). Human services and the information economy. *Computers in Human Services, 15*(2/3), 121-142.

Giffords, E. D. (1998). Social work on the internet: An introduction. *Social Work 43*(3), 243-251.

Hillman, D. C., Willis, D. J., & Gunawardena, C. N. (1994). Learner-interface interaction in distance education: An extension of contemporary models and strategies for practitioners. *The American Journal of Distance Education, 8*(2), 30-42.

Jennings, J., Siegel, E., & Conklin, J. J. (1995). Social work education and distance learning: Applications for continuing education. *Journal of Continuing Social Work Education 6*(3), 3-7.

Krueger, J E. & Stretch, J. J. (2000). How hypermodern technology in social work education bites back. *Journal of Social Work Education, 36*(1). Retrieved August 24, 2000 from EBSCOhost [38 paragraphs] on the World Wide Web: http://www.ebsco.com.

Marson, S. M. (1997). A selective history of Internet technology and social work. *Computers in Human Services, 14*(2), 35-49.

MayaQuest Expedition (1999). http://www.classroom.com/.

Peters, B. B. & Romero, F. W. (1998). Capability of practicing social workers to use the Internet for client services, information and referral, and professional development. *Proceedings of the Information Technologies for Social Work Education and Practice, USA* (pp. 259-265).

Petracchi, H. E. & Morgenbesser, M. (1995). The use of video and one-way broadcast technology to deliver continuing social work education: A comparative assessment of student learning. *Journal of Continuing Social Work Education 6*(3), 18-22.

Relan, A. & Gillani, B. B. (1997). Web-based information and the traditional classroom: Similarities and differences. In E. Khan (Ed.), *Web-Based Instruction* (pp. 41-47). Englewood Cliffs, New Jersey: Educational Technology Publications, Inc.

Siegel, E & Jennings, J. (1998). Distance learning in social work education: Results and implications of a national survey. *Journal of Social Work Education, 34*(1) 71-81.

Thyer, B. A., Polk, G., & Gaudin, J. G. (1997). Distance learning in social work education: A preliminary evaluation. *Journal of Social Work Education, 33*. 363-367.

Thyer, B. A. & Artelt, T. (1998). Evaluating distance learning in social work education: A replication study. *Journal of Social Work Education, 34*, 291-295.

Wan, D., & Johnson, P. (1994). Experiences with CLARE: A computer-supported collaborative learning environment. *International Journal of Human-Computer Studies, 41*, 851-879.

Implementing Web-Based Learning: Evaluation Results from a Mental Health Course

Alan J. Knowles

SUMMARY. This paper reports on the evaluation results of a web-enhanced mental health course. The instructional design of the course was based on the principles of constructivist and collaborative learning environments. Students strongly supported the use of web-based learning in this course and found that the online environment enhanced their learning. The benefits and disadvantages of web-based learning and the implications for future course development are discussed. Issues in implementing web-based learning in social work education are also identified. *[Article copies available for a fee from The Haworth Document Delivery Service: 1-800-342-9678. E-mail address: <getinfo@haworthpressinc.com> Website: <http://www.HaworthPress.com> © 2001 by The Haworth Press, Inc. All rights reserved.]*

KEYWORDS. Implementing web-based learning, evaluation and social work education, constructivist learning environments

Alan J. Knowles, MSW, is a full-time instructor in the Social Work Program, Grant MacEwan College. A doctoral student in the Department of Educational Policy Studies at the University of Alberta, his dissertation research focuses on the implementation of web-based learning in social work education.

Address correspondence to: Alan J. Knowles, Social Work Program, Grant MacEwan College, 10700 104 Ave., Edmonton, Alberta, Canada, T6L 1R9 (E-mail: knowlesa@gmcc.ab.ca).

[Haworth co-indexing entry note]: "Implementing Web-Based Learning: Evaluation Results from a Mental Health Course." Knowles, Alan J. Co-published simultaneously in *Journal of Technology in Human Services* (The Haworth Press, Inc.) Vol. 18. No. 3/4, 2001, pp. 171-187; and: *New Advances in Technology for Social Work Education and Practice* (ed: Julie Miller-Cribbs) The Haworth Press, Inc., 2001, pp. 171-187. Single or multiple copies of this article are available for a fee from The Haworth Document Delivery Service [1-800-342-9678, 9:00 a.m. - 5:00 p.m. (EST). E-mail address: getinfo@haworthpressinc.com].

Over the past two decades, social work education programs have gradually extended access to their programs through the use of distance education (Coe & Elliott, 1999; Raymond, Ginsberg & Gohagan, 1998; Seigel, Jennings, Conklin & Napoletano-Flynn, 1998). Although a variety of media and approaches have been utilized, social work distance education programs have primarily been offered through off campus site-based programs, print-based distance education, tele-conferencing, and interactive television (ITV). More recently, the availability and introduction of new information technologies (IT), coupled with a number of forces affecting higher education (HE), have contributed to an increased interest in web-based and distance learning. These forces include changing demographics, decreased funding, increased competition, and the globalization of HE (Hafner & Oblinger, 1998; Graves, 1997). The rapidly evolving context of HE is also requiring colleges and universities to re-examine their policies, cultures, and organizational structures (Bates, 2000; Duderstadt, 1997; Hanna, 1998; Graves, 1997; Turoff, 1997; Van Dusen, 1998).

WEB-BASED LEARNING IN SOCIAL WORK EDUCATION

Raymond et al. (1998) observe that "The use of web-based technology to provide a venue for teaching students outside of the traditional classroom environment is pushing the boundaries of distance education definitions" (p. 2). Becoming skilled in the adoption of IT in social work is also viewed as crucial for the profession and social work students (Butterfield, 1998; Miller-Cribbs & Chadiha, 1998). At the same time, social work educators have been reluctant to offer their programs in a distance format and have been suspicious of the use of technology in education and practice (Burton & Seabury, 1999; Butterfield, 1998; Marson, 1997; Siegel, Jennings et al., 1998). Kreuger and Stretch (2000) are especially critical of the impact of IT on social work education and suggest that asynchronous learning may negatively affect social integration, role modeling, mutual monitoring, and increase social distance.

A number of issues have been identified as important for social work educators implementing distance and web-based learning. These include concerns about academic performance, issues related to quality and accreditation standards, the loss of face-to-face (F2F) interaction, and the types of courses suited for web-based learning. They also include concerns about the impact of technology on experiential learning, relationship building, mentorship, socialization into the profession, student motivation, and student perceptions and adjustment to alternative learning. Faculty and implementation issues include the need for faculty education and training in distance education, pedagogy and technology. Access, technical problems, costs of development, release time, perceived threat to employment, recognition for developmental work, technical support, and institutional support are also important issues for faculty. Implementing web-based and other alternate learning environments also requires that programs examine and develop policies addressing these issues. Potential benefits include increased access for learners, responsiveness to changing demographics and learner needs, increased participation, promotion of self-directed learning, and the potential of enhancing relationships and mentorship. Web-based learning also provides the opportunity to integrate innovative, constructivist, experiential and collaborative learning strategies, and incorporate the capabilities of multimedia and the vast resources of the World Wide Web (Blakely, 1992; Burton & Seabury, 1999; Coe & Elliott, 1999; Freddolino, 1998; Forster & Rehner, 1998; Gasker & Cascio, 1998; Hick, 1999a; Jaffee, 1998; Stocks & Freddolino, 1998; Thyer, Artelt, Markward & Dozier, 1998; Wernet & Olliges, 1998; Wilkinson, 1999). A clear need for further research in social work distance education and alternative learning environments has also been identified (Freddolino, 1996; Falk, 1998; Haggenstad & Kraft, 1998; Hick, 1999a; MacFadden, Dumbrill & Maiter, 2000; Schoech, 2000; Seigel et al., 1988; Thyer et al., 1998; Wernet & Olliges, 1998; Wilkinson, 1999).

BACKGROUND OF PROJECT AND COURSE DESIGN

In this project, web-enhanced learning was introduced to a social work diploma course (Mental Health Intervention) as part of a longer-term strategy to convert the course to full web-based delivery. The web-enhanced version of the course was offered to on-campus students in the Fall of 1999, and to part-time evening students during the Spring of 2000. The web-enhanced portion of the course replaced the major assignment (research paper) and associated learning with three online modules, weighted at 35% of the final grade. WebCT was used as a software platform for the course. A number of course management tools were utilized to structure the learning environment and activities, including a course content area (course outline, description of modules, PowerPoint presentations), asynchronous forums, private mail, mental health links, synchronous chat, access to marks, and general tools (pass-word change, student websites). Postings and discussions for each mod-ule took place in designated asynchronous forums.

The instructional design of the modules was based on the principles of constructivist learning environments and provided a combination of self-directed learning, problem based collaborative learning, synchronous and asynchronous learning, and web research skills (Dijkstra, Collis & Eseryel, 1999; Harasim, Hiltz, Teles & Turoff, 1995; Honebein, 1996; Jonassen, Peck & Wilson, 1999; Mackeracher, 1998; Petraglia, 1998). In the first module, students were required to post their research on a men-tal disorder or issue, and then lead a discussion on their particular topic. In the second module, students worked in small groups (F2F and virtu-ally) on a case study and posted their responses and critiques to the module forum. In the third module, students the extended the learning initiated in module one by researching, posting, and leading a discus-sion on treatment approaches to specific mental disorders and the role of social workers in working with persons with mental health problems. In the Fall 1999 course, students also participated in an online synchro-nous chat with a "guest speaker." A non-weighted introductory module was included to assist students in becoming familiar and comfortable in negotiating the WebCT environment and gain experience in computer mediated communication. A forum was also provided for students to post feedback about learning online. Throughout all modules, the in-structor was active in structuring, facilitating, and participating in the online learning activities. Evaluation criteria for each module were based on both the content of students' postings and the quality and level of participation in the online forums.

Students who participated in the web-enhanced version of the course self-selected and also attended F2F classes. During the Fall of 1999, 11 of 22 students volunteered to participate; during the Spring 2000 term, 14 of 20 students participated. Both groups were offered a two hour training session to orient them to WebCT and computer mediated com-munication and conferencing. In the Fall of 2000, all students in the course will participate in web-based learning. As additional online modules are developed, it is expected that the course will be delivered to off-campus students in remote locations. Introducing web-based learning in this graduated way has provided the opportunity for the fac-ulty to learn from the experience and to evaluate students' perceptions and experiences of learning in an asynchronous virtual learning envi-ronment.

METHOD

At the end of each course, students were invited to complete an anonymous online survey to evaluate their experiences of learning online. Evaluations were completed and held independently, until after all grades were submitted. The evaluation was adapted from an instrument developed for another project in the college funded by the Office of Learning Technologies (Government of Canada) and Grant MacEwan College. The purpose of this evaluation was to guide the development and implementation of web-based learning and to evaluate students' perceptions of learning in the course (Kemp, Morrison & Ross, 1998). The evaluation included general questions about access and technical issues, questions exploring students' perceptions about learning online and course content, and open-ended questions asking students to comment on: their experience of learning in a web-based environment, advantages, disadvantages, and, recommendations. Additional demographic questions regarding age and employment were added to the Spring 2000 evaluation, as well as two questions that asked students about expansion of web-based learning in the course and whether or not they thought the course could be offered entirely online. In total, 22 of 25 students completed the online evaluation. Limitations of this approach are that the results are confined to these students learning in this course, the evaluation instrument was self-report and not standardized, and students who participated in the course self-selected and were interested in alternative ways of learning. The evaluation has provided valuable information for the implementation of web-based learning in this course.

RESULTS

Demographics and Access

Ninety-one percent of the students participating in the web-based learning were women, nine percent were men (n = 22). In the Fall of 1999, all were full-time students (n = 10). In Spring 2000, 75% of the students were between 30 and 40 years old, 8.3 % were between 25 and 29 and 16.7% were between 20 and 24; five students worked full-time, three worked part-time, and four were not working (n = 12). These demographics are consistent with the general demographics for the program. Twenty students owned their own computers and accessed the course from home, five students accessed the course from work, and three students accessed the course from both locations. Nine students connected via modems, three had cable connections and seven didn't know how the connection was made. All students in Fall 1999 accessed the course from home. Only one student (Fall 1999) had participated in online learning previously. Twenty-five percent of students described their computer skill level as "beginning;" 58.3% as having "some skills" and 16.7% as "computer literate." No students described their skills as "expert" (n = 12). In evaluating access and technical difficulties (5 = Often, 1 = Never) students had little difficulty in getting online or navigating WebCT and the course materials. They also were able to read materials and postings online, use the internal WebCT e-mail system, find Internet resources and print off desired course material (see Table 1).

Time

Students reported they were able to learn WebCT in a short period of time (M = 1.18 hrs, SD = .65, Range = .5-3 hrs [note: the mean was trimmed as one student reported 10 hours, which appeared to refer to numbers of hours spent/week online]. Students reported spending considerable time involved in online learning activities, in addition to regular class attendance and learning activities: M = 7.04 hrs/week SD = 3.29, Range = 3-14 hrs/week (n = 11). Students' responses to open-ended questions also identified the increased time demands of web-based learning in the course. Participating in the course was very time consuming for the instructor and involved the development of the modules, structuring the asynchronous conferencing and collaborative learning activities, customizing the WebCT environment for the course, uploading files, structuring and participating in the asynchronous discussion, participating in the chat, organizing and providing technical support to a guest speaker (Fall, 1999), responding to student e-mails, delivering two WebCT orientation sessions, and assessment of students' learning in the web-based environment.

Online Communication

Students' perceptions of online course communication were very positive (see Table 2). All students agreed or strongly agreed that e-mail facilitated communication with the instructor and other students. More importantly, approximately 81.8% strongly agreed and 18.2% agreed that online communication with the instructor and other students en-

TABLE 1. Access and Technical Difficulties (N = 22)

Statement During the course, I:	M	SD
Had trouble getting online	1.6	1.04
Read course material and postings online	4.59	.7
Printed off course material and postings to read	3.36	1.33
Found Internet resources suggested in the course material [a]	4.04	1.13
Had trouble navigating through online course material	1.9	1.23
Was able to send and receive e-mails	4.31	.87
Needed assistance with the technology required for the course	2.36	.73

Note. Responses were on a 5 point Likert-type scale where 5 = often, and 1 = never.
[a] n = 21.

TABLE 2. Student's Perceptions of Online Course Communication (N = 22)

Type of Communication	Percent of Total Respondents Agreeing/Disagreeing				
	Strongly Agree	Agree	Disagree	Strongly Disagree	Don't Know
E-mail facilitated communication with the instructor and other students	63.6	36.4			
The course conference (asynchronous) facilitated communication with other students	59	36.5	4.5		
The chat function facilitated communication with other students and the instructor (Fall 1999[a])	50	50			
The chat function facilitated communication with other students and the instructor (Spring 2000[b])	16.7	66.6			16.7
The online communication with the instructor and students enhanced my learning in the course	81.8	18.2			

Note. The chat function was encouraged but optional in the Spring 2000 course.
[a] n = 10.
[b] n = 12

hanced their learning. The majority of the students (95.5%) agreed or strongly agreed that the asynchronous course conference facilitated communication with other students. Students' evaluation of the chat function was also very positive. It should be noted that during the Fall 1999 course, participating in a synchronous chat (online guest speaker) was a weighted learning activity. The use of chat was optional during the Spring 2000 course due to time constraints.

Table 3 summarizes the total number of posts to all forums, the type of posts, and the number of articles read in the Spring course. Immediately evident is the intensity of the asynchronous discussions in the modules. Overall, there were 677 posts to the forums and a total of 6,825 articles read. There were 285 postings to module I, 70 to module II and 309 to module III (remainder of the posts were to the non-weighted forums). The number of original posts (M = 4.21) compared to follow-up posts (M = 44.14) is important to highlight, and consistent with the instructional design. In modules I and III, students were required to post their research and then lead a discussion on their particular topic. In module II, students worked collaboratively on a case study and posted their response as a group, followed by discussion. Participation in the asynchronous forums was highly interactive. Students posted their research, incorporated and linked Internet resources in their postings, shared personal and practice experience, provided support and suggestions to each other, and asked and responded to questions. This level of interactivity and discussion requires a shift in the role of the instructor to accommodate a conversational versus instructional approach to learning (Romiszowski & Mason, 1996). It also requires the ability to facilitate and support "emergent collaboration" (Nachmias, Mioduser, Oren & Ram, 2000).

Perception of Web-Based Learning Environment

The students' responses to statements about course design and learning strongly supported the use of web based learning in this course. All of the students agreed or strongly agreed that the learning activities were interesting and motivating, that learning objectives and expecta-

TABLE 3. Type of Posts and Number of Articles Read–Spring 2000 (N = 14[a])

Type of Post	N	M	SD	Range
Original Posts	59	4.21	1.31	2-7
Follow Up Posts [b]	618	44.14	15.54	23-72
Total Posts [c]	677	48.35	15.7	23-78
Articles Read (posts)	6825	487.5	187.5	190-717

Note. Total number of posts varies from Figure 1 as the tracking function for individual posts was re-set after the initial non-credit module.
[a] n = total posts for the Spring 2000 course.
[b] One student's posts were adjusted to reflect follow-up posts (as follow-up posts were posted inadvertently as original posts) .

tions were clear, and that the course content was suited to web-based learning (see Table 4). A majority of the students (91%) agreed or strongly agreed the modules contained an appropriate balance of assignments and learning activities and were well organized. Approximately 40% identified that the workload was too heavy, while 60% disagreed with this statement (time demands were also reflected in the responses to open-ended questions). More importantly, 86.4% strongly agreed and 9.1% agreed that the technology enhanced their ability to learn in the course and 100% felt the asynchronous conference facilitated learning. Support for learning in synchronous chat was also very strong with all Fall 1999 students agreeing that the chat function facilitated their learning while in the Spring course, 8.3% of students disagreed with this statement, and 25% didn't know. The use of chat in the Spring course was optional and unstructured, which may account for this difference in the responses. All of the students recommended web-based learning for other courses in the program, would take another course online, and would recommend web-based learning to others. Two questions added to the Spring 2000 evaluation specifically asked about expansion of web-based learning in the course and whether or not students thought the entire course could be offered online. Although 75% of the students felt that web-based learning could be expanded in the course, only 41.6% agreed that the course could be offered entirely online, while 41.7% disagreed and 16.6% didn't know (n = 12). Overall, 72.8% identified they would take an entire course online, while 18.2% disagreed and 9% didn't know (n = 22).

Responses to Open-Ended Questions

The students provided a substantial number of comments in response to the open-ended questions that asked about how web-based learning affected their learning, benefits, disadvantages and recommendations. Overall, comments were very positive and supported the responses to the survey questions. The following sections summarize the main themes identified and provide selected examples of the students' comments.

How Did Online Learning Affect Your Learning in This Course? Students appreciated the flexibility to learn on their own schedules. Although they identified that more time was required, they felt they learned more by participating in online learning. A key theme identified by many students was the high value of learning collaboratively from others, especially having the opportunity to read and respond to others'

TABLE 4. Course Design and Learning (N = 22)

Statement	Percent of Total Respondents Agreeing/Disagreeing				
	Strongly Agree	Agree	Disagree	Strongly Disagree	Don't Know
Overall the online course was appealing, interesting and motivating	77.3	22.7			
Module objectives were clearly stated	90.9	9.1			
Course modules contain an appropriate number of exercises, assignments & learning activities	45.5	45.5	9		
The workload was too heavy	13.6	27.3	40.9	18.2	
Learning activities were interesting and challenging	81.8	18.2			
The technology used in the course enhanced my ability to learn the course material	86.4	9.1			4.5
The course content was suited to online learning	77.3	22.7			
The course conference and activities facilitated learning	85.7	14.3			
The chat function and activities facilitated learning–Fall 1999 [a]	80	20			
The chat function and activities facilitated learning–Spring 2000 [b]	16.7	50	8.3		25
Web-based learning could be expanded in this course [b,c]	41.7	33.3			25
This course could be offered entirely online [b,c]	16.6	25	41.7		16.6
I would recommend web-based learning for other courses in the Social Work Program	68	32			
I would take another online course	72.7	27.3			
I would recommend online learning to others	68.2	31.8			
I would take an entire course offered online	36.4	36.4	13.7	4.5	9

Notes: [a] n = 10.
[b] n = 12.
[c] Questions added to evaluation for Spring 2000 course

research and writing online. The students also found web-based learning to be interesting and motivating. Typical comments included: "I think the most important effect it had on my learning was that it broadened what I have learned because I was able to see what others had learned, whenever I wanted to." "I was recently diagnosed with a learning disorder-the online modules were extremely effective in enhancing my learning." "I was able to learn from reading other students postings without having to be online at the same time." "Being able to access this course at any time is great. Online learning allowed me to work on my course material on my schedule." "I feel that online learning in this course enhanced my learning." "It was fun, it was different, and it was frustrating because of my computer skills, which were very limited." "I would do it again if it is offered in another course." "It was different from my other courses and sparked my interest."

Benefits of Online Learning? Students identified a number of benefits of online learning in the course. Many students commented that they had learned more than if they had attended only F2F classes and appreciated the flexibility of web-based learning. A major theme was that asynchronous learning enhanced depth in both communication processes and learning. Specific benefits included sharing knowledge, reading others' work, reflective learning, facilitating deeper levels of communication and intimacy, less procrastination, and more thoughtful responses. These results are especially relevant given the concerns identified about the loss of F2F communication and interactivity in web-based learning. Typical comments included: "Facilitates a deeper level of communication with fellow students, promotes sharing of knowledge and experience." "Not having the pressure of immediate responses–I also had the opportunity to think about opinions before I 'spoke' ." "It provided a window to express thoughts and ideas that may not have been expressed in person." "Incredible variety of constructive feedback." "As a new student in this group I got to know classmates faster by responding to postings and email." "It provided an example of others' research and writing styles." "It provided ongoing communication between the instructor and the students." "Prompted me to engage on the Internet, become more comfortable with the technology."

Disadvantages of Online Learning? Although students were very positive about their experience of learning online, they identified several disadvantages in their comments. Disadvantages focused on the time demands of learning online, the amount of reading and information overload, Internet access and computer ownership, technical limitations of WebCT, and reluctance to take an entire course online. Comments included: "Due to the amount of information posted, it took a long time to read." "I'm not sure I would want to take a course totally online, I value classroom discussions with my colleagues and instructor-face to face learning is important to me as well." "It was too much work and not enough time, considering we spent 3 hours in class and then came on-line." "Group dynamics are different." "Not that convenient when you don't own a computer." "I found responding to everyone's posting time consuming and felt like I wasn't responding with genuine comments." "The greatest challenge was to get connected to the Internet and comfortable with the technology."

Recommendations and Other Comments? Recommendations and general comments included increasing the weighting of the web-enhanced portion of the course due to the amount of work and learning involved, offering the course over a longer period of time (Spring students), placing limits on the numbers of postings, and providing a sample post. Students also recommended increasing web-based learning in the course, reducing F2F class time, increasing the number of courses offered online, and technical adjustments to the software environment (ability to draft posts off-line, spell checker). Typical comments were: "There was a lot more time involved than I initially thought-because of the amount of time, 35% was too low a mark for the online learning." "I think it is good for an added benefit, not a substitute for class work entirely." "I found this portion of the course so interesting, it was difficult to know when to stop!" "Combination between computer and class activities looks perfect to me." "I think that more social work courses should be offered online, after all, this is the way of the future." "I think we could have covered most of the (classwork) in a one or two day workshop and did the rest online." "I loved this experience and found it very exciting."

DISCUSSION

The students' evaluations strongly support the use and expansion of web-based learning in this course. Students had little difficulty accessing and negotiating the course and found that the learning environment facilitated communication and enhanced their learning. Virtually all of the students felt that the course content was suited for online learning and that the technology used in the course enhanced their learning. A key result was the strong support for asynchronous conferencing and learning activities in the course. This is especially important given that asynchronous conferencing and collaborative learning are core elements of web-based learning environments. Many students commented on the high learning value of reading and responding to each others' work online. Other benefits included flexible access, improved computer and IT skills, and enhanced knowledge of web resources for their practice. The results strongly support the use of constructivist and collaborative approaches to instructional design in this course. Students also recommended that web-based learning be integrated into other courses in the program. The intense level of discourse and personal sharing posed additional challenges for teaching online, as well as reinforcing the importance of security, confidentiality and privacy issues. Interestingly, the students did not express concern about these issues.

Although the students' experience of learning online was very positive, 41.7% of the Spring students disagreed and 16.6% did not know if this course should be offered entirely online. Overall however, all of the students would take another course online and 73% would take an entire course online. An important implication of these results is that while the students strongly endorsed web-based learning, they also prefer a mix of web-based and F2F learning in this course. This means that web-based learning will likely not replace F2F learning entirely in the course, but provide expanded, flexible and effective learning options for both on-campus and distance students. It is particularly well suited to adult students coping with multiple life demands who appreciate the flexibility web-based learning has to offer. It also means that additional demands will be placed on faculty who will need to develop the skills of teaching in multiple learning environments. As web-based learning expands in this course, a key challenge will be finding an effective balance of web-based and F2F interaction and learning strategies. In this regard, graduated implementation has been an effective way for faculty to gain experience in teaching online and to evaluate the suitability of this course for web-based learning.

Limited time and resources are a key faculty and program issue. Release time to develop the online modules was appreciated, but not sufficient given requirements of designing online learning activities, learning to use WebCT (robust, but not intuitive), and participating in online learning. Faculty who become involved in web-based learning need to be committed to the value of the pedagogy, learning needs of students and intrinsically motivated to experiment with web-based learning in order to be successful (Schifter, 2000). Related faculty and program issues include:

- computer and technical skills
- recognition for innovation
- knowledge of pedagogy and instructional design
- coping with changing IT, and forces affecting HE
- skills of teaching and learning online
- cost of development and maintenance

These issues have policy implications for programs and institutions hoping to expand the use of web-based learning and promote wider scale faculty adoption of alternative delivery of courses and programs. Given the cost of development and maintenance, there is a need to develop inter-program collaboration in developing web-based modules, learning objects and databases. Research in social work distance education has tended to focus on demonstrating comparability of alternative and traditional delivery, primarily as a result of accreditation concerns and requirements. Turoff (1999), among others, has noted the blurring of boundaries between distance and on-campus learning, and suggests "It is time to admit that separate distance learning programs are unnecessary. All such separate programs should be eliminated . . . Today, those distance students utilizing modern group communications in their distance courses may very well be getting a better quality education than the typical student in a face to face class" (para.1). The issues of competition, commercialization, and the globalization of HE also all pose particular philosophical, policy, and practical challenges for social work educators.

CONCLUSION

Students strongly supported the use of web-based learning in this course and found that the online environment enhanced their learning. Implementing web-based learning in a graduated fashion was an effective way to introduce and evaluate online learning. Although the evaluation results were very positive, there are a number of professional, pedagogical and policy issues that need further exploration. As web-based learning moves from innovative to mainstream, social work educators will need to find ways to address issues related to "pedagogy versus profit" and develop strategies to respond to demands for multiple learning environments in the context of diminishing resources in a highly competitive HE market.

REFERENCES

Bates, T. (2000). *Managing technological change: Strategies for college and university leaders.* San Francisco: Jossey Bass, Inc.

Blakely, Thomas, J. (1992). A model for distance education delivery. *Journal of Social Work Education 28*(2),214-221.

Burton, D., & Seabury, B. (1999). The "virtual" social work course: Promises and pitfalls. *New Technology in the Human Services, 12*(3/4),55-64.

Butterfield, W. H. (1998). Human services and the information economy. *Computers in Human Services, 15*(2/3), 121-142.

Coe, J. A., & Elliott, D. (1999). An evaluation of teaching direct practice courses in a distance education program for rural settings. *Journal of Social Work Education, 35*(3), 353-365.

Collis, B. (1996). *Tele-learning in a digital world: The future of distance learning.* London: Thompson Computer Press.

Dijkstra, S., Collis, B., & Eseryel, D. (1999). Instructional design for tele-learning. *Journal of Computing in Higher Education, 10*(2), 3-18.

Duderstadt, J. J. (1997). The future of the university in an age of knowledge. *Journal of Asynchronous Networks, 1*(2),78-88.

Falk, D. S. (1998). The virtual community: Computer conferencing for teaching and learning social work practice. *Conference Proceedings: Information Technologies for Social Work Education and Practice.* Columbia: College of Social Work, University of South Carolina.

Faux, T., & Black-Hughes, C. (2000). A comparison using the Internet versus lectures to teach social work history. *Research on Social Work Practice, 10*(4), 454-466.

Forster, M., & Rehner, T. (1998). Part-time MSW distance education: A program evaluation. *Computers in Human Services, 15* (2/3), 9-21.

Freddolino, P. P. (1996). Maintaining quality in graduate social work programs delivered to distant sites using electronic instruction technology. *Tulane Studies in Social Welfare, XX.* New Orleans: Tulane University

Freddolino, P. P. (1998). Building on experience: Lessons from a distance education M.S.W. program. *Computers in Human Services, 15*(2/3), 39-50.

Gasker, J., & Cascio, T. (1998). Computer mediated interaction: A tool for facilitating the educational helping relationship. *Conference Proceedings: Information Technologies for Social Work Education and Practice,* Columbia: College of Social Work, University of South Carolina.

Gibbs, William, J. (1999). Implementing online learning environments. *Journal of Computing in Higher Education, 10*(1),16-37.

Graves, W. H. (1997). Free trade in higher education: The meta university. *Journal of Asynchronous Learning Networks, 1*(1),97-108.

Haagenstad, S., & Kraft, S. (1998). Outcome measures comparing classroom education to distance education. *Conference Proceedings: Information Technologies for Social Work Education and Practice.* Columbia: College of Social Work, University of South Carolina.

Hafner, K., & Oblinger, D. (1998). Transforming the academy. D. Oblinger, & S. Rush (Eds.), *The future compatible campus: Planning, designing, and implementing information technology in the academy.* Bolton: Anker Publishing Co.

Hanna, D. E. (1998). Higher education in an era of digital competition: Emerging organizational models. *Journal of Asynchronous Learning Networks, 2*(1),66-95.

Harasim, L., Hiltz, S., Teles, L., & Turoff, M. (1995). *Learning networks: A field guide to teaching and learning online.* Cambridge, MA: The MIT Press.

Hick, S. (1999a). Learning to care on the Internet: Evaluating an online introductory social work course. *New Technology in the Human Services, 11*(4), 1-10.

Hick, S. (1999b). Rethinking the debate: Social work education on the Internet. *New Technology in the Human Services, 12*(3/4),65-74.

Hiltz, Starr, R. (1997). Impacts of college-level courses via asynchronous learning networks: Some preliminary results. *Journal of Asynchronous Learning Networks (1)*(2), 1-19.

Honnebein, P. (1996). Seven goals for the design of constructivist learning environments. B. Wilson (Ed.), *Constructivist learning environments: Case studies in instructional design.* Englewood Cliffs, New Jersey: Educational Technology Publications.

Jaffee, D. (1998). Institutionalized resistance to asynchronous learning networks. *Journal of Asynchronous Learning Networks, 2*(2), 21-32.

Jonnasen, D., Peck, K., & Wilson, B. (1999). *Learning with technology: A constructivist perspective.* Upper Saddle River, New Jersey: Prentice-Hall.

Kemp, J.E., Morrison, G.R., & Ross, S.M. (1998) *Designing effective instruction* (2nd ed.). Upper Saddle River: Prentice-Hall, Inc.

Kreuger, L.W., Stretch, J.J. (2000). How hypermodern technology in social work education bites back. *Journal of Social Work Education (36)* (1), 103-114.

Lancaster, K., Stokes, J., & Summary, L. (1998). The use of WebBoard conferencing in social work education. *Conference Proceedings: Information Technologies for Social Work Education and Practice.* Columbia, South Carolina: College of Social Work, University of South Carolina.

MacFadden, R., Dumbrill, G., & Maiter, S. (2000). Web-based education in a graduate faculty of social work: Crossing the new frontier. *New Technology in The Human Services, 13*(1,2), 27-38.

Mackeracher, D. (1998). What is learning all about? E. Burge & J. Roberts (Eds.), *Classrooms with a difference: Facilitating learning on the information highway* (2nd ed.). Montreal: Cheneliere/Mcgraw-Hill.

Marlowe-Carr, Lisa, C. (1997). Social workers on-line: A profile. *Computers in Human Services 14* (1), 59-69.

Marson, S.M. (1997) A selective history of Internet technology and social work. *Computers in Human Services* (14)(2), 35-49.

Miller-Cribbs, J., & Chadiha, L. (1998). Integrating the internet in a human diversity course. *Computers in Human Services, 15*(2/3),97-109.

Nachmias, R., Mioduser, D., Oren, A., & Ram, J. (2000). Web-supported emergent-collaboration in higher education courses. *Educational Technology & Society, 3*(3), 94-104.

Petraglia, J. (1998). *Reality by design: The rhetoric and technology of authenticity in education.* Mahwah, New Jersey: Lawrence Erlbaum Associates, Inc.

Raymond, F., Ginsberg, L., & Gohagan, D. (1998). Introduction-Information technologies: Teaching to use–using to teach. *Computers in Human Services, 15*(2/3), 1-5.

Romiszowski, A.,J., & Mason, R. (1996) Computer-mediated communication. D.H. Jonnasen (Ed.) *Handbook of research for educational communications and technology.* New York: Simon & Schuster Macmillan.

Schifter, Catherine, C. (2000) Faculty participation in asynchronous learning networks: A case study of motivating and inhibiting factors. *Journal of Asynchronous Learning Networks* (4) (1), 15-22.

Schoech, D. (2000). Teaching over the Internet: Results of one doctoral course. *Research on Social Work Practice, 10*(4), 467-486.

Siegel, E., Jennings, J., Conklin, J., & Napoletano-Flynn, S. A. (1998). Distance learning in social work education: Results and implications of a national survey. *Journal of Social Work Education, 34*(1), 71-80.

Stocks, J. T., & Freddolino, P. (1998). Evaluation of a world wide web-based graduate social work research methods course. *Computers in Human Services, 15*(2/3),51-69.

Thyer, B., Artelt, T., Markward, M., & Dozier, C. (1998). Evaluating distance learning in social work education: A replication study. *Journal of Social Work Education, 34*(2), 291-295.

Thyer, B., Polk, G., & Gaudin, J. G. (1997). Distance learning in social work education: A preliminary evaluation. *Journal of Social Work Education, 33*(2), 363-367.

Turoff, M. (1997). Alternative futures for distance learning: The force and the darkside. *UNESCO/Open University International Colloquium*: *Virtual Learning Environments and the Role of the Teacher.* Retrieved November 22, 1998 from the World Wide Web: http://eies.njit.edu/~turoff.

Turoff, M. (1999). An end to segregation: No more separation between distance learning and regular classes. Paper presented at Telelearning 99, November 1999, Montreal. Retrieved December 6, 1999, from the World Wide Web: http://eies.njit.edu/~turoff/Papers/canadapres/segregation.htm

Van Dusen, G. C. (1997). The virtual campus: Technology and reform in higher education. ASHE-ERIC Higher Education Report Vol.25, No.5. Washington: The George Washington University, Graduate School of Education and Human Development.

Wernet, S., & Olliges, R. (1998). The application of WebCT (Web Course Tools) in social work education. *Conference Proceedings*: *Information Technologies for Social Work Education and Practice.* Columbia: College of Social Work, University of South Carolina.

Wilkinson, A. (1999). Environments for social work learning in the learning age. *New Technology in the Human Services, 12*(3/4).

Ensuring That Course Websites Are ADA Compliant

Susan Sarnoff

SUMMARY. This paper explores how social work course websites can meet recommendations for ADA compliance. It addresses the current and expected rules for compliance, the types of disabilities that require accommodations and the accommodations that each requires. It discusses the software and hardware features and options available to students with disabilities. It also discusses software available to web authors to create accessible websites and identify noncompliant features. Following these guidelines will enable students with disabilities to fully benefit from online courses–and will offer benefits to users who do not have disabilities, as well. *[Article copies available for a fee from The Haworth Document Delivery Service: 1-800-342-9678. E-mail address: <getinfo@haworthpressinc.com> Website: <http://www.HaworthPress.com> © 2001 by The Haworth Press, Inc. All rights reserved.]*

KEYWORDS. Websites, disability, accommodation

Susan Sarnoff, DSW, is Assistant Professor at the Ohio University Department of Social Work, Morton Hall 522, Athens, Ohio 45701 (E-mail: sarnoff@ohio.edu). She teaches, in the classroom and online, Social Policy, Ethics and Writing for Social Work. She wishes to thank Kei Futamura for bringing this issue to her attention.

[Haworth co-indexing entry note]: "Ensuring That Course Websites Are ADA Compliant." Sarnoff, Susan. Co-published simultaneously in *Journal of Technology in Human Services* (The Haworth Press, Inc.) Vol. 18, No. 3/4, 2001, pp. 189-201; and: *New Advances in Technology for Social Work Education and Practice* (ed: Julie Miller-Cribbs) The Haworth Press, Inc., 2001, pp. 189-201. Single or multiple copies of this article are available for a fee from The Haworth Document Delivery Service [1-800-342-9678, 9:00 a.m. - 5:00 p.m. (EST). E-mail address: getinfo@haworthpressinc.com].

Social workers may not be at the forefront of website development, but are certainly at the forefront of ensuring that rights and services are available to all. That is why it is vital that social workers who develop websites understand how websites can be made accessible to people with disabilities.

Computers in general and web-based information in particular have been beneficial to many people, but have been particularly important to people with disabilities, who often find information less accessible by other means. Computer hardware has been customized to overcome the limitations of many handicapping conditions. For instance, alternative input devices, including one-handed keyboards; keyboards with ex-tra-large or braille keys; blow-tubes and eye movement scanners for those who cannot use standard keyboards; braille printers and software that converts text to voice, enlarges text, increases contrast and changes text commands to icons, enable people with various handicapping con-ditions to use computer technology (Cunningham and Coombs, 1999).

Conveniently, Windows, by far the most common operating system used with personal computers, incorporates options for use by people with a variety of disabilities, including text-voice and visual-sound conversion, enlarged fonts, high contrast, alternative access to the keyboard and mouse and features to compensate for spasticity or impaired movement. Further, vocational rehabilitation programs make specialized software and hard-ware available to disabled students who can benefit from programs and pe-ripherals (such as braille printers and fitted keyboards) that are not in general use. The Abledata website (http://www.abledata.com) offers infor-mation about many such assistive devices.

Yet some aspects of web design are incompatible with these assistive devices, or otherwise impede use for people with particular disabilities. For example, blinking or flashing features, including java script and even self-refreshing pages, can trigger seizures in people with epilepsy; and text-to-voice readers cannot translate uncaptioned graphics, tables or columns, the latter because the readers scan across the screen, failing to recognize column breaks.

Websites are not automatically rendered accessible by user-side soft-ware and hardware. Many accessibility features are only effective from the user's end if web authors have designed in usability features. It is these design features, and their many advantages to both disabled and non-disabled users, that are the focus of this paper. This paper also ex-plores how social work course websites can meet recommendations for ADA compliance by addressing current guidelines and expected rules for compliance, the types of disabilities that require accommodations and the accommodations that each requires. It also discusses the software and hardware features and options available to students with disabilities and to web authors to create accessible websites and to identify noncompliant features.

DISABILITIES AND COMPUTER USE

Fully 98% of current websites are inaccessible to people with disabilities that prevent them from using the full range of website design features. Even more shocking is the fact that 65% of 200 websites *devoted to disability issues* are similarly inaccessible (Olsen, 2000). These facts fly in the face of the vast number of laws requiring disability access and the facts that 20% of the American population have at least one disability and that half of them are between the ages of 16 and 64 (Cunningham and Coombs, 1999). Such inattention to website accessibility for one-tenth of the working population suggests one reason that 72% of disabled people are involuntarily unemployed (Cleaver, 2000).

Computer technology, if properly designed and adapted, can help people with many kinds of disabilities function in the workplace. The fact that three of four disabled people using computer technology to work from homes had their jobs before they were disabled (Cleaver 2000), however, suggests that employers tend to see adaptivity as a service to extend to employees who have proven themselves without disabilities, rather than a service that will make applicants with disabilities employable.

Therefore, making web courses fully accessible to students with the full range of possible disabilities would have far-reaching advantages, including:

- ensuring that universities comply with ADA guidelines;
- meeting the educational needs of existing students with disabilities;
- reaching out to a new pool of potential students who may not have considered higher education because they either do not expect it to meet their accessibility needs, or they do not expect to find employment even if they prepare by advancing their education.

Here, social workers can be of particular use to the disabled community, because by accepting students with disabilities into social work programs, the programs commit to placing them in field assignments where they obtain work experience and demonstrate their capabilities to employers. By understanding how technology helps in these situations, people with disabilities also demonstrate to the community how accessibility features can enable people with disabilities to work and train without limitations.

To do this, however, it is important to understand both barriers to accessibility and how they can be overcome. Ironically, much of the literature on computers and people with disabilities stresses the advantages of computers for people with mobility impairments. People whose only disabilities involve mobility can fully utilize computers without any need for specialized accessibility devices. Computers, in turn, enable these users (if employers do) to work from home, freeing them from the complications of commuting or dealing with the frustrations of a less-than-ideally-adapted workplace. However, disabilities differ in type and severity, and attention should be paid to web design to ensure that it is of maximum use to people with the full range of disabilities.

BARRIERS

The barriers to website accessibility are manifold, and depend on the type and severity of the disability of the user, as well as the degree of specialized skill needed by the user to operate adaptive technologies that require it. For instance, braille is one way that printouts and other features can be made accessible, but few people with sight disabilities can read braille. Morse code is used for some alternative input devices, but Morse code is also a skill unfamiliar to most people, with or without disabilities.

The most common forms of web design problems are unlabeled graphics, which cannot be read by text-to-voice converters; audio and video without text captions, which cannot be comprehended by people with hearing impairments; input that requires a mouse or trackball, with no keyboard- or single device-input alternative, which cannot be used by people with limited hand movement; websites that cannot be accurately viewed by the full range of browsers, including Lynx text-only browsers; charts and tables that are improperly marked up, so they become incomprehensible when read across the page by text-only browsers; and the use of flickering or strobing effects that can cause people with epilepsy to have seizures (Coombs, 1998).

Two other factors over which even designers do not have full control are advertising on web pages (which tends to make excessive use of moving and blinking images) and packaged course development tools, which have not, to date, integrated many accessibility features. For this reason, it is vital that social work educators advocate that course development tool authors meet accessibility guidelines and that advertisers offer accessible advertisements or the ability to turn off elements that impede use by people with disabilities.

Table 1 depicts the range of disabling conditions as they relate to computer use, and correlates them with adaptive devices and design considerations that make them usable by the range of users with disabilities. The "Adaptation Needed" column identifies hardware or software available to users to adapt computers to their needs. The "Design Consideration" column identifies the adaptive mechanisms that must be made by web authors in order to make websites accessible to users with the specified disabling conditions. Note that for people with some disabilities (color blindness, epilepsy and weakness/fatigue) there are no adaptive mechanisms that override website design, and they must rely on designers to incorporate the features that allow people with disabilities to access their websites. In other cases, adaptive mechanisms work less than optimally without appropriate design considerations. For instance, text-to-voice readers cannot interpret uncaptioned graphics. These factors explain why design-side accessibility considerations are so vital to website creation.

ACCOMMODATIONS

Many of the accommodations discussed above are self-explanatory, but a few require further clarification. Accommodations that make computers adaptable at the user end and require no design-end considerations include text-to-voice converters, voice recognition software and braille printers.

Alternative input devices include joysticks, sip-and-puff devices, optical/ultrasonic headpointers, and alternative or adapted keyboards. Alternative keyboards enable users with limited use of their hands to input information using a single mechanism, a rearranged keyboard (with keys moved to be more convenient to a one-handed user, for instance), and "sticky" keys that enable users to press keys individually for multiple-key operations, when pressing Ctrl-Alt-Del. Users with even less mobility may use sip-and-puff devices to enter letters in Morse Code, or to aim optical/ultrasonic headpointers at on-screen keyboards (Cunningham and Coombs, 1998). Note that these are the *only* accom-

TABLE 1. Website Accessibility for the Disabled: Problems and Solutions[1]

Disabling Condition	Adaptation Needed[2]	Design Consideration[3]
Blindness/Limited Sight	text-to-voice conversion voice recognition software enlarged text Braille keyboard/printer	alt = text captioned graphics global font increase option text only option
Cognitive/Reading/Learning Disability	text-to-voice conversion voice recognition software alternative (graphical/iconic) keyboard	simplified backgrounds or ability to remove backgrounds unlimited input time graphical/iconic alternatives to text option to turn on/off toolbar buttons current link markers
Color Blindness		alternative to color coding
Deafness/Limited Hearing	audio-to-text conversion	text alternative to audio
Epilepsy		elimination of, alternative to or ability to turn off flashing or strobing effects
Limited Dexterity	alternative input device adapted keyboard mouse alternative optical/ultrasonic headpointer abbreviation-expansion/word prediction software remappable keyboard	keyboard-only commands current link markers
Photosensitivity	screen filters	color options for background and foreground
Spasticity	large keys "sticky" keys	unlimited input time
Weakness/Fatigue		asynchronous communication mechanisms unlimited input time

[1]The information in this chart was obtained from Chisholm (1999), Gunderson (undated), Letourneau (2000) and Sullivan and Manning (1997), see Reference List. Note that unfamiliar terms are defined in the text.
[2]"Adaptation" refers to a hardware or software option available to the user.
[3]"Design Consideration" refers to an option that must be created by the website designer.

modations that can be retrofitted to computers by the end user; all others must be incorporated at the design stage.

However, Lynx (text-only) browser users, people with epilepsy who do not want to risk accessing moving images, and users of older, slower and newer, smaller devices rely on design features for usability (Letourneau, 2000). All such "Decaf" users (those who cannot access Java scripts, which activate movement, due to disabilities or equipment limitations) can be supported using captions on graphics and videos and transcripts on audio presentations (these features also make content more accessible to search engines and facilitate translation). Textual descriptions of graphics that can be read aloud are also useful–however, textual descriptions do not work with video which has its own audio track (Neilsen, 1999).

Accommodations that must be made at the design end include:

Asynchronous communication mechanisms, which enable people to share information quickly without having to be online at the same time. Examples include e-mail, discussion boards and video.

Color options consist of choices of foreground (text) and background (wallpaper) colors to increase contrast for those with limited sight; and offering means other than color for people who are colorblind to connect similar concepts.

Image maps create problems not only for text readers but also for keyboard-only users (those who cannot manipulate a mouse or trackball in addition to a keyboard). If they are used, a text-only equivalent, accessible with keystrokes, should be offered as an alternative means of access.

Markup refers to the HTML-coding used primarily to explain how text and graphics should be displayed on the web (Vanderheiden et al., 1997). However, markup can be used to explain to a disabled person using a text reader how to follow a table or what a graphic represents. When markup language uses relative rather than absolute units of measure ("larger" rather than "12 pt. font," for instance) software that enlarges fonts will present pages that appear in the proportions they were designed to reflect. *Global* markup rules enable users to change all instances of a particular feature at one time. For instance, a global font increase would enable a person with limited sight to enlarge all 12 pt. text to the same viewable size at one time.

Style sheets are rules that describe how documents are presented on the screen and/or in print (Vanderheiden et al., 1997). While it is best to create simple documents that do not require style sheets, if a complex document is necessary, style sheets are useful because they separate content (text) from layout (position, tabulation, color). This enables users to change layouts to accommodate their needs and equipment without affecting text (W3C, 2000).

As Coombs (1998) observes, good design is a solution for all these problems. Creating alt = text (markup text for graphics) makes sense because it is used by so many users for so many purposes. Offering a text only option is an even more useful feature. Unless the purpose of the website dictates otherwise, eliminating tables and using simple designs and colors with good contrast make websites easier for all users to access, and make it unnecessary to "retrofit" pages for the use of people with disabilities. Conversely, documents that rely on one type of hardware will be inaccessible to many users, including users of older equipment, and will soon become outmoded (W3C, 2000).

As a general rule, designers should ensure that they provide clear and consistent navigation mechanisms; ensure that text and graphics are understandable when viewed without color; use features that enable activation of page elements (such as navigation mechanisms) via a variety of input devices; and provide context and orientation information to help users understand complex pages or elements (Cunningham and Coombs, 1999). While these features all increase accessibility, they also make for good design that will remain accessible to most users and most devices over the long term.

GUIDELINES

There is not yet a set of clear, specific rules that website designers must follow to make websites accessible–which should be obvious from the huge proportion of websites that are not fully accessible. A private group, made up of experts from the government, academia and software concerns, has developed a set of guidelines for authors to follow in making sites accessible. This group, known as W3C, issued its most recent accessibility recommendations (as of this writing) in February 2000. They are available at www.w3.org/TR/ATAG10.

However, the guidelines fall short of rules and no specific enforcement mechanisms have been developed in any case. The guidelines have three levels of priority: developers *must* satisfy the first level, *should* satisfy the second level and *may* satisfy the third level (W3C, 2000). It is not clear which level of priority will eventually be established as the standard that must be met, but in this interim period it is important for web authors to familiarize themselves with all levels, because it is easier to design an accessible website than to re-engineer an inaccessible site to meet accessibility guidelines.

Absent specific guidelines, campuses are still required to conduct self-evaluations of their ADA compliance, and could be cited for failing to consider accessibility in their website designs (Cunningham and Coombs, 1999). That is to say, while no specific guidelines have been translated into rules for website design that must be followed, designers who ignore accessibility altogether could, indeed, be cited for failing to meet ADA standards.

The first level priorities require that web authors:

- provide a text equivalent for every nontext element, known as (ALT = text);
- ensure that all information conveyed with color is also available without color [as the sole identifier];
- identify changes in the natural language of a document's text and any text equivalents such as captions;
- organize documents so they may be read without style sheets;
- ensure that equivalents for dynamic content are updated when the dynamic content changes;
- avoid causing screens to flicker [which includes auto-refreshing as well as moving and flashing effects];
- use the clearest and simplest language for a site's content.

Specifically in regard to images, web authors should:

- provide redundant text links for each active region of a server-side image map;
- supply client-side image maps instead of server-side image maps except when the areas cannot be defined with an available geometric shape.

Specifically in regard to data tables, web authors should:

- identify row and column headers [for text browsers that do not recognize row and column breaks];
- use markup to associate data cells and header cells when two or more logical levels of row or column headers are not present; [when tables are used stylistically, although it is preferable to avoid such use of tables altogether] ("Electronic Access Rules Proposed," 2000; W3C, 2000).

It should be noted that even these accommodations, and their second- and third-level counterparts, do not ensure that all users will be able to use all aspects of all sites. Second- and third-level priorities recommend that web authors follow formal rules to make it easier for people with non-standard text browsers to comprehend text breaks caused by tables, graphics and other features that they may be unable to view. Style sheets, defined above, are one such set of rules.

In particular, people with epilepsy, who can have a seizure triggered by flickering or strobing features, need to be careful every time they link to a new site. Even designers who ensure that none of the sites to which they link include such features cannot be sure, unless they test each daily, that none have been altered to include these mechanisms or carry advertising that include them.

DETERMINING ACCESS

All website authors should check their web pages in a variety of browsers and on a variety of screens to ensure that their users can see what their designers want them to see (Cunningham and Coombs, 1999; Nguyen, 1996). Similarly, website authors should ensure that webpages are "backward compatible," that is, that they are viewable on older hardware and earlier versions of common browsers.

There are now several tools which enable authors to determine whether their websites are accessible. For instance, "Bobby," available at www.cast.org/bobby, tests a website for adherence to all of the first level priorities in the W3C guidelines. Many more such tools and more information on accessibility features and guidelines are available at: "Designing More Usable Web Sites," www.trace.wisc.edu/world/web/index.html. These help website authors to see how their pages will look when viewed or interpreted by a range of accessibility softwares and hardwares, and will identify inaccessible features so they can be corrected prior to publication.

ADVANTAGES FOR OTHER USERS

Finally, it is important to note that making websites accessible to those with disabilities offers advantages to the non-disabled population, as well. Most obviously, fully accessible websites allow access to users with older, slower equipment and older software. Until recently, some social work educators have argued against requiring computer literacy among students, no less against courses taught over the web, because they disenfranchised poorer students. Today, however, computers have become so ubiquitous in social agencies and on campuses that computer access is no longer an impediment to students at most universities and the convenience of a home computer as opposed to campus access only is the primary technical distinction between poorer and richer students.

Even that will change soon. Given that half of all American households had at least one computer in 1999 (Samuelson, 1999), the next generation of computer purchases will make used computers available to the households currently without them. However, those older computers may not have the capacity to sustain all types of software or features, and their slower speed will make it frustrating for users to wait for elaborate graphics to load. As a result, competent web authors will design pages that load quickly with text-only, or text-only options, to increase access to their sites.

Ironically, the newest hardware, such as pocket-size display units often integrated with cellular telephones and other hand-held devices, also access websites that are text-only, so these features increasingly appeal to "high-end" users. Such hardware is proliferating and filling other uses. For instance, automobiles are being equipped with computers, but for safety drivers are encouraged to access text-only sites and to access them using speech-to-text conversion that enable drivers to watch the road as they access online information.

Other users find these features preferable if not necessary. For instance, some users find that they so dislike the mouse alternatives available on laptops that they prefer to use keyboard-only input features whenever they are available. Fast keyboarders also note the delay caused by moving between the keyboard and the mouse.

Finally, search ease is facilitated by good design. Web authors who want many users to read their pages, and to find their pages through all methods of searching, benefit from good design features that translate all website content into simple, searchable text (Rowan, 1998).

FUTURE DIRECTIONS

The fact that high-end users are beginning to demand the same functions that low-end users and those with special needs have long required suggests that these design elements will become more common in the future. They will be spurred, too, by the move toward enforceable rules for website accessibility. Already, many software manufacturers are voluntarily developing means to meet these guidelines. For instance, Adobe has made its Acrobat software more accessible (Adobe, 2000). And at least one course development tool manufacturer has begun to explore methods of making its product accessible (Blackboard, 2000). Coombs (1998) notes that increased research and development by software developers will make it easier to make software accessible, and rating and certification will create further impetus to create websites that meet the highest standards for accessibility.

Social workers must be part of the advocacy effort toward these ends. We must also ensure that web course development tools, that enable non-programmers to create course websites, integrate these features. By doing so we not only increase web access, but help to make education available to people with the full range of disabilities, as well as to people with less powerful computers.

CONCLUSIONS

Few websites, including course websites, are currently accessible to people with the full range of disabling conditions, despite ADA guidelines for educators. Ensuring that course websites are ADA compliant will make websites more accessible to all users, increase the ability of users to access the web using new handheld equipment as well as older, less powerful hardware and software, facilitate searching and fulfill the mission of the ADA technologically. While these issues should be important to all educators, they are doubly vital to social work educators, who as social workers are ethically committed to making services accessible to all. As more and more education, work, commerce and social interaction takes place online, social workers must ensure that these services are accessible to all people, regardless of the disabling conditions they may have or the limitations of the equipment they may use.

REFERENCES

Adobe. (2000). "Adobe Enhances Accessibility of Acrobat Software for the Disability Community." Adobe.

Blackboard. (2000). "Blackboard Accessibility FAQ," Washington, DC: Blackboard.

Chisolm, Wendy. (August 30, 1999). "Enabling Your Website," *Web Techniques,* available online at designshops.com/pace/ds/pub/1999/08/able.html.

Cleaver, Joanne. (March 2000). "Homeward Bound," *Home Office Computing,* 68-71.

Coombs, Norman. (1998). "The Campus Web: A Connecting Device or a Trap?" *Campus-Wide Information Systems,* 15, 1, 16-21.

Cunningham, Carmela and Norman Coombs. (1999). *Information Access and Adaptive Technology.* Phoenix: Oryx Press,.

"Designing More Usable Web Sites." (Undated). www.trace.wisc.edu/world/web/index.html.

"Electronic Access Rule Proposed," (May 2000). *Section 504 Compliance Handbook,* Washington, DC: Thompson Publishing Group, 1, 4-5.

Gunderson, Jon. (Undated). "World Wide Web Browser Access Recommendations," Urbana, IL: University of Illinois, available online at www.staff.uiuc.edu/~jongund/access-browsers.html.

Letourneau, Chuck. (February 29, 2000). "Accessible Web Design–A Definition," *Starling Access Services*, www.starlingweb.com/webac.htm.

Neilsen, Jakob. (August 8, 1999). "Disabled Access," *Alertbox*, www.useit.com/alertbox/990808.html.

Nguyen, Kevin. (1996). "The Accessible Web: Web Access Through Adaptive Technology," presented at the 1996 NEADS Conference, available online at www.utoronto.ca/atrc/rd/library/papers/WebAccess.html.

Olson, Walter. (May 2000). "Access Excess," *Reason*, 49-51.

Rowan, Murray. (1998). "Disability and Information Systems for Higher Education," *Interim Report*. Dundee: Digital Media Access Group.

Samuelson, Robert. (April 5, 1999). "The PC Boom–and Now Bust?" *Newsweek*.

Sullivan, Terry and Krystyn Manning. (August 15, 1997). "Could Helen Keller Read Your Page?" www.pantos.org/atw/35412.html.

Vanderheiden, Greg C., Wendy A. Chisholm, Neal Ewers and Shannon M. Dunphy. (June 1997). "Unified Web Site Accessibility Guidelines, Version 7.2." Madison, WI: Trace R & D Center, trace.wisc.edu/archive/html_guidelines/version7.htm.

W3C. (2000). "Web Content Accessibility Guidelines 1.0," www.w3.org/TR/ATAG10, MIT, INRIA, Keio.

Older Adults and the Digital Divide: Assessing Results of a Web-Based Survey

Laural Opalinski

SUMMARY. This study used an on-line, web-based survey to assess the significance of computer and Internet technology in the lives of adults over age 60. A convenience sample of 110 individuals from the United States, Canada and other countries responded to a 20-question survey regarding individual use, opportunities for learning, family and social connectivity and preferences for and barriers to effectual use. Particular focus was made on the self-described perceptions of personal control and life satisfaction within the responding population. *[Article copies available for a fee from The Haworth Document Delivery Service: 1-800-342-9678. E-mail address: <getinfo@haworthpressinc.com> Website: <http://www.HaworthPress.com> © 2001 by The Haworth Press, Inc. All rights reserved.]*

KEYWORDS. Computers, Internet, seniors, older adults

Access to information, connection to resources, and affiliation with others are all fundamental concepts throughout the life span in the

Laural Opalinski, MSW, is a Geriatrics Program Specialist in the Greater Los Angeles Healthcare System coordinating a distance education/information technology program for advanced geriatrics.

Address correspondence to: Laural Opalinski, 1424 Dalmatia Drive, San Pedro, CA 90732 (E-mail: lopalinski@sprintmail.com or laural.opalinski@med.va.gov).

[Haworth co-indexing entry note]: "Older Adults and the Digital Divide: Assessing Results of a Web-Based Survey." Opalinski, Laural. Co-published simultaneously in *Journal of Technology in Human Services* (The Haworth Press, Inc.) Vol. 18, No. 3/4, 2001, pp. 203-221; and: *New Advances in Technology for Social Work Education and Practice* (ed: Julie Miller-Cribbs) The Haworth Press, Inc., 2001, pp. 203-221. Single or multiple copies of this article are available for a fee from The Haworth Document Delivery Service [1-800-342-9678, 9:00 a.m. - 5:00 p.m. (EST). E-mail address: getinfo@haworthpressinc.com].

maintenance of independence and continued self-determination as well as mobility and interaction within one's environment. The intention of this investigation was to describe Internet and computer technology for information access and communication by adults age 60+. Respondents' commented on the role of these technologies in their perceptions of control, life satisfaction, levels of communication, enhancement of leisure pursuits and also the barriers to as well as the effective use and suggestions for improving technology. The author discusses how these perceptions might contribute to older adults' striving for the ideal of successful aging as well as the challenges faced in the interim. Greater understanding of the process by which older adults may be empowered through information access and learning and skills acquired through computer technology will help towards the elimination of barriers that decrease the level of contact with the outside systems that may promote disengagement and isolation.

LITERATURE REVIEW

As of December 11, 2000, population estimates indicate there were 276,308,381 people living in the United States and 6,114,899,216 in the world. Data indicate that the number of individuals over age 60 has increased substantially and will continue to rise through the year 2030 at which time individuals age 65+ are expected to comprise 20% of the population (U.S. Census, 2000). In 1994, the world's population consisted of 357 million or (6%) of individuals 65 or older. Between now and 2050, the elderly population is expected to double in size to 80 million.

In August 2000, 51% of U.S. households had computers (U.S. Census, 2000). These same data indicate that 5.7% of individuals over age 65 regularly use computers. Of those 50 years and older, 29.6% of the population and 9.3% of individuals over age 65 have access to the Internet as opposed to 44.4% of the rest of the population. Educational attainment, as well as income, appears to be related to the percentage of individuals who own computers. AARP (2000) reported that of users age 65 and older, "less affluent users and less educated users are generally less proficient and less confident than those who are younger, more affluent, and more educated." AARP further stated that older adults are "at risk in an increasingly technology-driven commercial environment." Although the Internet is currently being used by one in five Americans, only 7.9% of adults over age 65 use the Internet. Of those who use the Internet, the most common uses are e-mail and finding government, business, health, or education information (AARP, 2000).

In 1997, it was estimated by a Harris Poll that almost 20 percent of Internet users were older than 50 (Richtel, 1999). This number is rapidly increasing. Glen Gilbert, former Director of SeniorNet, stated "the net brings the world into your home" and he has helped to introduce over 100,000 seniors to the Internet across the United States (Harper, 1999). Laura Fay, SeniorNet's assistant director of development states that 13 million older adults are on-line and that "one of the most compelling reasons for an older adult to learn how to use a computer is so many others are already doing it" (Westbrook, 1999). Further, Furlong (1995) believes that communities for seniors are becoming less geographically based and more of communities of the mind. David Lansdale, geriatrics expert of Stanford University termed computers as an "elixir" for older adults; he believes that computers help to overcome the "four plagues of institutionalized elders, including loneliness, boredom, helplessness, and decline of mental skills."

TECHNOLOGY AS A LINK TO HEALTHY AND SUCCESSFUL AGING

Successful aging is a term that is constantly being re-evaluated by gerontologists. This term may depend on finding a comfort level within one's life and relationships or may depend on an individual's ability to adapt to his/her environment. Personal growth is continuing and important as one faces mortality in later life. As individuals age, they often deal with the loss of friends, parents, and other family members. This is a time of life when individuals recognize this mortality, and may question the time left to accomplish these goals. Continuing growth can offer relief from a feeling of stagnation, thus resiliency and adaptation may be key throughout the life process of successful aging. Pfeiffer (1977) discussed the importance of replacing some of the losses in late-life with new relationships, and the importance of creating new roles and of retraining lost capacities. Technology can host an avenue for new relationships, provide a means for continued learning, facilitate personal growth, provide an outlet for hobbies and new experiences, or re-define careers and roles in retirement as losses increase. Communication rated as a primary importance in computer ownership and communication often can become even more important as individuals age (Ashford, Lecroy, and Lortie, 1997).

Healthy aging is described by Coughlin (1999), as "more than good physiological health; when disease and natural aging process are managed, healthy aging is the ability of the individual to live at the limits of their own capacity, not at the limits of which they live." He further states, "There are no precedents to help predict the future physical needs of older adults living and working in multiple housing, work, education, leisure, and caregiving settings." Moreover, today's older adults are not adequate predictors of the lifestyle of seniors in the future. Our aging society and the problems that they may face in future years have not yet been assessed on a large scale.

HEALTH CARE

Computers are being used in a variety of ways for both mental and physical health care needs. A variety of resources are available to patients and their caregivers on chronic and acute conditions, diseases, treatments, health practices. Technology can allow patients/clients to be informed and self-directive in their care and decision-making processes. With large growth rates in our aging population chronic and degenerative diseases are going to be a huge concern in the future. One individual interviewed by *Forbes* magazine (Noer & Wandvez, 1995) found that connecting to the Internet brought him more relief than pain medication and stated, "I am absorbed for hours and completely forget myself."

Of some interest is the movement of popular American culture to adopt Eastern standards and ideals of health. Of importance in this philosophy is to find and promote balance between physical, social, emotional, and intellectual systems. As the mind-body connection brings a new dynamic into social work, aging, and health care, it is relevant that we look for complementary means of increasing independence and slowing decline. Many websites are being organized to help seniors adjust to physical decline or avoid injury, and the needs and issues as related to caregivers are additionally addressed. These conveniences create solutions for isolated seniors and other adults with the added benefit of helping combat loneliness, depression, and the physical deterioration of inactivity that may foster dependence. Coughlin (1999) admitted that "all age groups will pay higher health care costs if a larger portion of the population is unable to access preventative care on a routine basis.

Of interest is a move to healthcare programs that incorporate telemedicine. Efforts to use technology for home health care, patient research and interaction and physician interchange are currently underway though there are many barriers to overcome before effective systems are in place. Currently, the American Accreditation Healthcare Commission is working to create a process to evaluate and monitor the credibility of on-line healthcare (AMA, 2000) and continually working to increase the reliability of this form of service.

LEARNING

Thousands of adults are enrolling in computer courses throughout the world. In a study by Eilers (1989), it was found that older students have several reasons for enrolling in computer courses. In order of importance these include learning; mental challenge and memory improvement; keeping up with the times and communicating with other computer users; practical applications including business, personal accounts, investments, and graphics; and a new pastime. Notable gerontologist, Jeanne Bader (1999) stated that "most older persons are not computer literate today" but believes that "tomorrow's elders will search the Internet and other electronic data banks before using other search methods" and that "some baby boomers will use high tech devices to maintain their independence and their life styles." Gerontologist Ken Dychtwald predicted "explosive growth in adult education in the years ahead, as boomers look to stay current with the world around them. Learning is going to be one of the great businesses of the future as people have more time" (Kennedy, 2000). Limited research done with older adults has found that computers are effective in increasing skills, increasing levels of life enjoyment and willingness to learn, and can provide the additional benefit of decreasing levels of depression (McConatha et al., 1995; Sherer, 1997; McNeely, 1991).

Seniors with a passion for life-long learning are evident in the numbers of seniors demanding educational opportunities, as well as the number of colleges who are responding to the needs of these individuals are growing. At California State University, Long Beach, many seniors are registering for and participating in college course work in computers and other courses to obtain degrees or enrich their lives. The recently established Senior University computer classes are full and in many cases have a waiting list. David Lowe (2000), senior computer lab director, stated, "I think our classes have been wildly successful and we continue to sell out most classes." He believes that communication between seniors is an important mode of promoting normalcy and of getting the word out about technology applications for seniors. He expressed "I think word of mouth must play a large part in the continuing interest from new students. The demand is kept current as we also try to provide slightly more advanced subjects to our graduates as the need arises. Most of our students have had no in depth acquaintance with the computer before, and some big hurdles for our new students are to break the fear of harming the computer, become at ease with the mouse, and to learn where the letters are on the keyboard."

EMPLOYMENT/CAREER GOALS

AARP has numerous articles and guidelines on technology applications touting the benefits of keeping marketable through increasing levels of technological skill. A growing program in Madison, Wisconsin, Over 50 Employment Services, is helping older adults become economically efficient and supplement social security. There are current initiatives to help find employment for individuals with newly acquired technology skills. Thus far, clients have ranged in age from age 40+ to 89 (Sandell, 2000). This trend may continue to grow. Ken Dychtwald (1986) stated "By 2020, the traditional 'linear life' paradigm in which people migrate through education, then work, then leisure/retirement, will be replaced by a new 'cyclic life' paradigm in which education, work, and leisure are interspersed repeatedly throughout the life span. It will become 'normal' for 50-year-olds to go back to school and for 70-year-olds to start new careers." Further, as it is expected that increased longevity will put additional strain on our economic and societal resources, we must fervently research avenues of prevention. Older workers may continue to work as hobbies or for pleasure, but economic realities are also a likely factor of continuing late life employment.

COMPUTER DESIGN AND CONFIGURATION

To help eliminate barriers, computer configuration and design fit well with the needs of the elderly and for those individuals with chronic health problems or disability. According to the 1990 U.S. Census, 20.1% of adults over age 65 have a mobility limitation. Environmental design should accommodate the special needs of older adults, including adequate lighting, reduction of glare, trackball installation, large font, and adequate color selections. Computers are becoming less expensive and more portable and have been designed to include a large variety of assistive devices available to enhance learning and accommodate disability. Some of these enhancements include volume control and hearing devices to combat presbycusis and tinnitus, large screen/type and special applications for vision impairment and glare reduction to combat decrease in acuity, voice enhancement systems, and a variety of enhanced keyboards and tracking devices that will help to accommodate arthritic/movement problems.

SUMMARY OF BENEFITS

Numerous studies have evaluated the effects of activity, learning, personal goals, and continuing self-development, and have found that generativity and levels of life satisfaction and meaning are enhanced and positively correlated with increased feelings of control, self-esteem, and self-efficacy (Neikrug et al., 1998; LaPierre, Bouffard, & Bastin, 1997; Fisher, 1995; Courtney & Truluck, 1997). Additionally, those individuals who pursue intellectual pursuits are more involved in the positive self-direction of their lives (Neikrug et al., 1998). Ryff and Essex (as cited in LaPierre, Bouffard, & Bastin, 1997) identified several criteria of psychological well being to include: autonomy, environmental mastery, feelings of competence, purpose in life, positive relations with others, self-acceptance, and personal growth. LaPierre, Bouffard, and Bastin (1997) further found that the elderly participants in their studies believed that continued self-development was as important as leisure activity and that by pursuing individual aspirations, needs for well-being, meaning in life and continued contribution to society were met.

RESEARCH METHODS

This research employed an on-line survey designed by the author to elicit the importance of computer use and Internet access as a tool for empowerment, in increasing quality of life and in providing a sense of control. To employ this technique, an electronic convenience survey was utilized with a series of 20 questions on demographics and qualitative responses. The data set is comprised of 110 respondents. This was a purposive, convenience sample that was available worldwide through the Internet on the World Wide Web at www.csulb.edu/lopalinski/oasurvey.htm. The participants were recruited through senior listserves and the website was advertised in several major search engines. The participants were notified that the research was a graduate student study for a social work thesis.

RESEARCH FINDINGS

The respondents consisted of 80% females and 19.1% males (see Table 1). The ages ranged from a minimum of age 60 to at least age 90. As expected, the greatest number of respondents fell into the 60-65 age range (47.3%). The next highest response was in the 66-70 age range at 27.3% and 20.0% were in the 71-75 age category. Only 0.9% of the respondents were 90 or older. The majority of the respondents were self-described as Caucasian (92.7%) with the remainder being comprised of 1 African American (0.9%) and 1 Asian (0.9%). The majority of the respondents lived in the eastern United States (40.0%), 28.7% lived in the western United States, and 13.9% of the respondents were from the central United States; 7.0% from Canada and 5.2% were from other countries. Of the respondents, 17.0% had between 6 and 12 years of education, 36.4% had at least some college, 25.5% had a college education, and 20.0% had a post-graduate degree. Nearly all (94.5%) of the respondents lived within one city block of their nearest neighbor with 1.8% living between one to five blocks and 2.7% living more than five blocks (see Table 2). Regarding employment status, 18.2% of the respondents were employed and (see Table 2) 81.8% were unemployed. To the question pertaining to periods of computer use, 3.6% used computers one to five times per month, with an overwhelming 96.4 using their computers 15 or more times per month. Five individuals (4.5%) rated their skills on the computer as poor while 17 (15.5%) rated their skills as excellent. The majority of respondents self-rated skills as either fair (40.0%) or good (40.0%). One half stated that they have attended computer classes (see Table 3).

COMMUNICATION AND SOCIAL NETWORKING

Overwhelmingly, 100% of the respondents described the computer as an important source of communication and interaction with others

TABLE 1. Demographic Characteristics of Respondents: Age, Gender, Ethnicity, Geographic Locale (n = 110)

Characteristic	Number	Percent
Age		
60-65	52	47.3
66-70	30	27.3
71-75	22	20.0
76-80	2	1.8
81-85	2	1.8
86-90	1	.9
90+	1	.9
Gender		
Female	88	80.0
Male	21	19.1
Did not state	1	.9
Ethnicity		
Caucasian/European	102	92.7
Asian	1	.009
African American	1	.009
Did not respond	6	.05
Geographic Locale		
West Coast	33	30.0
Middle States	16	14.5
East Coast	46	41.8
Canada	8	7.3
Other Countries	6	5.5

and 57.3% used chat rooms and other forms of on-line communication. Responses regarding communication indicated the enormity of the importance of the convenience of the computer to keep in touch with families and friends as well as establish new relationships. All individuals (100%) had something positive to say about correspondence and the benefits of communication in this manner, including the additional opportunities for connection.

Increased Contact: Responses often stated the importance of the increased level of contact with family members and friends. Statements such as "prior to e-mail I might write three letters per year; now I have a network of 23 family members to spread news." "E-mail has made life

TABLE 2. Demographic Characteristics of Respondents: Living Arrangements, Proximity, Education, Computer Use (n = 110)

Characteristics	Number	Percent
Living Arrangements		
Alone	25	22.7
With Spouse	81	73.6
With Other Family	1	.9
With Friends	2	1.8
Did not indicate	1	.9
Proximity to Neighbor		
Less than one city block	104	94.5
One to 5 blocks	2	1.8
More than 5 blocks	3	2.7
Did not respond	1	.9
Educational		
Less than 6 years	0	
6-12 years	19	17.3
Some College	40	36.4
College Degree	28	25.5
Post-Graduate Degree	22	20.0
Did not respond	1	.9
Employment		
Employed	20	18.2
Unemployed	90	81.8
Where Computer is Used		
At Home	110	100.0
Office/Business	15	13.6
Library	13	11.8
School	5	.05
Other	2	.02
How Often Uses the Computer		
1-5 times per month	4	3.6
6-15 times per month		
More than 15 times per month	106	96.4

TABLE 3. Demographic Characteristics of Respondents: Self Rating, Areas of Use, Classes, Use of Chatrooms and Satisfaction Levels (n = 110)

Characteristic	Number	Percent
Self Rating of Computer Skills		
Poor	5	4.5
Fair	44	40.0
Good	44	40.0
Excellent	17	15.5
Areas of Computer Usage		
Employment	13	11.8
E-mail	110	100.0
Internet	104	97.2
Word Processing	83	75.4
Finances	43	39.0
Graphics	46	41.8
Shopping	46	41.8
Hobby	74	67.2
Other	20	18.1
Computer Classes		
Yes	56	50.9
No	54	49.1
Use of Chat Rooms		
Yes	63	57.3
No	47	42.7
General Satisfaction with Computers		
Very Satisfied	89	80.9
Somewhat Satisfied	18	16.4
Not Very Satisfied	3	2.7
Not at all Satisfied	0	0.0

richer and fuller by providing me with additional ways to communicate with family and friends . . . it has also provided me with ways to communicate and exchange ideas and information." "I am not alone, yet I am private."

Grief: Others used this form of communication to ease the grief of losing a loved one. "Since my husband's death 5 years ago, computers have helped me keep my sanity by keeping in touch with my children and I have made new friends all over the world."

Geographical Boundaries: Still others appreciated e-mail's ability to cross geographical boundaries that often separate families. "I have eight children and keep in touch more often with e-mail than the phone." "I now maintain a relationship that would not have likely continued as closely were e-mail not available." At least one individual was able to locate long-lost friends. "I have located people I went to school with in Europe in the late 50's." Many people indicated their levels of isolation in statements such as "A great boon during the long winter months." "I would be very, very lonely without this new technology in my life. It has opened up doors to a new world for me." "I live in a very small town. We moved here from the big city in California. I felt so isolated so my husband got me the computer and said 'here! Learn how to use it.' I have and now don't know how I lived without it." Others lived in areas where it was difficult to get out. "We live in a very rural area with no public transportation, so the computer helps me to get out." "I am in good health and walk everywhere, but it is handy for shopping as I live in New York City and don't own a car."

HOBBIES AND LEISURE PURSUITS

Many respondents 79 (72%) were very interested in having the Internet as a tool to pursue leisure activities and a surprising variety of hobbies were addressed in the responses. Individuals used the computer to keep genealogical records and do research as well as process and organize photographs. Many respondents used computerized sewing machines in their leisure pursuits. This hobby often required a computer and Internet access to download digital design files. "I customize, digitize, and create numerous designs through the Internet with my designer 1 sewing machine." One individual commented, "Thousands around the world are learning to use a computer because their hobby or interest or the fact that they are shut in requires it." Games provided a source for passing time. On-line Bridge games were popular and some games were played across the country. Others made friends and pen pals in foreign countries. Some individuals enjoyed making greeting cards, shopping, or reading interest/news digests. Common responses revolved around connecting with others with similar interests.

EDUCATION AND INFORMATION

Forty-three percent of the respondents used their computers and the Internet to obtain information, increase their skills, or take classes.

Many discussed the importance of keeping their minds active in order to stay healthy, or of having stimulating work available.

Education/New Careers: Some of the respondents talked about having the computer: "To complete educational requirements, to learn a second career as a tax-preparer," or to track investments "to check on my stocks." Regarding reference as a purpose they made statements such as, "It's great when I need info about something to just look it up," "libraries where I live are poor so I use the Internet for reference and research . . . here I have the whole world at my fingertips." Some individuals placed great importance on having stimulating activities for a greater level of mental health. "I have a great need to learn and without a computer I would be in dire straights and sunk in depression." "For an older person keeping the mind healthy is a very important matter."

Challenge/Stimulation: Others found convenience in their searches for insight. "I can find a wealth of information with just a single search click." "love a challenge and am determined to make something work if I find it interesting and satisfying." One individual indicated the computer as a source of "Informational socialization."

Generation Gap: Many respondents were able to find common interests with younger, computer literate individuals. "There is a whole new world out there. It is keeping my mind active and I'm able to understand what my children and grandkids are talking about.

PHYSICAL DIFFICULTIES AND IMMOBILITY

A significant number of respondents (22%) reported physical characteristics that made the computer of importance.

Acute Accident/Illness: Those who reported physical challenges or disabilities stated "I'm disabled and have not been able to work for the last 6 years due to an auto accident and I use my computer to keep up with people and what is going on in the world." "I have overcome two catastrophic illnesses and the computer helped me to understand what I had and put me in touch with support groups." "Had a stroke in July 1999 that originally caused paralysis in right side and speech. Getting a lot of use of right hand back, but unable to write so the computer helps me in therapy and also to communicate."

Chronic Illness: "With my rheumatoid arthritis, physically going to the law library or a public library is sometimes daunting for me." Others used their computer to replace activities in which they could no longer participate. "I am deaf and have cancer, it is almost my only interaction with the outside world." "I have lived in 15 countries and traveled in a hundred more. Can no longer travel, the computer gives me mobility and interaction." "I am unable to walk well, especially in the winter when sidewalks are snowy and slippery." "I suffer from loss of eyesight and it (the computer) has replaced much of the time I used to spend reading, being easier to use and see." "I have been deaf for more than 40 years. I have also been rendered mute by cancer in more recent times. As a deaf mute, my computer is my most valuable contact with the rest of the world." One individual explained that "many of the people I communicate with are deaf and it is much easier to use the computer than the TTY or Relay Services.

COMMENTS ON DEVELOPMENTS

Many participants in the survey were explicit about what they would like to see in technological advances for their personal systems.

Tutorials/Instructions/Simplicity: Simplicity was a theme that came up repeatedly: "Better tutorials with more pictures to explain steps." "Simplified instructions, larger font, better keyboards and monitors." "Simplicity, simple directions write directions in easy plain language!" "User-friendly programs."

Issues of Cost: Some individuals stressed the barriers of cost. "Less expensive computers." "PCs for poorer people." "My economic status limits me to free ISP and a text-only PC."

Comfort Level/Adaptability: Others wanted to increase their physical comfort level: "Better keyboards or letters for visually impaired people with stiff fingers." "Keyboards for those who have large fingers." "Video connections to see family members." or "Mounted cameras. I will have a new grandbaby and would like to see this baby grow." "Affordable high resolution monitor that is low enough to read when you are using bifocals." Increased level of function was important to others. "Voice to print." "High speed internet, and more video messaging." This included "Clear help screens and stable operating systems and low cost applications." "Enlarged font!"

Ease of Repair: One individual expressed the important of having a system that could be easily repaired. "I would like to feel confident that when the computer gulps, I could fix it. Tech help usually helps but spending a couple of hours on the phone is a bit much. I like appliances to WORK!"

DISCUSSION

Information access, access to services, and connection with others throughout the life span are fundamental in maintaining levels of independence and self-determination in choices related to one's self and one's level of interaction with the environment. Information technology allows older adults to maintain links and connections. The American Psychological Association (1999) stated that the potential for increasing levels of empowerment will be promoted through the acquisition of new skills to access to information and computer technology, helping to negate aspects of isolation by inviting new opportunities for learning, communication, and socialization via the Internet and the Web. This technology was found to be of significant importance in terms of the ability for individuals to be able to communicate effectively with each other, whether for sources of pleasure and family sharing, for linking individuals with similar interests, or for sharing the tragedy of grief and loss.

In this study, it was obvious that individuals found the computer of great use as a tool for communication. All of the respondents put great emphasis on technology and it is significance as an instrument in increasing levels of family and social support. Many found the computer invaluable in allowing increased and enhanced levels of communication, particularly with large families separated by distance. Additionally, networking through like-minded activity groups allowed individuals to develop new relationships, and maintain friendships, which appeared particularly important for individuals limited by mobility. Isolation appeared to be reduced significantly, regardless of geographical inhibition or immobilization.

According to the findings, leisure activities also play an important part in the lives of the mostly retired people who responded to the survey. Hobbies through technological media brought enjoyment, relief from pain, friendships and information. This offered opportunities for one to be expressive through one's crafts, to be intellectually stimulated, and to pursue something intrinsically valuable to each individual. Education was also an important aspect of computer usage for almost half of the respondents. This provided a source of stimulation from what sometimes was described as a non-stimulating existence. Individuals found growth and knowledge, were able to immerse themselves in mind-strengthening activities, and found enhancement through their pursuits. They found resources to help others as well as themselves, found opportunities for expansion, and found empowerment through having information available on demand.

The future of health care is heavily dependent on technology to disseminate information, to organize information, for triage, and simply for the effective and efficient functioning of the health care system. The computer can provide not only patients and families information regarding acute or chronic disease, but recommended treatments as well as new research are available, thus allowing patients/clients to be informed and self-directive in their decision making processes. Vulnerable, at risk, and isolated individuals can benefit from technology. Because isolation is one of the greatest risks in aging, communication via computer can help to limit the levels of isolation by providing a means for friends and families to keep in contact.

Computers are often accessible in a variety of different human service facilities and educational institutions. Creative thinking by staff could afford many opportunities to decrease the digital divide between technology and our population of older adults. Older computers can be recycled and upgraded and placed in community facilities or individual residences, agencies could share space and help to design programs for the populations that they serve and individual practitioners could incorporate computer applications and help their clients to reduce levels of anxiety and become more comfortable in our technologically oriented world.

IMPLICATIONS FOR POLICY

Policymakers are currently addressing the importance of the need to provide information to the general public as quickly as possible. Closing the "Digital Divide" is an important aspect of current policy. Technology can help in meeting the goals of the Older American's Act 1998 Reauthorization (Department of Health and Human Services, 1998). The results of the study were in alignment with the goals of this act. The Act expressed the importance of increasing independence; removing personal and social barriers, promote employment opportunities, and empowering individuals to contribute to their communities through volunteer services. All of these goals and many additional, were found to be enhanced through the use of computer technology. Additional policy is constantly being developed at a federal level that will benefit individuals who are typically underserved. In a paper presented at the Annual Meeting of the American Sociological Association in August 1999, Robert Kominski and Eric Newburger of the Population Division of the U.S. Census Bureau stated:

> The impact of technology on human society can be far-reaching and pervasive . . . In less than two decades, personal computing devices have gone from being interesting playthings of the technically capable and financially able to practical, useful, and sometimes essential tools of the general public. . . . the march forward into a "computer facile and literate" society is not one in which all persons participate equally. Despite sizable reductions in cost, and considerable improvements in technical efficiency, not all people have access to or use of computers. A piece of this unequal access may be due to choice alone, an issue not examined in these data. However, despite improvements of differentials from our first survey measurement in 1984, there are still serious gaps in computer ownership and use, especially across racial, age, economic, and educational levels . . . Those late starting the race will find it difficult to catch up; still others may not be given the opportunity to enter the race at all.

The results of this study may enhance the knowledge base of gerontological social work and allow individuals to develop policies, strategies, and activities for the isolated elderly to help these individuals develop a sense of control and positive and fulfilling direction in their lives. Of central importance is the challenge in combating the anxiety that is often associated with computer use and of finding affordable, available, and easy to use equipment to provide to this underserved population.

REFERENCES

AARP (2000). *National Survey on Consumer Preparedness and E-Commerce: A Survey of Computer Users Age 45 and Older. Executive Summary.* [On:line] Available: http://research.aarp.org/consume/ecommerce1.html.

American Medical Association (2000). Seal of approval for on-line health sites may be coming. American Medical News. Nov. 27, 2000. [On-line] Available: http://www.ama-assn.org/sci-pubs/amnews/pick_00/tesb1127.htm.

American Psychological Association. (1999). *Psychological problems of older Americans.* [On line] Available: http://www.apa.org//pi/aging/older/psychological.html

Ashford, J.B., LeCroy, C.W., and Lortie, K.L. (1997). *Developmental Psychology, Social Psychology.* Pacific Grove, CA. Brooks Publishing.

Bader, Jeanne E. (1999). *Ca.boom*. Presented at California Council on Gerontology and Geriatrics, Long Beach, California.

Couglin, J.R. (1999). Setting a national policy agenda for technology and healthy aging. *The public Policy and Aging Report. National Academy on an aging society. A policy institute of the Gerontological Society of America*. Spring, 10,1. 3-6.

Courtenay, B.C. & Truluck, J. (1997). The meaning of life and older learners: addressing the fundamental issue through critical thinking and teaching. *Educational Gerontology, 23* (2). 175-195.

Department of Health and Human Services (1998). *Side by Side Comparison Chart of 1996 Older Americans Act Reauthorization Bills and Proposals: Title I—Objectives*. [Online] Available: http://www.aoa.dhhs.gov/oaa/98reauth/title1.html.

Dychtwald, K. (1998). *PressRoom: Quotes from Ken Dychtwald, Ph.D.* Agewave, LLC. [On-line]. Available: http://www.agewave.com/agewave/quotes.html

Eilers, M.L. (1989) Older adults and computer education: Not to have the world a closed door. *The International Journal of Technology and Aging*. 2(1). 56-76.

Fisher, B.J. (1995). Successful aging, life satisfaction, and generativity in later life. *International Journal Aging and Human Development*. 41, (3) 239-250.

Furlong, M. (1995). Communities for seniors in cyberspace. *Ageing International*. March.

Harper, T. (1999). Wired Seniors. *Cybersurf*. September 22-26.

Integrated State Health Information Systems. Workshop Summary, July 9-11, 1997, User Liaison Program. Agency for Health Care Policy and Research, Rockville, MD. http://www.ahcpr.gov/research/ulpinfos.htm

Kennedy, M. (2000). Boomers to revisit education as seniors. *Times Union*. June 4, E1.

Kominski, R and Newburger, E. (1999). *Access denied: Changes in computer ownership and use: 1984-1997*. Population Division U.S. Census Bureau. Paper presented at the Annual Meeting of the American Sociological Association, Chicago Illinois, August 1999.

LaPierre, S, Bouffard, L. & Bastin, E. (1997). Personal goals and subjective well-being in later life. *International Journal Aging and Human Development*, 45, (4) 287-303.

Lowe, D. (2000). SeniorNet Program Director at California State University, Long Beach. Personal Conversation.

McConatha, J.T., McConatha, D., Deaner, S.L. & Dermignny, R. (1995). A computer-based intervention for the education and therapy of institutionalized older adults. *Educational Gerontology, 21*(2). 130-138.

McNeely, E. (1991). Computer assisted instruction and the older adult learner. *Educational Gerontology*, (3). 229-237.

Neikrug, S. (1998). The value of gerontological knowledge for elders: A study of the relationship between knowledge on aging and worry about the future. *Educational Gerontology*, (3). 287-296.

Noer, M and Wandvez, K. (1995) Senior Cybernauts. *Forbes 156,*(7) 240.

Pfeiffer, Eric. (1977). Psychopathology and social pathology. Book Chapter in *Handbook of the Psychology of Aging*. Van Nostrand Reinhold Company New York.

Richtel, M. (1999). When even grandma is more cyber-savvy than you. New York Times on the Web. *Technlogy Cybertimes*. November 7.

Sandell, D. (2000). Over 50 Employment Services Inc. *Madison Capital Times*. June 14, 1B.

Scheidt, R.J. and Humpherys, D.R. Successful aging: what is not to like? *Journal of Applied Gerontology*, Sept 88, V 18,3 277.

Sherer, M. (1997). Introducing computers to frail residents of homes for the aged. *Educational Gerontology*, *23* (4). 345-358.

U.S. Census (1997). *Computer Use in the United States: Population Characteristics*. Issued September 1999. US Department of Commerce Publication.

U.S. Census (1999). Census Data. United States Census. [On-line], Available: http://www.census.gov/prod/1/pop/p23-190/p23190-d.pdf

U.S. Census (2000). Census population estimates 60+ by 5 year age group. [On-Line] Available: www.census.gov.

Westbrook, D. (1999). Welcome to the computer age. *Get Up and Go: New Ideas for the Mature Years*. June.

Index

Abledata website, 190

Academic performance, effect of distance education and web-based learning on, 172

Access (Microsoft), 7,9,10
use with patient medical database, 27,28,29,31

Accreditation standards, effect of distance and web-based learning on, 172

Administrators, attitudes toward distance education, 103-104

Adobe Acrobat, 199

Adoption and Safe Families Act (1997), 135

Adult Classroom Environment Scale (ACES), 73

Advertising, on Web pages, 192-193,197-198

Advocacy groups, influence on use of integrated clinical information systems, 55-56

African-American social workers, 89

American Association of Retired Persons, 204-205

American Dream Policy Demonstration, 20-21n

American Psychological Association, 217

American Sociological Association, 218-219

Americans with Disabilities Act, guidelines for compliance of website design with, 196-198

Asian-American social workers, 89

Assessment, technology-enhanced, 118

Assets for Independence Act (1998), 19

Assistive devices, for computer use, 190

Ball State University, televised courses of, 68

Blackboard (training development software), 118

Blindness. *See also* Visual impairment cataract-related, 242-5

"Bobby," 198

Braille keyboards, 190

Braille printers/printouts, 190,192

Browsers, use by disabled people, 192,194

Bulletin boards, Internet-based, 147

Cataract surgery eye camp, patient medical database of, 23-40
data collection and reporting for by clinical statistics team, 32
data capture procedures for, 32-36
evaluation of, 36-38
development of, 29-32
implication for social work practice, 38-39
Microsoft Access use with, 27,28, 29,31
Microsoft Office Professional use with, 28,38
Novell Network use with, 27-28
organizational and technological context of, 26-29

CD-ROMs, use in distance education, 71

Child protective services, multimedia-based supervisory competence assessment for, 117-131
background of, 117-120
design and development of, 121-124